Ervin Laszlo's new map of reality encompasses baffling pro-
ms and paradoxes in various disciplines of modern science.
a tour de force extended over half a century and culminat-
in the present book, a phenomenal achievement. . . . Laszlo's
sdisciplinary understanding . . . summarized in his opus mag-
What Is Reality? The New Map of Cosmos and Consciousness
ges and integrates science, philosophy, metaphysics, and spiri-
ty. However, its potential significance reaches even farther; the
pt of the Akasha dimension has important implications for
pplication in ecology, economy, sociology, politics, and reli-
Laszlo's articulation of the new map of reality could become
eless instrument in solving the problems brought into the
by the industrial system, and could show us the way toward
inable global civilization."

From the introduction by **Stanislav Grof**

a spiritual dimension to our lives? Is there purpose behind
tion of the universe, beyond space and time? Laszlo's map
challenges the materialistic view, pushing mainstream
o explore beyond its existing boundaries. We should be
o Ervin Laszlo, one of the great thinkers of our time, for
cinating, thought provoking, and inspirational book."

Jane Goodall PhD, DBE
Founder the Jane Goodall Institute
UN Messenger of Peace

lo, preeminent philosopher of our time, has pioneered
books and activism a new path for humanity beyond
crises of limited perception and understanding. As
educator and political activist, he has guided the lives
including myself, to become active agents of ethical

Advance Praise for

What Is Realit
The New Map of C
and Consciousn

". . . there's every reason to value highly
Ervin Laszlo. His new map of reality en
consciousness aims to change our core b
change how we lead our daily lives. . . .
fork in the road. One signpost says 'co
the other signpost says 'matter is the s
deepest mysteries of reality, Ervin L
to choose. And with his description
inspires us with the courage to actual

From the

"Ervin Laszlo's map of reality off
tific concept to replace the most c
world. It is a revolution in the scie
of Isaac Newton. It is a powerful
fully spacious ways of approachi
our role in It. . . . an emerging s
intellect and the limitations of t
heart and accounts for the full
that are becoming the substar
Laszlo's wonderfully open par
into a great future tree."

F

". .
ble
It i
ing
tra
num
brid
tuali
conc
and a
gion.
a pri
world
a susta

"Is there
the crea
of realit
science
grateful
such a fa

"Ervin Lasz
in his man
our curren
an inspired
of millions,

change beyond reductionism, materialism, GDP-fetishism, mindless consumerism, and narrow-minded sectarianism. This book does indeed succeed in providing a new map of reality, for millions of aspiring global citizens to see beyond today's conflicts and ideological and religious factions, grounding our spiritual and instinctive vision of wholeness, the inseparable oneness of our human family with all life on this planet."

Hazel Henderson

President, Ethical Markets Media

Author of *Building a Win-Win World* and *Paradigms in Progress*

"This book will be read by this and future generations with awe. It is the equivalent of a twenty-first century Copernican Revolution, setting the stage for a convergence in mind and in reality of all facets of the Cosmos and the Biosphere we Homo Sapiens call home. A work of sublime synthesis and feeling, articulated with many lifetimes of wisdom."

Michael Charles Tobias

President, Dancing Star Foundation

"There is a growing realization that our view of the world and the nature of consciousness is not merely a matter of personal philosophy, but is also a critical factor in our survival as a species. Our age has suffered greatly from the deadening effects of the grim ideology of materialism. In contrast, the resplendent vision of the new map of reality offers a new dawn of hope, meaning, direction, and purpose."

Larry Dossey, MD

Author of *One Mind: How Our Individual Mind Is Part of a Greater Consciousness*

"Laszlo's new map of reality provides real hope for the planet at a time of imminent crisis and encourages all of us to wake up to reality in order to play our part in this new era of shared consciousness. Dr. Laszlo's insights offer us a new way of thinking about our place in the universe and a new multi-dimensional approach to the way we view science and the search for truth. This book provides a blueprint for all readers to rediscover the potential of the human mind to solve problems and invites us to join together on an evolutionary journey in order to live 'as if everything is a miracle.'"

Mirela Sula

Chief Editor, *Global Woman Magazine*

"In his compelling latest book, *What Is Reality?*, Dr. Ervin Laszlo . . . offers a cogent and cohesive framework from which emerges, with justifiable confidence, an enlarged empirically-driven comprehension about the nature of reality. His stimulating forward-looking analysis provides invaluable insights into the greatest questions of human existence. His reasoning is well-positioned on the frontier of breakthrough knowledge, which predictably may ultimately transform science itself as it reluctantly parts company with the last remaining vestiges of the embattled materialist model of creation. For lay persons probing life's really big questions, this book is highly recommended reading. For mainstream scientists looking for a sound basis to adopt a post-materialist view of reality, look no further than the brilliantly crafted arguments Dr. Laszlo offers in this gem of a book."

Raymond A. Moody, PhD, MD

Author of *Life After Life*

"Ervin Laszlo has been a long-term participant in the awakening of humanity that is just now truly breaking the surface, becoming apparent to millions more as it progresses. His insights concerning the nature of this awakening are profound, and of great value to those who are deeply steeped in the elements of the awakening, as well as to those who are just beginning to glimpse its implications. As Ervin states, there is "remarkably robust evidence that consciousness is not confined to the brain." In the midst of that profound realization, birthed from the tsunami of evidence concerning the reality of nonlocal consciousness, lie the seeds for the most profound revolution in recorded human history, the outline of which is provided in his remarkable essay on the nature of reality."

Eben Alexander
Author of *The Gates of Heaven*

New Paradigm Books of
The Laszlo Institute of New Paradigm Research
Kingsley L. Dennis, Series Editor

What Is Consciousness? Three Sages Look Behind the Veil
(June 2016)

What Is Reality? The New Map of Cosmos and Consciousness
(October 2016)

The Laszlo Chronicle: A Global Thinker's Journey from Systems to Consciousness and the Akashic Field
(January 2017)

What Is Reality?

The New Map of Cosmos and Consciousness

Ervin Laszlo

with Alexander Laszlo

Foreword by Deepak Chopra

Introduction by Stanislav Grof

A New Paradigm Book of
The Laszlo Institute of New Paradigm Research
Kingsley L. Dennis, Series Editor

SelectBooks, Inc.
New York

This edition published by SelectBooks, Inc.
For information address SelectBooks, Inc., New York, New York.

First Edition

ISBN 978-1-59079-391-6

Library of Congress Cataloging-in-Publication Data

Names: Laszlo, Ervin, 1932- author.
Title: What is reality : the new map of cosmos and consciousness / Ervin Laszlo, Alexander Laszlo ; Kingsley L. Dennis, editor ; foreword by Deepak
Chopra ; Introduction by Stanislav Grof.
Description: first [edition]. | New York : SelectBooks, Inc., 2016. | Includes bibliographical references and index.
Identifiers: LCCN 2015046974 | ISBN 9781590793916 (hardcover book : alk. paper)
Subjects: LCSH: Cosmology. | Philosophical anthropology. | Consciousness. | Civilization--Forecasting.
Classification: LCC BD511 .L3735 2016 | DDC 113--dc23 LC record available at https://lccn.loc.gov/2015046974

Book design by Janice Benight

Manufactured in the United States of America
10 9 8 7 6 5 4 3 2 1

Contents

Preface

In one form or another, the question "What is truly the nature of reality?" has been asked by thinking people throughout history. They realized that reality is not necessarily as we see it, and that there could be more to reality than what we can see, hear, and touch. There were many answers, but they were either framed by the then-current systems of belief, or rooted in the personal insight of a prophet or another charismatic individual. Today we can attempt to give an answer based on science—an answer distilled from findings coming to light in the relevant fields of scientific inquiry.

This is a meaningful enterprise, but it needs to be periodically revisited. Scientists do not have privileged access to reality. They make observations, create theories based on their observations, and form an idea of the nature of reality in light of their theories. Physicists make observations and create theories regarding the physical aspects of reality; life scientists investigate the biological aspects; human and social scientists look at the psychological, social, and sociocultural aspects. The theories they come up with are the best approximation of the scheme that Einstein said scientists seek to tie together the observed facts. These schemes can change. As new observations are made and new experiments are performed, new schemes are developed, and new features of the world come to light.

The reality now coming to light in science moves ever further beyond the world we can see, hear, and touch. The latest theories are not collections and catalogues of elements of sensory experience, but high-level extrapolations. They do not describe pebbles and planets; they postulate coherently interrelated patterns of events. The observation of pebbles and planets is reinterpreted. In physics the reinterpretation often takes the form of differential equations; these reconstruct the basic structure of pebbles and planets and relate it to the structure that underlies the observation of other things in other fields. Physicist Sir Arthur Eddington once remarked that in the scientific perspective even one's wife is a complex differential equation. (But, he advised, it would not be wise to introduce this idea into domestic life.)

Theories in science reinterpret the "observed facts" in a form that permits their integration as integral elements of a coherent reality. The reality that now emerges at the cutting edge of science supersedes the reality envisaged by classical physics, where particles of matter interact in passive space and indifferently flowing time. The new reality perceives embracing interconnection among all things in the universe. It is not based on matter, and it incorporates space and time in the embracing interaction that defines evolution in the integral system of the world. This is not a radically new concept; it has been intuitively known for millennia.

Plato said that all knowledge is recollection. Today we can recollect that we are part of an integral reality in which we co-evolve with all things around us. Connection and co-evolution are the core of the new map of cosmos and consciousness, the map that promises to give us the best insight we ever had into the true nature of reality. This book describes and discusses the essential features of that map. Connection and co-evolution are the core of the new map of cosmos and consciousness: the newly rediscovered concept that is the best and now also the most trustworthy insight we have ever had into the nature of the reality that frames our life and lends meaning to our existence.

Foreword

Deepak Chopra

What you did today has nothing to do with the nature of reality and the meaning of life, and yet it has everything to do with the nature of reality and the meaning of life. That's the paradox of the greatest mysteries. We don't spend time thinking about them. When deciding between a Cobb salad or a tuna sandwich for lunch, my choice doesn't depend on the meaning of life, the origin of the universe, or what happens after I die. Life is too demanding, its hard realities too hard, to expend energy on imponderables. But everything you did today depended on a hidden force inside you, the force of your core beliefs.

Core beliefs are so fundamental that no one needs to consult them. They function like unstoppable Energizer Bunnies, fueling our thoughts, emotions, actions, and reactions. If you deeply believe that you don't matter in the larger scheme of things, there is no doubt that your day isn't going the way it's going for people who believe that the whole world revolves around them. Pessimism versus optimism, empathy versus indifference, service versus selfishness, peace versus violence—all of these issues get settled, for better or worse, at the level of core beliefs.

I recently talked to a CEO who had founded an organization devoted to near-death experiences (NDE), and his attitude toward public acceptance was very mixed. "No one is interested in big issues, Deepak. They only think about themselves, which is why nothing ever changes. But promise them eternal life, and maybe you can inspire people to be more compassionate and loving. Their whole conception of themselves has to change before the world can change."

He was addressing, in his own words, the level of core beliefs that fuel our daily life. NDEs already have enough popular support, I imagine, so that "going into the light" may replace Heaven as the accepted notion of an afterlife. Devout believers would probably be shocked to learn that according to the *Catholic Encyclopedia*, Heaven isn't an actual place but a state of grace in which the soul joins God. This brings up the second important point about the greatest mysteries of existence. If you ask them what happens after we die or what is the ultimate meaning of life or anything of that magnitude, the automatic answer is "Nobody knows."

Yet, in reality the answers to the greatest mysteries are lodged in convenient pigeonholes in almost everyone's head. A huge majority of people will either go to Heaven when they die or will go nowhere. There isn't much wiggle room between casual religious belief and casual atheism, the two compartments most people fall into.

If my description of the situation seems credible, there's every reason to value highly a profound thinker like Ervin Laszlo. His new map of reality encompassing cosmos and consciousness aims to change our core beliefs, which in turn will change how we lead our daily lives. Science does not exist in a vacuum. It must serve the evolution of consciousness. Only the evolution of consciousness can produce a better world.

On the way to proposing a new map of reality as the need of the planet, Laszlo refuses to be pigeonholed into believer or atheist, taking the rare course of free and open thinking. His working assumptions are the following:

> The mind is deeply mysterious, but it has the capacity to figure itself out.

> Since all experience occurs in consciousness, the key to every mystery ultimately goes back to consciousness.

> We mustn't assume, out of petty arrogance, that consciousness is solely a human quality.

> Imponderable questions can be pondered, once you expand your conception of reality.

> Any discovery made "in here" through thought and insight can be verified "out there" in the material world. Science is amenable to wisdom and can be expanded to encompass it.

Each of these assumptions is arguable except for the last one. There are dedicated, stubbornly convinced materialists who would toss out any attempt to settle imponderable questions through science. Anyone who has worked seriously in the field of consciousness—never mind cosmic consciousness—knows what it is like to be told that your endeavors aren't "real science." Laszlo has persisted long enough to enjoy the present moment, when consciousness studies are not only accepted but form one of the most exciting frontiers in science.

What led us to this turn-around was reality itself. Finally, we are compelled to go wherever reality leads us. Einstein famously said, "There are two ways to live: you can live as if nothing is a miracle; you can live as if everything is a miracle." This echoes the notion that deeply held beliefs covertly guide everything we do. But by implying that for him, everything is a miracle, Einstein unwittingly let science off the hook. Science doesn't investigate miracles, yet as long as *everything* falls into that category, it doesn't matter what you work on. Finding the next new industrial plastic is on an even playing field with discovering the source of consciousness in the universe.

But this is a cop out—as Einstein well knew, being someone who respected spiritual perspectives—and reality eventually pressed the issue. It became imperative, once the quantum field was established, to know where the field originated, which meant discovering the origin of space and time, and this in turn led to the investigation of beyond-spacetime. By the same token, since the brain is made up of atoms that can be reduced to subatomic particles, and these in turn disappear into the infinite, invisible quantum field, one has to ask how consciousness emerged from the same "nothing"—the ground state of the cosmos—as the universe itself did.

Laszlo has gathered these issues together in an "all-roads-lead to-Rome" map that I believe is absolutely appropriate, in fact necessary. The present situation in science has come down to one of two possibilities. Either matter came first and originated mind, which would make materialistic explanations valid for everything. Or mind came first, producing the panoply of outer existence, in which case everything is traceable back to consciousness. The time for splitting the difference between these two choices has passed. Gone, too, is the assumption that consciousness can be set aside as irrelevant to the real business of science, which is measurement, experimentation, data collecting, and verifying facts.

We live in a hazy transition zone that this book attempts, with considerable success, to transcend. The epoch of naive realism (the belief that the world of the five senses can be simply accepted as a given) is quickly drawing to a close. The apple cart was overturned a century ago, when quantum pioneers like Erwin Schrödinger could assert the following:

> To divide or multiply consciousness is something meaningless.[i]

> I venture to call it [the mind] indestructible since it has a peculiar timetable, namely mind is always now. There is really no before and after for the mind.[ii]

> There is obviously only one alternative, namely the unification of minds or consciousness . . . . [I]n truth there is only one mind.[iii]

As you can see, there's a rich history of thinking about imponderable questions and expanding science to encompass them. For a long time the direction of physics veered away from Schrödinger's line of inquiry. Now we find ourselves completing the circle by going back to a basic assertion made by another quantum pioneer, Max Planck: "There is no getting behind consciousness."[iv]

Because it maps experiences of life as well as afterlife, this book can be—and will be—accused of muddling science and mysticism. Behind such an accusation is the need to protect hidebound ideas. One of these concerns the brain, which supplies our interface with reality (about this there is no disagreement). If you are a staunch physicalist, someone who refuses to accept any explanation outside materialism, the brain must be the creator of the mind, and the world we perceive must be registered faithfully by the brain. But there's no doubt that the human brain is fallible. Its mechanisms are easily fooled, by optical illusions, for example. Its fixed neural pathways constantly distort even basic perceptions, as when a person suffering from anorexia looks at her starved and wasted body but sees it as "too fat."

Leaving aside its fallibility, the human brain processes only a fraction of the billions of bits of sensory data bombarding it every day. Through a process of filtering and reduction, it creates a map of the world that is acceptable for everyday navigation, nothing more. It has been rightly said that the "real world" is actually a reflected image of how the brain works. It is an abstraction built up from mechanical manipulation at the neural level.

To simplify, our map of reality is like a fenced-in corral that includes only what is acceptable and permissible while shutting out what is not. Acceptable and permissible are personal terms—we all know people who are blind to aspects of their lives that are glaringly obvious to others. But these are also social and cultural terms. The brain can shut out what society refuses to see. Sometimes this refusal runs deep into the unconscious. The historical denigration of women and African Americans, for example, was created by a complex mélange of beliefs, attitudes, perceptions, received opinions, and willful blindness. All of these ingredients changed the brains of the people who participated in them, including of the victims.

A scientific map of consciousness must reach beyond the conventions of brain-based acceptable and permissible reality. Physicists find doing this impossible except in a limited way. They insist that the brain must be delivering reality, because for them there is no other alternative. Thus the brain is given a privileged position. Rocks, trees, clouds, hydrogen atoms, and quarks are not conscious, but even as it sits in the middle of the scene, with no qualities to distinguish its "thingness" from the "thingness" around it, we are supposed to view the brain as totally unique. This is pure animism, the belief that spirits live inside material objects, verging close to religiosity, turning the brain into a three-pound god.

By abandoning physicalism, we would not be returning to an age of superstition (the favorite straw man of the skeptical camp). We would be expanding the fence of science, allowing in *more* of reality. Until there is an understanding of how the mind interfaces with reality, no viable explanation exists for any experience, much less the mystical.

The new map described in this book explores reality beyond the brain, not just as it applies to the afterlife but as the only path that leads to the source. Mind outside the brain was a routine belief in the age of faith (when God was the cosmic mind); it was always a workable hypothesis in philosophy from the ancient Greeks onward. It was pushed to the fringes by the scientific revolution of the modern age, and until yesterday, it was scientific heresy. Reality didn't care. Whatever our shifting attitudes, reality has brought us to a fork in the road. One signpost says "consciousness is the source," the other signpost says "matter is the source." By investigating the deepest mysteries of reality, Ervin Laszlo indicates which road to choose. And with his description of the new map of reality he inspires us with the courage to actually take it.

Introduction

STANISLAV GROF

In 1962, after fifteen years of intensive study of the history of science, Thomas Kuhn, one of the most influential philosophers of the twentieth century, published his groundbreaking book, *The Structure of Scientific Revolutions*.[v] He demonstrated that the history of science is not a process of gradual accumulation of data and formulation of increasingly accurate theories. It breaks into distinct periods, each of which is governed by what Kuhn called a *paradigm*—a constellation of basic metaphysical assumptions, beliefs, values, and techniques shared by the members of the academic community. Scientific activity during such periods ("normal science") is essentially problem-solving within the conceptual constraints of a paradigm, comparable to a chess game.

This situation continues until observations reveal new facts that seriously question the basic assumptions of the leading paradigm. After mainstream scientists concede that the challenge to the existing belief system cannot be handled by questioning the expertise, integrity, or sanity of those who present it, original thinkers formulate daring alternatives to the established way of thinking in an attempt to resolve the conceptual crisis. This period of "abnormal science" ends when one of these alternatives is accepted as the paradigm that governs thinking and theory-construction in the next historical period.

It has become increasingly clear that we are currently experiencing a major paradigm shift comparable in its scope and importance to the Copernican revolution. In the course of the twentieth century, various disciplines of modern science amassed an extraordinary array of observations that cannot be accounted for or adequately explained in terms of the materialistic worldview. These "anomalous phenomena" came from a wide range of fields: astrophysics, quantum-relativistic physics, and chemistry to biology, anthropology, thanatology, parapsychology, and transpersonal psychology. A very good definition for "anomalous phenomena" is "what is left after we apply a bad theory." The fact that so many scientific disciplines constituting the current materialistic worldview are plagued by these baffling observations and paradoxical findings indicates urgent need for a radical paradigm change.

Pioneering researchers formulated revolutionary new theories in an attempt to solve the disconcerting enigmas in their respective fields. Over a period of several decades, a radically different map of reality and of human nature started to come into view; it became known as the emerging paradigm. Among these new perspectives were David Bohm's theory of holomovement, Karl Pribram's holographic model of the brain, Rupert Sheldrake's theory of morphogenetic fields, Ilya Prigogine's theory of dissipative structures, transpersonal psychology, and others.[vi]

However, these attempts constituted a mosaic of attempts to address specific problems that have emerged in the context of individual disciplines. They lacked mutual cohesion and remained disconnected enclaves in the tapestry of the materialistic worldview.

Ervin Laszlo's interdisciplinary and transdisciplinary research, extended over a period of over a half-century and culminating in this book, has accomplished something that none of the earlier revolutionary approaches were able to do. His connectivity hypothesis and his concept of the Akashic field or Akasha dimension provided plausible explanation for the anomalous phenomena, paradoxical observations, and paradigmatic challenges plaguing a wide range of disciplines and made it possible to integrate them into a comprehensive theory of the universal information field, a "theory of everything."[vii] In his unique systemic and interdisciplinary approach to problem solving, Laszlo now succeeded in producing a map that dissolves the boundaries between natural science and the study of mind and spirituality. In this Introduction I will focus on this last aspect of Ervin Laszlo's work.

I had the pleasure and privilege to be at the cradle of transpersonal psychology, a discipline attempting to integrate the best of modern science with authentic spirituality, and have been involved for over a half-century in consciousness research. My special area of interest has been the exploration of a large and important subcategory of nonordinary states of consciousness that have unique healing, transformative, heuristic, and even evolutionary potential. I have coined for these states "holotropic"—literally "moving toward wholeness" from the Greek *holos* (whole) and *trepo/trepein* (moving in the direction of something).[viii]

Novice shamans experience holotropic states during their initiatory crises and later in life induce them in their clients for therapeutic purposes. Ancient and native cultures have used these states in their rites of passage and healing ceremonies for millennia. They were described by mystics of all ages and initiates in the ancient mysteries of death and rebirth. Procedures for inducing them ("technologies of the sacred") were also developed and used in the context of major world religions—Hinduism, Buddhism, Jainism, Taoism, Islam, Judaism, Zoroastrianism, and Christianity. Additional important categories of holotropic states are experiences induced by psychedelic substances, near-death experiences (NDEs), and UFO-related events and phenomena.

My own introduction to holotropic states of consciousness happened in November 1956 when, as a beginning psychiatrist, I volunteered for an experiment with LSD-25, a new investigational substance that was sent to the Psychiatric Department of Charles University in Prague by Sandoz Pharmaceutical Company in Basel. In my session, I had a magnificent experience of cosmic consciousness, which had an enormous impact on my professional and personal life. Following it, the study of holotropic states of consciousness became my profession, vocation, and passion.[iix]

I started using psychedelics as adjuncts to psychotherapy after three years of laboratory research of these substances in the context of a large multidimensional interdisciplinary project. The extraordinary inter- and intra-individual variability in the reactions of our experimental subjects was unprecedented in the world of pharmacology. It made clear that these substances were not ordinary pharmacological agents with reasonably predictable effects. Rather, they were potent catalysts of the unconscious processes that enabled the material from the depth of the psyche to emerge into consciousness. I realized we were not doing psychopharmacological research, but exploring the human psyche with the help of extraordinary new tools. It was not an exaggeration to compare the potential significance of psychedelics for psychiatry to the crucial role the microscope plays in biology and medicine or the telescope in astronomy.

From the very beginning, the use of serial sessions with psychedelics for self-exploration and psychotherapy brought about experiences and observations that challenged the existing paradigm. In the early sessions of the series my patients were experiencing colorful geometric (fractal-like) visions and reliving memories from childhood and infancy. However, when the sessions continued or the doses were increased, a new phenomenon emerged: the same clients now discovered in their psyche a transbiographical domain that is not recognized by mainstream academicians or clinicians. They started reliving episodes from their biological birth and releasing the emotions and physical feelings that they had held back since the time they came into this world. Although this challenged the belief of traditional psychiatrists that it is not possible to have a memory of birth because the brain of the newborn is not completely myelinized, it did not represent a major conceptual challenge. ("Myelinized" refers to the development of the myelin sheath of proteins and phospholipids that surrounds healthy nerve cells.)

The myelinization argument is unconvincing and even absurd considering that prenatal research has demonstrated sensitivity of the fetus already *in utero*. In addition, memory exists in primitive organisms that do not have a brain at all, and there is general agreement in professional circles that the quality of nursing and even *bonding* (exchange of looks between the mother and the newborn) has profound effect on postnatal life. The illogical denial of the importance of birth is likely due to repression of the frightening memory of a very painful and potentially life-threatening situation. However, as psychedelic research continued, more formidable conceptual challenges emerged. In the sessions appeared memories of various stages of prenatal life, fast experiential replays of the entire embryogenesis, and even cellular memories of spermatozoids and ova during the process of fertilization.[x]

Further probing of the depth of the unconscious revealed another vast transbiographical and transexperiential domain for which I chose the term *transpersonal.* It comprises a rich array of experiences in which consciousness transcends the boundaries of the body/ego and the usual limitations of linear time and three-dimensional space. It took me three years to map this territory before I felt that the new cartography included the most important categories and types of transpersonal experiences and phenomena. By that time I realized that this understanding of the psyche was not new at all. Certain parts of it had been described by psychoanalytic renegades Otto Rank, C.G. Jung, and Sandor Ferenczi, while others bore resemblance to the great spiritual systems of the East that Aldous Huxley included in his *Perennial Philosophy.*[xi] My map integrated all these disconnected insights into the human psyche and complemented them with new observations from modern consciousness research.[xii]

Transpersonal phenomena have an extraordinary property that undermines the basic metaphysical assumptions of Western science. They can provide access to accurate information about various aspects of the universe that reaches far beyond the knowledge of the subjects involved. In many cases, it was possible to confirm that these individuals had not received this information through the ordinary channels; other times it was information of a kind that no media can offer (e.g., the body image of animals, olfactory, gustatory and tactile sensations, or species-specific experience of sexual arousal).

Interested readers will find many specific examples in my previous publications.[xiii]

For example, experiential identification with another person can provide deep insights into that person's personality, emotional life, thoughts, and sometimes even personal memories. Becoming an eagle, bat, or dolphin can convey information about these animals' body images and the unique way they experience the world. People who encounter archetypal beings and visit archetypal domains can obtain information about mythologies of which they had no previous intellectual knowledge.[xiv]

Past-life experiences can accurately portray costumes, weapons, architecture, and other aspects of the cultures and historical periods involved and in rare instances even specific historical events.[xv]

The transcendence of consciousness within spacetime begins with the experience of dual unity when the boundaries of the body/ego dissolve and the individual seems to become one with another person while also retaining his or her own identity. Experiences of this kind are common between a pregnant mother and her fetus or nursing mother and her baby. Conversely, adults in holotropic states experiencing regression to the breast or the womb can have a sense of fusing with their mothers. The practice of *maithuna*, sexual union in *Vamamarga Tantra*, is designed to induce experiential fusion of the partners reaching the spiritual level.

In mediumistic experiences the identification with the other person is so strong and pervasive that the individual loses his or her identity. The dissolution of consciousness can extend further and result in experiential identification with entire groups of people (e.g., all mothers of the world or all suffering or dying individuals), and even in the experience of the field of consciousness of the entire human species. Experiences in this category can also reveal the interior of the subject's body down to the microscopic level—its organs, tissues, and even cells. The transcendence of spatial boundaries can cross the species barrier and lead to authentic identification with animals and plants from any level of the evolutionary tree. Less frequent is experiential identification with inorganic materials and processes, such as granite, amber, diamond, or an exploding volcano.[xvi]

Incredible and absurd as it might seem to a Westerner committed to a monistic materialistic worldview, these experiences suggest that everything we can experience in the everyday state of consciousness as an object has a corresponding subjective representation while we are in holotropic states of consciousness. These observations support a basic tenet of Hindu spiritual philosophy (Brahman, Satchitananda) that the material world is a manifestation of Absolute Consciousness.

Reliving of episodes from infancy, birth, or prenatal life can be understood as examples of the transcendence of linear time rather than the reliving of memories in the conventional sense. The reason for this is that they represent an integral part of an uninterrupted line of historical replays that includes sequences for which it is difficult or even impossible to find a material substrate. Here belongs identification with spermatozoids and ova during the process of conception experienced on the cellular level of consciousness; sequences of ancestral, racial, collective, and karmic experiences; and those portraying events in the evolution of the animal and botanical kingdoms. Temporal transcendence can also involve inorganic objects and processes, such as the evolution of the universe or the early history of our planet.

Some transpersonal experiences are related to a dimension that is radically different from consensual reality. It is immaterial and lies beyond spacetime; within it there are no boundaries and everything seems to coexist in the eternal Now. It is a realm that harbors archetypes, cosmic principles that form and inform the material world: these can manifest either in their universal form or in the form of specific culture-bound entities. It is the realm Laszlo in this book calls the deep dimension, the domain of the cosmos beyond space and time.

The experiential spectrum of holotropic states includes encounter and communication with deceased persons and discarnate entities such as spirits, shamanic power animals, and spirit guides. In its farthest reaches, individual consciousness can identify with the Universal Mind or Cosmic Consciousness, the creative principle of the universe. The most profound experience available in the holotropic state is immersion in the Supracosmic and Metacosmic Void, the primordial emptiness and nothingness that is the source of existence. The Void has a paradoxical nature. It is a vacuum, in the sense that it is devoid of any concrete forms, but it is also a plenum, since it seems to have the potential—all the information and energy—necessary to manifest the material universe.

Another category of transpersonal experiences comprises phenomena that seem to occur in a twilight zone between consciousness and the material world. C.G. Jung called it *psychoid*, borrowing the term from the founder of neovitalism, Hans Driesch. The most common of them are synchronicities, meaningful connections between intrapsychic experiences and events in spacetime. Additional examples are supernormal physical feats of athletes, the siddhis, physical mediumship in spiritistic seances, UFO experiences, poltergeist and intentional psychokinesis.[xvii]

The existence and nature of transpersonal experiences violate some of the most basic assumptions of materialistic science. They imply such seemingly absurd notions as the relativity and arbitrary nature of all physical boundaries, nonlocal connections in the universe, communication through unknown means and channels, memory without a material substrate, the nonlinearity of time, or consciousness associated with all living organisms, and even inorganic matter. Many transpersonal experiences involve events from both the microcosm and the macrocosm, realms that unaided human senses normally cannot reach, or from historical periods that precede the origin of the solar system, formation of planet Earth, appearance of living organisms, development of the nervous system, and emergence of *Homo sapiens.*

The totality of the experiences and observations described above represents a formidable challenge to materialistic science, something that cannot be handled by minor conceptual patchwork (*ad hoc* hypotheses), but asks for major paradigmatic overhaul. After more than a half-century of research into holotropic states of consciousness, I am convinced of the ontological reality of the transpersonal domain and its pivotal gnoseological importance. Mainstream scientists tend to deal with this challenge by denying or misinterpreting the existing evidence. This stalwart resistance, based on radical incompatibility of the new data with the dominant paradigm in science, is further fomented by a tendency of scientists to "confuse the map with the territory" alluded to by Thomas Kuhn and discussed at length by Alfred Korzybski and Gregory Bateson.[xviii] The inclination to mistake the existing paradigms for an accurate and definitive description of reality has been pervasive in the world of science.

Ervin Laszlo's new map of reality encompasses baffling problems and paradoxes in various disciplines of modern science. It is a tour de force extended over a half-century and culminating in the present book—a phenomenal achievement.[xix] The importance of his new map is truly groundbreaking. I briefly outline here the radically new perspective that his map offers on the problems encountered in the research on holotropic states, particularly those connected with a wide range of transpersonal experiences.

The most important general conclusion that one can draw from various avenues of modern consciousness research is that consciousness is not a product of the neurophysiological processes in the brain, but an essential and integral part of existence. This realization is also the basic tenet of Laszlo's map of reality. According to this map, consciousness does not originate in the brain, but in the Akashic field. The information in this field forms and informs all entities and phenomena in spacetime.

The Akashic Holofield harbors the *logos* of the cosmos; it contains the information, rules, and regularities that govern events in the manifest world and the behavior of its constituents. It also conserves a complete holographic record of the history of the universe and of our planet, including the patterns of consciousness that it created. Since this domain has no boundaries and partitions, all the information contained in it is present in all its points. The consciousness of three-dimensional entities in spacetime is localized but intrinsically nonlocal: it is a manifestation of the higher-dimensional vibrational regime of our coherence domain.

Many problems related to transpersonal experiences can be resolved if we accept Laszlo's postulate of the Akashic Holofield with all the characteristics that he describes and consider the possibility that localized consciousness is a manifestation of the information contained in this field.

One of the most astonishing observations in holotropic states of consciousness is the possibility of what appears to be time travel to other historical periods and countries. I have in my records many reports of individuals who were convinced that they experienced events that took place in ancient Assyria or Babylonia; Japan at the time of the samurai; in the French Revolution; colonial Africa; and many other times and places. I have personally experienced what appeared to be convincing past-life experiences in ancient Egypt and Czarist Russia and similar sequences from ancient and more recent historical periods and various geographical locations.[xx] The possibility that information about events in spacetime remains holographically recorded in the cosmos at a higher-dimensional regime of vibration is a basic assumption of Ervin Laszlo's new map. The existence of these experiences can be seen as the empirical validation of this map.

Experiential identification with other people, animals, plants, and inorganic materials, for which it is impossible to find horizontal communication channels, becomes understandable if we accept the possibility that the connection is mediated by information from a holofield beyond space and time. This would also account for Jung's "a-causal connecting principle" underlying synchronicities and for such ESP phenomena as telepathy, clairvoyance, psychometry, and astral projection. Psychoid events could be seen as situations in which localized consciousness reaches beyond spacetime and appropriates the capacity of orchestrating the behavior of various constituents of spacetime, as it does in the creation of the phenomenal world itself. The shift of localized consciousness in spacetime to the higher-dimensional regime of our coherence domain could account for many experiences and events occurring in near-death situations, during the dying process, or following biological death. Examples would be out-of-body experiences (OBEs), veridical OBEs in congenitally blind people ("mindsight"); the *bardo body* and *bardo realms* described in the Tibetan Book of the Dead; apparitions of recently dead relatives and friends; the "welcoming committee" of deceased people appearing to those who are close to death; auspiciously timed physical events in the lives of survivors; communication with deceased people; haunted houses and castles; as well as visions of astral planes and spirits.

Laszlo's map of reality based on theories and findings on the cutting edge of science offers an elegant solution for the dilemmas and paradoxes in a number of scientific disciplines that have remained and persisted even after earlier revolutionary attempts provided partial corrections. I am referring here to David Bohm's theory of holomovement, Karl Pribram's holographic theory of the brain, Rupert Sheldrake's concept of morphic resonance and morphogenetic fields, Ilya Prigogine's discovery of dissipative structures, Alfred North Whitehead's process philosophy, Gregory Bateson's generalist worldview, and others.[xxi]

Laszlo's new map also achieves something that previous generations of modern scientists would have considered impossible. It explains and illuminates a number of seemingly obscure and absurd assertions and tenets found in mystical and esoteric literature. For example, the Jain religion describes all beings in the universe as self-deluded separate units of consciousness (*jivas)* that misperceive themselves as autonomous units.

The jivas have an important characteristic that seems fantastic and incredible: each of them has the information about all the others. Vedic mythology describes a pearl necklace in Indra's heaven in which the pearls are arranged in such a way that each of them reflects all the others; this necklace symbolizes the universe. In the remarkable philosophy of mutual interpenetration found in Avatamsaka (Huayan) Buddhism, the essence of the universe is succinctly captured in four statements: One in One, One in Many, Many in Many, and Many in One.

The ancient Emerald Tablet (*tabula smaragdina*) attributed to Hermes Trismegistus states: "That which is below is like that which is above and that which is above is like that which is below to do the miracles of one only thing." The idea that the macrocosm is contained in every microcosm can be found in many esoteric systems: Tantra, Kabbalah, the Gnostic tradition, and others. The concept that each of us is identical with the entire universe is graphically represented in the images of Purushakara Yantra, Adam Kadmon, and the Gnostic Cosmic Man. Research into holotropic states has brought empirical validation for this idea, if it is properly understood. Each of us is identical with the entire universe—not in terms of what can be weighed and measured, but because we have the potential to experientially identify with any of its parts.

Laszlo's map of reality subsumes ideas from various philosophical systems. Thus in the monadology of the great German mathematician and philosopher Gottfried Wilhelm Leibniz, the universe consists of monads, essential forms of being that are eternal and indestructible. Each of them contains the information about all the others and reflects the entire universe in a pre-established harmony.[xxii] According to Alfred North Whitehead the universe is made up of momentary events of experience rather than enduring material substances. Each of these moments ("actual events" or "actual occasions") contains the entire history of the universe and is internally related to all the others.[xxiii]

Ervin Laszlo's transdisciplinary understanding of cosmos and consciousness summarized in his magnum opus, *What Is Reality? The New Map of Cosmos and Consciousness,* bridges and integrates science, philosophy, metaphysics, and spirituality. However, its potential significance reaches even farther. The concept of the Akashic holofield and a higher-dimensional regime in the manifestation of our cosmic coherence domain has important implications for and application in ecology, economy, sociology, politics, and religion.

Laszlo's articulation of the new map of reality could become a priceless instrument in solving the problems brought into the world by the industrial system, and could show us the way toward a sustainable global civilization.

PART ONE

The New Map

CHAPTER 1

Cosmos

Paradigm Shift

Paradigms shifts come about in science from time to time—fundamental shifts in the way scientists perceive reality. Major shifts occurred throughout the twentieth century. The paradigm that emerges in the second decade of the twenty-first century differs as much from the preceding paradigms as those differed from the pre-scientific speculations that dominated traditional thinking about the world. The emerging paradigm suggests a radically new conception of the nature of reality.

The Waning of the Classical Paradigm

The current and now obsolete, but in some respects still dominant paradigm is the inheritance of classical physics. It views the world as consisting of individual bits of "matter" that interact in passive space and indifferently flowing time. This concept has been challenged by the relativity revolution in the first decade of the twentieth century, and by the quantum revolution in the third. The new paradigm at the dawn of the twenty-first century consolidates these revolutions. It sees the world as a whole system where all things interact and together constitute an entangled, quantum-like system in which all thing are intrinsic elements in an integral whole.

The "global realism" of the emerging paradigm contrasts with the "local realism" of the classical conception. In the latter, real things occupy unique positions in space and time and are only affected by local forces transmitted by mechanistic interaction.

Global realism is supported by observational and experimental evidence. It discloses that things may be at any finite distance in space and time, but remain nonetheless connected. Such action-at-a-distance is an anomaly for the classical paradigm—even Einstein called it "spooky."

The first evidence of space- and time- transcending "nonlocal" interconnection came from physics. It shows that pairs of particles that originate from the same source but have opposite spin remain intrinsically interconnected. Measuring one particle has an instant effect on the other, no matter how far they may be from each other. This surprising (and, for the classical paradigm, anomalous) finding was reported by Alain Aspect and his collaborators in 1982.[1] They tested the Einstein-Podolski-Rosen (EPR) thought-experiment published in 1935 under the title "Can quantum-mechanical description of physical reality be considered complete?"[2] Aspect and collaborators came up with experimental evidence for nonlocal interconnection, even though this was not the purpose of the experiment (Einstein intended to demonstrate that the quantum mechanical description of the physical world is essentially incomplete). Since then a large number of experiments have been testing interconnection among particles at various distances and came up with evidence that it is real. Skeptics objected that the tests may have disregarded the presence of classical interconnections, but in 2015 physicists Hensen, Bernien, Dreau, et al., reported a "loophole-free" experiment that provided nearly indubitable evidence that distant interconnection does exist in nature.[3]

At least on the quantum level, reality proved to be interconnected, entangled, nonlocal. This did not and does not suggest that there would not be distinct entities in the microscale world, only that the entities are "entangled"—intrinsically interconnected. By the second decade of this century, entangled interconnections surfaced in the living world and even at the macro-dimension of astrophysics and cosmology.

The Nature of the New Paradigm

In the second decade of the twenty-first century we can describe the basic tenets of the new paradigm. Particles are not corpuscular entities, and they do not exist independently against a passive background. The fundamental reality is not matter but energy, and the laws of nature are not rules of mechanistic interaction but "instructions" or "algorithms" coding patterns of energy.

Ever since Thomas Young performed his famous double-slit experiments in 1801, particles have been known to possess both corpuscular and wave properties. According to the standard version of quantum theory, these different and in some respects contradictory properties appear according to the kind of experiments one performs to observe them. This intrinsic dualism at the heart of nature is overcome in the new paradigm. Reality is fundamentally waveform. Integral wave packets appear as corpuscles, but they are assemblies of interacting waves. The furnishings of the world are clusters of standing and propagating waves.

The standing waves we know as particles are observable and measurable. They have mass, reflect light, and obey the action of local and universal forces. Yet they are not material entities, but relatively stable clusters of interfering waves. The same holds true of atoms and molecules and the structures they constitute. The definition of real-world things must be revised. In the old-paradigm definition we would say that a living body vibrates, for example, at 10^{15} Herz, meaning that there is a material body in space and time that resonates at 10^{15} vibrations per second. In the new paradigm definition we say that interfering standing waves vibrating at 10^{15} Herz constitute a living body.

"If you want to find the secrets of the universe," said the maverick genius Nikola Tesla in 1942, "think in terms of energy, frequency and vibration."* This insight was seconded by the great physicist Max Planck in 1944. He said,

---

* *Reflection* magazine No. 9, July/August 1998, p. 22.

> As a man who has devoted his whole life to the most clear-headed science, to the study of matter, I can tell you as a result of my research about atoms this much: There is no matter as such. All matter originates and exists only by virtue of a force which brings the particle of an atom to vibration and holds this most minute solar system of the atom together.*

Planck followed this with a statement that is just as astonishing as the negation of matter. "We must assume," he said, "behind this force the existence of a conscious and intelligent Mind. This Mind is the matrix of all matter."

Tesla's proposition, that to find the secrets of the universe we must think in terms of energy, frequency, and vibration, together with Planck's statements—that there is nothing in the world we can call "matter," and that what there is, presupposes the presence of a conscious and intelligent Mind—are the premises of the basic scheme that, according to Einstein, scientists seek to tie together the observed facts. In this case they are the premises of the simplest possible scheme that can tie together all (or at least the representative majority) of the observed facts. Explored and elaborated, it gives us the most faithful map we have ever had of the fundamental nature of reality.

---

* *Das Wesen der Materie* (*The Nature of Matter*), speech in Florence, Italy, 1944. Archiv zur Geschichte der Max Planck Gesellschaft, Abt. Va, Rep. 11 Planck, Nr. 1797.

The Map of the Cosmos

"Cosmos," in the sense of the Greek *Kosmos*, stands for the ordered totality that encompasses all things in the world. A scientific theory of the cosmos integrates all the things in an optimally consistent and economical whole. This is the intention of the map we now draw of the cosmos. This map is a radical innovation in regard to the established and now transcended classical paradigm, while it is but a "re-cognition" of insights that hallmarked human intuitions of reality for millennia.

Basic Tenets

In the new map of the cosmos there is no such thing as "matter." There are only "matter-like" entities constituted of clusters of coordinated vibration.

The material things we consider elements of the real world are bits and clusters of vibration, oscillating standing waves at various scales of size and complexity. Planck-size bits configure into clusters of coordinated vibration, and their interaction creates the manifest world. The clusters, superclusters, and hyperclusters compose the particles, atoms and molecules; the organisms and ecologies; and the stars, stellar systems, and galaxies that are the furnishings—the "matter content"—of the world. They constitute individually distinguishable but not categorically separate entities. They are intrinsic elements of the field of vibration in which they appear.

The vibrations that furnish the world appear in the "excited" (as contrasted with the "ground") state of the cosmos. Our universe can be defined as a coherence domain in the general wave field of the excited state of the cosmos. All things in it are clusters of coordinated vibration.

The following points describe the basic principles of the map of reality based on this concept of the cosmos.

Intelligence at the Ground State of the Cosmos

The things that furnish space and time are coordinated patterns of interfering waves. The manifest world is a set of clusters of coordinated vibration in the excited state of the cosmos. The coordination of the clusters of vibration indicates nonrandomness at the heart of reality. The clusters are "in-formed" by a factor we identify (as does Planck) as an underlying cosmic intelligence.

The presence of intelligence at the heart of reality is a familiar tenet in religious and spiritual systems. In the Old Testament of the Abrahamic religions it is the *logos*—"the Word"— that is not just *of* God, but *is* God. ("In the beginning was the Word, and the Word was with God, and the Word was God." (John 1:1). For the Chinese belief system the cosmic intelligence is the Tao; for the Hindu system it is Brahman, for Buddhism it is Dharmakaya, and for African and pre-Colombian belief systems it is the Great Spirit that resides at the heart of all things in nature.

The Excitation of the Ground State

The ground state of the cosmos is vibration centered at the zero point of that state. It is pure potential that, when realized, creates the coordinated vibration that constitutes the universe. The vibration of the ground state in-forms the resulting clusters of vibration.

The vibration of the ground state is eternal and immutable, but it is capable of excitation. Its excitation produces the manifest universe. The cosmic ground state appears to have been last excited 13.8 billion years ago with the influx of energies liberated by the singularity we know as the Big Bang. The cosmos entered the excited state where it is a universal field of vibration producing waves of diverse amplitude, phase and frequency. The interaction of the waves creates patterns of interference, of which the clusters and higher-order superclusters are the matter-like entities of the universe.

Manifest Entities in the Excited State

The excitation of the ground state produces multifold patterns and clusters of patterns of coordinated vibration. It produces propagating waves such as streams of photons (EM waves), short-range attraction and repulsion waves (nuclear forces), and waves of long-range attraction (gravitational waves). It produces standing waves: stationary nodes in the excited-state wave field. Their coordinated vibration appears as quarks and particles constituted of quarks, including leptons, hadrons, baryons, bosons, fermions, and a variety of short-lived virtual particles.

The interference of nucleons and electrons creates more complex coordinated vibrations: the atoms of the elements. The coordinated vibration of atoms in turn produces molecules and multimolecular systems. The synchronous presence of these entities introduces space into the wave field of the excited-state cosmos, and their diachronic succession introduces time.

Some standing wave interference patterns comprise waves of coordinated frequency. (Phase coordination, as it is known, does not call for introducing additional energies; it is an intrinsic phenomenon in complex wave fields.) In-phase waves are mutually reinforcing rather than destructive, and in consequence the clusters they create are relatively stable. Some of the correlations are long-range and encompass vast regions of the excited-state wave field.

Some of the in-phase wave interference patterns constitute self-regenerating "autocatalytic" cycles. Those that create, or enable the creation of, other autocatalytic cycles are particularly stable: they constitute "cross-catalytic" cycles. These patterns and clusters of patterns of coordinated vibration constitute a domain of coherence in the excited-state wave field: our universe.

Two Kinds of Manifest Entities

The manifest entities of the universe are clusters of long-range coordinated in-phase standing waves. They are real-world Gestalts: "figures" that stand out against the "ground" of chaotic, less coordinated wave configurations.

Two types of wave interference clusters are particularly noteworthy. One type appears as physically real objects, and the other type as phenomena of mind or consciousness. The former corresponds to the Cartesian concept of *res extensa:* they are quanta, atoms, molecules, and multiatomic and multimolecular systems. The latter are *res cogitans*, elements of mind. Both physical and mind phenomena are clusters of comparatively stable wave interference patterns in the wavefield of the excited-state cosmos. Their presence indicates diversity, but not duality, in the universe.

Neither matter nor mind is the basic reality. The basic reality is the intelligence that coordinates the clusters of vibration that appear as object-like and mind-like phenomena. This accords with Wolfgang Pauli's prophecy: "It is my personal opinion that in the science of the future reality will neither be 'psychic' nor 'physical' but somehow both and somehow neither."[4]

Frequency Domains, Temporal Endurance, and the Manifestations of Entities

Object-like clusters of waves vibrate at a band of relatively high-frequency vibration in the spectrum of vibrations, and mind-like clusters vibrate at a lower frequency band. However, frequency levels cannot be univocally determined, since the waves that compose the clusters vibrate at variable, context-dependent frequencies. This is true of the matter-like clusters at the high-frequency band where biomolecules, for example, have been found to resonate at extremely high bandwidths. The frequency of patterns that create mind-like Gestalts cannot be measured with current instrumentation, but it is known that the waves produced by the brain when such phenomena appear are at the lower end of the EEG spectrum, in the Delta, Theta, and Alpha range.

Complex object-like clusters, including those we recognize as living systems, have been building up in the universe. The more complex among these clusters oscillate across a wide band of frequencies and embrace both high-frequency object-like clusters and low-frequency mind-like clusters.

High-frequency object-like clusters have a finite existence. With the possible exception of electrons, all quantum particles decay in time. Some virtual particles "tunnel" below the level of manifest reality, and atoms above the weight of uranium radiate off their elements. Complex molecules are subject to decomposition, and cells composed of molecules, although capable of indefinite division, encounter *apoptosis,* programmed cell-death.

In the high-frequency band, object-like clusters are composed of high-amplitude waves and are relatively manifest, whereas in the low-frequency band the waves are of lower amplitude and the Gestalts they create are correspondingly less defined: ideas, intuitions, and ineffable sensations.

The Nonlocality of Manifest Entities

The comparatively stable clusters of wave interference that constitute the manifest entities of the universe are phenomenologically distinct, but they are not ontologically separate.

They are "nonlocal" manifestations in this coherence domain of the cosmos.

Nonlocality and entanglement are recognized in regard to the microscale entities that appear at the ultrasmall region of the high-frequency band. Quarks and the quantum particles composed of quarks appear as intrinsic parts of the fields in which they manifest. An electron, for example, is a high-density configuration of fields around the nucleus; it manifests where the field configuration is densest. However, clusters above the quantum-scale manifest as separate objects.

Due to the presence of complex, in-phase self-stabilizing long-range clusters of interfering standing waves, the universe is populated by a variety of object-like as well as mind-like entities: physical objects ranging from quanta to galaxies, and individual minds or consciousnesses at various levels of articulation and evolution. These are individually real, but not individually separate, entities.

The In-Formation of Manifest Entities

In its ground state, the cosmos is a coherent sea of vibration; a pure potential. The waves that emerge in its excited state are the actualization of this potential, and they convey the vibration of the ground state. Consequently the clusters that constitute the manifest entities of the universe are in-formed by the vibration of the cosmic ground state. Object-like patterns and clusters of patterns in the high-frequency band are in-formed by the constraints and degrees of freedom that constitute the laws of nature; and mind-like patterns in the low-frequency band reflect and resonate with the intelligence that permeates the wave field of the excited-state cosmos.*

The Deep Dimension

In contemporary physics, the ground state of an object is its lowest energy state, and this state is sourced in the quantum vacuum. The quantum vacuum, however, despite its denomination is not empty space; it is filled with fluctuating fields. Given that the fields fluctuate around the expectation value of zero, the quantum vacuum is a zero-point field. It is more than an energy field: it is the domain David Bohm called the implicate order, the dimension into which manifest entities "enfold," and from which they "unfold."

The quantum vacuum is the deep dimension of the cosmos: the source of the in-formation of the clusters that manifest in the dimension of the excited state. The closer the clusters vibrate to the deep dimension, the more they are in-formed by the intelligence intrinsic to the cosmos.

---

* This tenet conflicts with the conventional spiritual view: that the higher vibrations are vibrations at a higher frequency (the commonly voiced aspiration is to "raise the frequency of one's vibration"). It is more correct, however, to maintain that the vibrations we can regard as higher are vibrations of a lower frequency. High-frequency vibrations constitute highly excited states of intense but narrowly focused consciousness. The wave-clusters vibrating at these frequencies are short-range and relatively short-lived. The low-frequency clusters, on the other hand, have a longer range and are comparatively enduring. They allow contact and communication with a wider range of consciousness phenomena and are the truly "higher" vibrations. The Beatles had it right when they sang "the deeper you go, the higher you fly." The meaningful aspiration is thus to lower rather than to raise the frequency of one's vibration, for example, by entering a state of deep meditation, prayer, aesthetic enjoyment, or unconditional love.

The Deep Dimension in Classical Philosophy and in Modern Science

The creation stories of the world's religious and spiritual systems speak of a primordial domain out of which the manifest world would have emerged. In some Eastern metaphysics this domain is a cosmic egg, whereas in the Old Testament it is a dark and formless sea. "In the beginning God created the heaven and the earth; and the earth was without form, and void; and darkness [was] upon the face of the deep. And the Spirit of God moved upon the face of the waters" (Genesis 1:1–2). From this spaceless and timeless void God created light, the firmament, day and night, and all the things that exist the world.

The recognition of a deep dimension beyond space and time is a recurrent feature in the history of philosophy. Plato called it the sphere of Forms and Ideas, and identified it as the seat of the Soul. The Hellenic philosophers gave it various names: Pythagoras called it *Kosmos*, and Plotinus *The One*.

A century before Plato, Pythagoras spoke of the "aether" as the fifth element of the world, in addition to earth, air, fire, and water. Aristotle pointed out that this element does not have any properties; it does not become hot or cold, as the other elements do. Plotinus elaborated this concept in the fourth treatise of his *Second Ennead*. Based on first principles, he reasoned that matter must exist in two forms: one that makes up the material world where things have form and can change form, and another that is devoid of form. The creative principle of the cosmos gives rise to formless matter, and formless matter in turn gives rise to shifting, form-changing matter.

Plato illustrated the idea of the two dimensions in his famous parable of the cave. Think of a cave, he said, filled with prisoners chained to the floor in such a way that they can only see the wall in front of them. The opening of the cave is behind them, and the light that enters casts shadows on the far wall of the cave. The prisoners see only the shadows and begin to give names to what they see. They come to believe that it is the real world, yet the real world is behind them. It takes an enlightened mind not to mistake the shadow-world for the real world.

The Chinese sage Lao-Tse offered the same basic insight. All things originate in the Tao (also known as the Dao), and all things return to the Tao. The Tao is the creator of everything—of Heaven, Mother Earth, and countless planets, stars, galaxies, and universes. It is both the source of all things and the destination of all things. It is not observable in itself, and not even nameable. Lao Tse said, "Tao cannot be seen by our eyes. Tao cannot be heard by our ears. Tao cannot be touched by our hands." It has no shape and no space and no time. What is it, then? The Tao is the "blurred reality"—the veiled realm of the world.

This concept held sway also in India. In the Hindu concept Brahman is the eternal and eternally unchanging reality. The world of space and time is *lila*, the unceasing play of appearance and disappearance, of forming and dissolution. It is a surface manifestation of the deeper, beyond-space and time reality of Brahman.

The idea that the observed world is informed by a higher or deeper dimension is present in cultures both East and West. It is present in the animistic-naturalistic cultures of indigenous societies as well.[5]

The *rishis* ("seers") of India named the deep dimension of reality "Akasha." A Sanskrit term, Akasha stands for the fifth element of the world, beyond *vata* (air), *agni* (fire), *ap* (water), and *prithivi* (earth). Akasha holds all the elements within itself, but it is also outside of them. In his classic *Raja Yoga,* Swami Vivekananda wrote that at the beginning of creation there was only Akasha, and at the end of the present cycle the solids, liquids, and gases all melt into the Akasha again, to arise in the next cycle. The Akasha cannot be perceived; it can only be seen when it has become gross, has taken form. It is "the omnipresent, all-penetrating existence. Everything that has form, everything that is the result of combination, is evolved out of this Akasha."[6] In more recent times Paramahansa Yogananda said that the Akasha is the "subtle background" against which everything in the universe becomes perceptible.

The Akasha is an intuitive, yet remarkably up-to-date concept of a deep dimension underlying the universe. At the dawn of modern science this dimension was considered to be a space-filling substance, the ether. The heavenly bodies are not fixed points on the crystal spheres of Aristotelian and Ptolemaic cosmology, said modern science pioneer Giordano Bruno, but move under their own impetus through the substance called *spiritus* or *aether.*

In the nineteenth century the idea of the ether entered the mainstream of science. According to the theory of French physicist Jacques Fresnel, the ether fills all space. It is not observable in itself, but produces observable effect.

Fresnel claimed that his materialist conception of the ether is testable: the friction created by movement through the ether must be measurable. At the turn of the twentieth century Albert Michelson and Edward Morley created an ingenious experiment involving the rotation of the earth in relation to the sun to test the ether-drag hypothesis. However, the predicted effect did not materialize. Michelson warned that the experiments did not disprove the existence of the ether, only of a particular theory of it, but physicists discarded the hypothesis of a space-filling ether and embraced Einstein's relativity theory in its place.

However, the concept of a beyond-spacetime dimension came back to physics in the second half of the twentieth century. John Wheeler reported that at the Planck-scale (10^{-35} meter in space and 10^{-44} second in time) the energy levels of the universe exceed the known dimensions of spacetime. Spacetime could not be the entire reality of the universe.

As already noted, David Bohm called the dimension of reality beyond space and time the implicate order. In that enfolded dimension, space and time no longer determine the relationship between different elements. There is a deeper, more fundamental connection, and it is from that dimension that our concepts of space and time and of separately existing entities derive.

A dimension beyond spacetime is also implied by the Schrödinger wave equation. This equation incorporates a series of variables within a wave function that defines all the possible states of a system in the form of distributed probabilities. It permits the extrapolation of the evolution of the probabilities through time. The probabilities "collapse" into a classical state when the system is observed or measured, but prior to its observation or measurement the state of the system is probabilistic. In that state the system is not in spacetime, but in a so-called complex plane that embraces the superposed probabilities of its state.

Until recently, physicists considered the complex plane a mathematical device, useful for predicting the behavior of quantum systems over time, but not an element of physical reality. This view is being reassessed. The complex plane appears to be a dimension or domain of the physical world beyond spacetime.

Recognizing the existence of this domain resolves puzzles that have plagued quantum physics from the beginning. It is the key, among other things, to the so-called "measurement problem." How does the abstract wavefunction of a particle turn into, or generate, the observed and presumably real wavepacket? The wavefunction describes the pristine state of the particle, prior to interaction or measurement. The wavepacket is what results when interaction or measurement takes place: then the wavefunction "collapses." The wavefunction itself is abstract (it is made up of imaginary numbers), whereas the wavepacket is real; it is an observable/measurable entity. But how can abstract information generate physical events? Without recognizing a dimension that is part of the cosmos (but is not the dimension of spacetime), this question cannot be answered.

The answer is not the "many worlds" hypothesis (that a new universe is split off at every collapse of the wavefunction), but that there is a dimension of the cosmos that is beyond the reach of observation and measurement. The wavefunction of the particle, as all laws of nature, originates in the deep dimension—in the "quantum vacuum," "zero-point field," or "implicate order." An integral part of the cosmos, that dimension interacts with the observable/measurable dimension. It "in-forms" the manifest universe, providing the cosmic "quantum information" that defines phenomena in spacetime and, by creating manifest entities, creates spacetime itself. As the new map of the cosmos maintains, clusters of vibration in the manifest high-frequency domain of spacetime are in-formed by the beyond-spacetime constraints and degrees of freedom that we know as the laws of nature (see "the in-formation of manifest entities," above).

The as yet not fully understood "tunneling" of particles beyond the reach of observability/measurability likewise suggests the existence of a deep dimension. A wormhole is said to be a shortcut between two separate points in spacetime, but travel ("tunneling") through a wormhole is not travel in spacetime. When a particle passes through a wormhole it is traveling in what Haramein among others calls "the spacetime-memory micro-wormhole network"—a network that is beyond spacetime.

The wavefunction of quanta and of higher-order systems constituted of quanta, the same as all laws of nature, is beyond spacetime. A striking recent addition to the repertory of these beyond-spacetime realities is the geometrical object known as the amplituhedron. The work of Nima Arkani-Hamed of the Institute for Advanced Study and his former student Jaroslav Trinka, the amplituhedron simplifies the calculation of scattering amplitudes in particle interactions in reference to a geometrical object that has as many dimensions as the interaction it describes.*

Arkani-Hamed noted that beyond making calculations easier and perhaps leading the way to understanding quantum gravity, the discovery of the amplituhedron may cause a profound shift in our concept of reality: We may have to give up the idea that space and time are the fundamental elements of reality. Space and time would have originated from a ground of pure geometry; in a deep dimension that is not *in* spacetime, but *in-forms* spacetime.

* Previously, the number and variety of the particles that result from the collision of two or more particles (their scattering amplitude) were calculated by diagrams created by Richard Feynman in 1948. But the number of diagrams required for the calculation was so large that until supercomputers came on line even simple interactions could not be fully calculated. (Describing the scattering amplitude in the collision of two gluons, for example, which results in four less-energetic gluons, required 220 Feynman diagrams with thousands of terms.) A few decades ago a better approach emerged. Patterns were discerned that suggest a coherent geometrical structure. This structure was initially described by BCFW (Ruth Britto, Freddy Cacharo, Bo Feng and Edward Witten) recursion relations. The BCFW diagrams abandon variables such as position and time and substitute for them strange variables—called "twistors"—beyond space and time. They suggest that two fundamental tenets of quantum field physics do not hold: locality and unitarity. Particle interactions are not limited to local positions in space and time, and the probabilities of their outcome do not add up to one. The amplituhedron is a further development of the BCFW twistor diagrams.

Postscript: Is the Deep Dimension a Hologram?

The vibration of the ground state of the cosmos, we said, in-forms the clusters of vibration that appear in its excited state. Given that this vibration in-forms all phenomena in the universe, the question arises whether the deep dimension would be a hologram.*

The idea that the phenomena we encounter in the world are projections of holographic codes is widely discussed in physics. The holographic theory of the universe was originally proposed by David Bohm in 1980,[7] and it gained support when astrophysicist Jakob Bekenstein calculated the informational content of a black hole. Surprisingly, the "Bekenstein bound" corresponds not to the volume of a black hole, but to its boundary. This prompted Gerard 't Hooft to suggest that the information of any 3D volume in space is equivalent to 2D information at the periphery of that space. The 3D objects we observe are projections of 2D codes at the spacetime periphery.

Experimental confirmation of the theory came in 2013, when Fermilab physicist Craig Hogan offered a hypothesis that could be tested by observation. He suggested that the fluctuations observed by the German gravity wave detector GEO600

* A hologram is an image produced by the interference of two sets of waves: a set of object waves and a set of reference waves. The object waves are directed towards the object. They encode the intensity changes and phase shifts reflecting the features of the object as the waves reach it and are reflected away from it. When the reference waves are directed back toward the remodulated object waves, they create an interference pattern that records the phase shifts of the object waves relative to the reference waves. This pattern codes the phase shift information from which a static three-dimensional image of the object is constituted through a so-called Fourier (more exactly Gabor) transform.

may be due to the graininess of space (according to string theory, as the supersmall scale space is not smooth but patterned by minuscule ripples: it is "grainy"). It turned out that the inhomogeneities found by GEO600 are not gravity waves, as first hypothesized by the experimenters—the instruments capable of registering such superminute waves became available only in early 2016—but they could be ripples in the fine structure of space. This would be the case if they were 3D projections of the 2D Planck-dimensional codes that paper the periphery of spacetime. If the grains found by GEO600 were precisely the size that 2D Planck-dimensional codes at the surface of spacetime would produce in the volume of spacetime, Hogan's hypothesis would be confirmed. Subsequent observations showed that they are precisely of the required dimensions.

Further experimental support for the holographic theory was produced by Yoshifumi Hyakutake and colleagues at Ibaraki University in Japan. They computed the internal energy of a black hole, the position of its event horizon, its entropy and several other properties based on the predictions of string theory and the effects of virtual particles. Hyakutake, together with Masanori Hanada, Goro Ishiki and Jun Nishimura, then calculated the internal energy of the corresponding lower-dimensional cosmos with no gravity. They found that the two calculations match. The internal energy of a black hole and the internal energy of the corresponding lower-dimensional cosmos are the same. Black holes, as well as the cosmos as a whole, appear to be holographic.

In collaboration with Leonard Susskind, Gerard 't Hooft suggested that if a 3D star can be encoded on a black hole's 2D event horizon, the same may be true of all things within the area of spacetime. (The area of spacetime is calculated as the area covered by light waves—streams of photons—since the Big Bang 13.8 billion years ago. Its growing periphery is now 42 billion light years from the Earth. It is said to be a 2D surface "papered" by the 2D codes that create 3D structures within the volume of spacetime.)

On first sight, the idea that the 3D things we encounter in the world are holograms seems preposterous. Yet significant evidence is surfacing in support of this hypothesis. Self-similar (fractal) patterns, suggesting that they may be projections of holographic codes, are discovered in field after field of investigation, from the spacing of galaxies to the frequency and energy of earthquakes (which appear to follow the Gutenberg-Richter power law), even to the Milankovitch cycles that describe changes in the planet's orbital eccentricity, axial tilt, and precessional wobbles.

Fractal processes are also found to underlie the morphology of biological systems. The processes of differentiation of the 256 different kinds of cells in the human body appear to be governed by multifractal attractors, and it appears that the thousand trillion connections in the human brain are compacted into fractally folded and branching structures. The developmental paths of both individual growth and species evolution (ontogeny as well as phylogeny) exhibit fractal self-similarities.

Holographic information is not only decodable by the brain; the brain may actually operate on the basis of such information. The cerebral mechanisms for the decoding of holographic signals has been outlined by Karl Pribram. According to Pribram's "holonomic brain theory," dendrites attached to neurons in the brain branch in complex patterns and form the dendritic arbor. Information is encoded in the interference patterns of waves throughout the synapto-dendritic web. This is distributed information, where every part of the dendritic arbor processes all the information captured by the system as a whole.[8] Initially Pribram advanced the holonomic brain theory to account for holographically coded information originating in Bohm's explicate order, but in collaboration with Bohm he then explored the possibility that the holographic information received by the brain originates in the implicate order—the deep dimension of the cosmos.

Presently the idea that the deep dimension would be a hologram, and the things we observe in space and time would be its projection, is a hypothesis. It is a plausible hypothesis, however, given that it explains the entangled, nonlocal character of physical as well as mind-like phenomena in the universe, overcoming the outdated materialism and local realism of the classical paradigm.

CHAPTER 2

Consciousness

Classical physics maintained that all phenomena in the world originate in the interaction of particles of matter. Everything we observe, ourselves included, is the outcome of this interaction. There is no place for mind in the world. Mind and consciousness, if not entirely illusory, are the by-product of the interaction of neurons in the brain.

The truth of the brain-production theory of mind and consciousness is said to be borne out by observation. When the brain stops functioning, consciousness stops. This does not admit of exceptions: a dead brain cannot produce consciousness. Phenomena of consciousness beyond the brain must be fantasy. However, a different view of consciousness is coming to light. It appears that on occasion consciousness is present in the absence of a living brain.

Reports of consciousness without cerebral activity come from a variety of sources. They come from people who arrived at the portals of death and returned. They also come from spiritual masters as well as ordinary people, who enter a meditative, prayerful, deeply loving or otherwise extraordinary state of consciousness. They also come from psychic mediums who "channel" what appears to be the consciousness of people who are no longer living. Many such reports have been examined by scientists, medical doctors, physicists, and neurosurgeons, and a rapidly growing number among them affirm that they are veridical: there is reason to believe there is consciousness beyond the brain.

THE CONVENTIONAL THEORY

The currently generally accepted "conventional" theory holds that the human brain generates the consciousness that appears for us. It acts much like a turbine does. When a turbine functions, it generates electricity, which is a stream of electrons. When the brain functions, it generates consciousness, which is a stream of sensations. When the turbine shuts down, the electric current vanishes, and when the brain shuts down, the stream of sensations ceases. Already when brain functions are impaired, consciousness is distorted. And consciousness can be manipulated by interacting with the functioning of the brain, for example, by drugs, hypnosis, or surgery. All this is said to prove that consciousness is produced by the brain.

Challenges to the Conventional Theory

Evidence for the conventional brain production theory of consciousness appears strong, but it is circumstantial. The observation of the brain does not disclose consciousness; all it discloses are networks of neurons firing in complex sequences.

We observe a stream of sensations, feelings, volitions, and intuitions and ascribe them to the activity of the brain.

The brain production theory predicts that when the brain stops functioning, consciousness will vanish. This is a key prediction, and it can be tested by observation. We can observe the behavior of people whose brain stopped functioning and see whether they behave as we expect people without consciousness would behave, which is without awareness of themselves and of their surroundings. The prediction does not allow for exceptions. On the theory that the brain produces consciousness we could no more account for the presence of consciousness in a dead brain than we could account for electrical charge in a stationary turbine. An observation to the contrary would be critical counter-evidence for the conventional theory.

Counter-evidence did surface, however. In some cases, consciousness did not cease when the brain stopped working. Here we cite some of the many widely reported and *ipso facto* robust cases that lend substance to this claim.

Near-Death Experiences

One strand of evidence for the presence of consciousness in the absence of a functioning brain is furnished by people who have reached the portals of death and returned to the living. In some cases, critically sick people become temporarily brain dead, but then regain normal cerebral functions.

Near-death experiences (NDEs) are not as rare as most people think. Some investigators claim that at least six million people have reported near-death experiences, but the number may be as high as thirteen million in the US alone.[9] Brain-dead periods are not particularly rare. Brain function normally stops fifteen seconds after the cessation of heartbeat, and it takes about a minute for the life-support equipment in mobile ambulances and intensive care departments to come online. Thus there is often an interval when the patient is alive but without brain function. In that interval consciousness should be absent. But this is not always the case.

Some reports of NDE are surprisingly robust. The case of Pamela Reynolds, who died on May 29, 2010 at the age of fifty-three, is a case in point.[10] Pamela effectively died on the operating table before she truly died—nineteen years earlier. Her quasi-defunct condition was induced by a surgical team who attempted to remove an aneurism in her brain stem.

During her operation Pamela was clinically dead, with a flat EEG and no bodily functions. However, when her brain returned to normal functioning she described in detail what had taken place in the operating theater, including a description of what music was playing ("Hotel California" by the Eagles). She described a whole series of conversations among the medical team. She reported having watched the opening of her skull by the surgeon from a position above him, and described in detail the "Midas Rex" bone-cutting device and the distinct sound it made.

As she heard the bone saw activate about ninety minutes into the operation, Pam saw her body from the outside and felt herself being pulled out and into a tunnel of light. Yet there was a specially designed ear speaker in each of Pam's ears that shut out all external sounds. The speakers were broadcasting audible clicks, to confirm that there was no activity in her brain stem. She had been given a general anesthetic that should have assured that she was fully unconscious. She should not have been able either to see or to hear anything.

NDEs occur in every part of the world, in people young and old. It is critical counter-evidence for the old paradigm theory of consciousness. There is no known physiological mechanism that could account for conscious experience in a nonfunctioning brain. The consciousness that then occurs cannot have been a product of the brain.

Out-of-Body Experiences

Veridical perceptions in the absence of brain function are not limited to people who are close to death; they also occur in meditative states of consciousness and in states triggered by accidents and other traumatic events.

In some cases, people have perceptions that locate them beyond their brain. This is known as the OBE: the out-of-body experience. OBEs are at least as frequent as NDEs. In a recent survey of a cross-section of the US population, ten percent of the people who were interviewed said that they found themselves outside of their body at least once in their lives.[11]

Kenneth Ring investigated hundreds of cases of OBEs and came up with surprising findings. It appears that in an OBE, blind people can "see." It is not a restored eye function that produces the vision—the visual experience is fundamentally different from normal eyesight. In an OBE people experience a kind of perception Ring describes as "transcendental awareness." It occurs also in people with highly impaired vision and even in the congenitally blind. Overall, eighty percent of persons who were either blind from birth, became blind, or had seriously impaired vision reported vision-like impressions during their out-of-body experience. They described their surroundings, sometimes in great detail, with a sense of sharp, subjectively perfect acuity.[12]

As reported by Kenneth Ring, Vicky, a young woman who has been blind almost since birth, gave this description of her experience while she was in a near-death condition.

> When I was going into the dining room or into the dormitory generally, of course, I would perceive the things by bumping into them, or by touching them, or whatever. This time I could see them from a distance. It was not like I had to be right on top of them, touching them, or sitting on them or whatever, before I was aware of them. I don't imagine things very well in my mind until I get there. I have a lot of trouble dealing with images of things when I am not directly there. This time, it was like I didn't have to be right there to be aware of the chairs. I saw the metal chairs that we sat on as children and the round tables in the dining

> room, and they had plastic tablecloths on them. I didn't have to touch the plastic tablecloths to be aware of them.[13]

This kind of visual awareness, Ring concluded, has nothing in common with dreams, and is not a retrospective reconstruction of prior experiences or just a vague sensing of the surroundings. Nor is it restored eyesight, for it occurs even when the perceived object is shielded from the eyes. This "transcendental awareness" is reported in visual terms because the language of vision is the only language available to the perceivers to describe them.

Remote Viewing

Perception of the "transcendental" kind has been reported also in remote viewing experiments. In these experiments individuals demonstrate the ability to give detailed descriptions of persons, places, and objects even when they are shielded from them by time or space, or both.

Studies have shown that the precision and accuracy of the viewer's perception is influenced by his or her state of mind. Stephan Schwartz, one of a small group of cognitive scientists who created the Remote Viewing protocols, explored the issue exhaustively and found that personality as such is not the important factor.[14] The ability to engage in remote viewing, like other human abilities, is spread throughout the population in a bell-shaped curve: There is a small group at one end of people who are unusually gifted and a small group at the other end of people who either cannot or do not want to have the experience. In between there is a large majority of ordinary people who under certain conditions can engage in remote viewing. These conditions do not improve a person's native ability, but enhance the chances that it is being used. In this regard sustaining a relaxed but intentioned, focused awareness is a factor. Meditators usually do better than nonmeditators in performing tasks calling for nonlocal awareness.[15]

Schwartz reported that two other factors can be used to enhance the outcome of remote viewing sessions: numinosity and entropic process.[16] Numinosity is meant in the Jungian sense as a kind of information enriching process that occurs as the result of intentioned, focused awareness. An ancient spiritual shrine is easier to perceive than a warehouse: one has been the focus of untold thousands of individual acts of focused awareness while the other goes largely unnoticed. In turn, by entropic process a transition in an informational state is intended, such as a boiling kettle compared to a cold one or a person dying compared to a person merely lying in bed. Repeated experiments have shown that targets that are emotionally engaging and depict sudden, substantial, and unexpected changes elicit the strongest and most accurate non-eyesight–based "transcendental" awareness.

Channeled Experiences

There is also a distinctly esoteric form of evidence challenging the conventional theory. It appears that consciousness can exist independently of brain function not just under special circumstances, and not only during the temporary cessation of brain activity, but even in the permanent absence of brain function—when the individual is fully and irreversibly dead.

This claim is made by psychic mediums who, usually in a state of trance, "channel" contact with the consciousness of people who are no longer alive. Channeling can occur through various forms of extrasensory or nonsensory perception: by clairvoyance (seeing apparitions), clairaudience (hearing voices), clairsentience (physical sensations), or by a combination of the above. The authenticity of these experiences has encountered various objections, among them that the mediums themselves invent them, or that they pick them up from living persons.

There are cases, however, in which these possibilities can be effectively ruled out, because the experiences contain information that neither the mediums themselves could have accessed nor could any living person with whom they could have been in touch. The following is one case where the evidence is particularly robust. It is a game of chess played by a living chess grandmaster with a grandmaster who has been dead for decades.[17]

Wolfgang Eisenbeiss, an amateur chess player, engaged the medium Robert Rollans to transmit the moves of a game to be played with Viktor Korchnoi, the world's third-ranking grandmaster. His opponent was to be a player whom Rollans was to find in his trance state. Eisenbeiss gave Rollins a list of deceased grand masters and asked him to contact them and ask who would be willing to play. Rollins entered his state of trance and did so. On June 15, 1985, the former grandmaster Géza Maróczy responded and said that he was available. Maróczy was the third-ranking grandmaster in the year 1900. He was born in 1870 and died in 1951 at the age of eighty-one.

Rollans reported that Maróczy responded to his invitation as follows:

> I will be at your disposal in this peculiar game of chess for two reasons. First, because I also want to do something to aid mankind living on Earth to become convinced that death does not end everything, but instead the mind is separated from the physical body and comes up to us in a new world, where individual life continues to manifest itself in a new unknown dimension. Second, being a Hungarian patriot, I want to guide the eyes of the world into the direction of my beloved Hungary.

Korchnoi and Maróczy began a game that was frequently interrupted due to Korchnoi's poor health and numerous travels. It lasted seven years and eight months. Speaking through Robert Rollans, Maróczy gave his moves in the standard form: for example, "5. A3 – Bxc3+". Korchnoi gave his own moves to Rollans in the same form, but by ordinary communication. Every move was analyzed and recorded. It turned out that the game was played at the grandmaster level and that it exhibited the style for which Maróczy was famous. It ended on February 11, 1993, when at move 48 Maróczy resigned. Subsequent analysis showed that it was a wise decision: five moves later Korchnoi would have achieved checkmate.

In this case the medium Rollans channeled information he did not possess in his ordinary state of consciousness. And this information was so expert and precise that it is unlikely that anyone Rollans would have known would have possessed it. This is one case among several others that suggests that it is possible to communicate with entities that have a sense of self, carry memories of physical existence, and manifest a wish to communicate. Yet they are not associated with a living brain and body.

Instrumental Transcommunication

Deceased individuals cannot only communicate through psychic mediums; they seem able to leave messages also on electronic instruments. Known as Instrumental Transcommunication (ITC, including EVC, Electronic Voice Communication), it consists of anomalous voices appearing on audio recorders, radios, and even on ordinary telephones. Anomalous images may also appear on TV receivers tuned to the white noise of an empty channel. Hundreds of controlled experiments on ITC have been reported in various parts of the world, and they testify that, although it lacks a satisfactory explanation, the phenomenon is real.[18]

Alternative Conceptions

If consciousness beyond the brain is not a chimera but a bona fide phenomenon, the conventional theory of consciousness is incorrect. Although most modern people think so, the consciousness that appears for us is not entirely the product of our brain.

There are cogent alternatives to the conventional brain-production theory of consciousness. A widely discussed alternative was suggested by William James already in his 1899 Ingersoll Lecture on Immortality.[19] James spoke of a "veiled" domain from where information would be transmitted by the brain. The transmission theory, he said, is a good alternative to the "production theory" because it can account for a phenomenon that is anomalous for the production theory: consciousness beyond the brain.

The transmission theory is embraced today by a growing number of investigators. Astrophysicist David Darling wrote:

> The brain does not produce consciousness at all, any more than a television set creates the programs that appear on its screen. . . . On the contrary, the brain filters and restricts consciousness, just as our senses limit the totality of experience to which we might otherwise have access.[20]

Neurosurgeon Eben Alexander, previously an outspoken sceptic about NDEs and related consciousness phenomena, became convinced of the truth of the alternative theory after undergoing a week-long NDE. He wrote a book on his changing views and founded the Eternea organization, on the website of which he posted seven core statements.[21]

1. The enduring essence of consciousness extends beyond the brain, transcending it and capable of existing independently of it;

2. This aspect of consciousness is eternal in nature, unbounded by space, time, and matter, and is able to manifest in other forms and places throughout the spectrum of eternal existence;

3. All things in the cosmos are interconnected at the quantum level, influencing each other nonlocally and instantaneously, implying that all things are one in the grand web of creation;

4. The meaning and purpose of all existence and the organizing principle of the cosmos which drives the evolution of all things is to become greater expressions of harmony and love . . . loving all things unconditionally, including oneself;

5. There is a profound Intelligence or Source underlying the creation and evolution of the universe from which all things originate and to which all things return;

6. In an interconnected universe an intricate matrix of cause-effect relationships exists, suggesting that what we do to others we do to ourselves, which means that we reap what we sow; and

7. The good of the one and the good of the whole are mutually enhancing, affirming the ancient wisdom that the quality of both individual and collective existence is enhanced by bringing every aspect of creation into a state of complete unity, harmony and love.

Stephan Schwartz summarized the gist of the alternative views in the form of four conclusions addressing "the emerging paradigm incorporating nonlocal consciousness."

1. Only certain aspects of the mind are the result of physiologic processes.

2. Consciousness is causal, and physical reality is its manifestation.

3. All consciousnesses, regardless of their physical manifestations, are part of a network of life which they both inform and influence and are informed and influenced by.

4. Some aspects of consciousness are not limited by the spacetime continuum, and do not originate entirely within an organism's neuroanatomy.[22]

The Manifesto of the international summit on Post-Materialist Science, Spirituality and Society held at Canyon Ranch in Tucson, Arizona (February 7–9, 2015) outlined the substance of the alternative theory.

- Mind represents an aspect of reality as primordial as the physical world. Mind is fundamental in the universe; i.e., it cannot be derived from matter and reduced to anything more basic.
- There is a deep interconnectedness between mind and the physical world.
- Mind (will/intention) can influence the state of the physical world, and operate in a nonlocal (or extended) fashion; i.e., it is not confined to specific points in space, such as brains and bodies, nor to specific points in time, such as the present. . . . .
- The shift from materialist science to post-materialist science may be of vital importance to the evolution of the human civilization. It may be even more pivotal than the transition from geocentrism to heliocentrism.[23]

The Map of Consciousness

A credible alternative to the conventional theory of consciousness must explain how consciousness could exist beyond the brain. The map of the cosmos outlined in this book provides an answer. It tells us that "Object-like patterns and clusters of patterns in the high-frequency band are in-formed by the constraints and degrees of freedom that constitute the laws of nature; and mind-like patterns in the low-frequency band reflect and resonate with the intelligence that permeates the wave field of the excited-state cosmos" (Chapter 1). The mind-like patterns resonate with the ground-state intelligence of the cosmos. They are constituted of in-phase waves of low frequency and amplitude, hence they appear as "numinous," "spiritual," "dreamlike," or "ineffable," contrasting with the high frequency and high amplitude waves that manifest as physically real objects.

There is no such thing as color or sound in the universe, any more than there is matter. All that exists is vibration, clustering into patterns producing matter-like and mind-like Gestalts. Some clusters are received by sensory organs and are conveyed as electrical impulses to the brain, where they are decoded and give rise to the sensation of color, sound, texture, odor, and taste. In regard to sound, for example, waves in the air bring to vibration thousands of cilia (thin hairs) according to their frequency. The vibrations are compressed and amplified and then conveyed to the cochlea in the inner ear where the Corti organ transforms them into neural signals. The human ear decodes frequencies spanning about ten octaves. The human eye, in turn, responds to a smaller but likewise specific range of vibrations in the electromagnetic spectrum. The cornea acts as a convex lens that conveys streams of photons to the retina, where optical cells convert them into electrical impulses. Each human eye has more than 125 million optical cells, six or seven million of which are responsible for the sensation of color. The lowest frequency that produces visual sensation is in the region of 375 trillion Hertz; this produces the perception of red. The highest frequency is about 750 trillion Hertz, giving the color blue.

The vibrations that gives us the sights and sounds of the everyday world are of a relatively high frequency. There are, however, vibrations also of a lower frequency. Their decoding offers glimpses of a nonphysical but equally real world: the deep-dimensional world of mind or consciousness. These vibrations are not processed by specialized sensory organs but reach the organism through quantum-level resonance in a whole array of subneuronal networks. They do not produce Gestalts of physical objects, but forms and elements of consciousness. They are elements of the "transcendental awareness" that comes to light above all in NDEs, OBEs, after-death experiences, and in meditative and other nonordinary states of consciousness.

The vibrations that produce object-like and mind-like Gestalts in human consciousness exist objectively in the excited-state wave field of the universe. They do not vanish when they are not transmitted and decoded whether by us, or by any other system in space and time.

Object-like and mind-like clusters of interfering waves are distinct but not separate: they interact and may be part of the same complex cluster. That cluster is a high-order pattern of wave interference. The living cell is an organization of molecules and molecular assemblies: a wave-interference *supercluster.* A human being is a multicellular system, a cluster of superclusters: a wave-interference *hypercluster.* It oscillates across a wide range of frequencies, some of which create object-like Gestalts, and others mind-like Gestalts. "Objective" physical phenomena and "subjective" mind phenomena are distinct but not categorically different phenomena. The map of consciousness and the map of the cosmos maps the same reality, it only focuses on different manifestations of it.

Both the high-frequency, object-like and the low-frequency, mind-like clusters evolve in the course of time. The matter-like clusters evolved from the entities we know as quanta to atoms, to molecules, and to complex multiatomic and multimolecular superclusters. Consciousness evolved in turn from the basic sensitivity exhibited by cells and simple multicellular organisms to the complex perceptive and cognitive systems investigated in contemporary psychology and consciousness studies. An evolved consciousness is a mind-like hypercluster of interfering low-frequency, low-amplitude waves.

In the low-frequency band, some in-phase and hence comparatively enduring wave-interference clusters maintain their identity in the welter of change around them: they appear as individual minds or consciousnesses. In the high-frequency band, object-like Gestalts typically have a shorter time span: they emerge and vanish in quicker succession.

In evolved organisms the high- and the low-frequency clusters conjugate and jointly form a psycho-physical hyper-cluster. The high-frequency component of that cluster—the body—is discontinuous, whereas the low-frequency component—the mind or consciousness—is, as we shall see, more persistent. In human beings, relatively continuous consciousness is associated with discontinuous bodies.

Both consciousness and body are in-formed by the vibration of the ground state of the cosmos. The body and the brain, and the organism as a whole, receive and resonate with the intelligence that permeates the universe.

Postscript: The End of Dualism

For the classical paradigm, mind is an epiphenomenon produced by the workings of the brain. Matter is fundamentally real, and mind is not. They are entirely different phenomena.

This dualist view is the heritage of the distinction introduced by Galileo in his theory of "primary" and "secondary" qualities. Primary qualities, he said, are properties of objects that are independent of the observer, such as solidity, extension, motion, number, and figure. Secondary qualities are introduced by the observer. These include, among others, color, taste, sound, and other "qualia." In *The Assayer* (1623) Galileo wrote that he considers secondary qualities mere names as far as the objects in which we locate them are concerned, since they are in the subjective consciousness of the observer.

There is no place for mind in in this dualistic world concept. Everything that exists is the product of random interactions among bits of matter ("mass-points") moving in accordance with mechanistic laws in passive space and indifferently flowing time. Life itself is the result of an unusually serendipitous sequence of random interactions among bits and configurations of mass points, constantly weeded for efficiency by the inexorable laws of natural selection. Mind is an epiphenomenon resulting from a natural selection among networks of neurons in the brain.

In the second decade of the twenty-first century, the mechanistic-materialistic view of reality and the dualistic concept of the world have run their course. The map emerging at science's cutting edge does not depict the world as a giant mechanism, but as a unitary realm of in-formed clusters of vibration. What we have been calling space is the origin as well as the destination of the clusters that emerge in the universe, and information, something we believed was only a product of the human mind, turned out to be a basic element of the cosmos. In the final count all things—mind and consciousness, as well as what we have been calling "matter"—are clusters of vibration in the excited-state wavefield of the universe.

CHAPTER 3

Existence

C*ogito ego sum*, said philosopher René Descartes. If I think, comprehend, then I exist. I can doubt nearly everything, but this I can believe without a shadow of a doubt.

We can pursue this reasoning in the context of a map of reality that recognizes that consciousness is a part of the cosmos. If I think, comprehend, then I am conscious—and if I am conscious, then I exist; I am part of the cosmos. This, too, I can believe with good reason.

We can go still further. I exist when, and as long as, I am conscious, and if I continue to be conscious beyond my brain, then I continue to exist beyond my brain. As far as logic is concerned, this conclusion is impeccable. But do I, do we, remain conscious beyond the brain? Do we survive the body?

In Chapter 2, we have seen that in cases of NDE and OBE consciousness transcends the living brain. We have also seen that there are *ipso facto* credible reports that consciousness persists beyond the life of the organism itself. In this chapter we look at the evidence for the survival of consciousness in light of some surprising, and surprisingly articulate, accounts. They are accounts of conscious experience by people who have died, and should not have had conscious experience—or experience of any kind at all.

SURVIVAL

The wisdom traditions are unanimous in affirming that the mind survives the body. Beyond the demise of the body, there is a "soul" or "spirit" that continues to exist, even if it does not exist on the same Plane as the body. The Planes of existence are not limited to the Physical Plane, where consciousness is associated with the body. There are also transcendent Planes such as the Astral, the Mental, the Causal, and the Etheric. On these Planes the soul or spirit continues to exist beyond space and time.

The Astral Plane is the closest to the Physical Plane. It is said to be the first that consciousness enters after the demise of the body. The next higher Plane is usually identified as the Mental Plane, although some shamanic traditions claim that the next Plane is the Causal, and the Mental follows thereafter. Most traditions agree, however, that the highest Plane is the Etheric. It is the doorway to the eighth chakra and therewith to the opening of the transcendental realm of cosmic consciousness.

The insights of the wisdom traditions were not born yesterday: They repose on millennia of experience handed down in the world's great cultural traditions. The doctrines that convey the insights are authoritative, but their acceptance is a matter of faith. There is evidence for the claims, however, that can be independently investigated. It is in the form of reports of consciousness beyond death. They are not, as we said, firsthand reports from the person with this consciousness, because when the experiences took place the individual was dead. Yet that individual could, it seems, communicate his or her experience to the living.

In the following we review some of these reports, beginning with those that indicate the presence of consciousness immediately following the death of the body of the individual.

Existence After Death

Reports of consciousness beyond the body are channeled by psychic mediums. According to these reports, existence after death is not a descent into nothingness. It is also not merely a sleep-like subsistence, awaiting an ultimate trumpet call. It is a conscious journey on the transcendental Planes of existence that begins at the moment of death. In the following we sample some of the more robust and articulate of these reports.

Rosemary Brown's Report of the Experience of Philosopher Bertrand Russell

Bertrand Russell was a lifelong champion of thinking free of speculative, "metaphysical" accruements. He did not hesitate to say that he did not believe in life after death. Yet, after his death, the trance-medium Rosemary Brown channeled a number of messages that came purportedly from him.

After announcing that he now believes in God "without equivocation and with a positive intellectual comprehension which was and is the sole acceptable proposition," Russell said,

> You may not believe that it is I, Bertrand Arthur William Russell, who am saying these things, and perhaps there is no conclusive proof that I can offer through this somewhat restrictive medium. Those with an ear to hear may catch the echo of my voice in my phrases, the tenor of my tongue in my tautology; those who do not wish to hear will no doubt conjure up a whole table of tricks to disprove my retrospective rhetoric.

Russell said that mind-to-mind communication is the way to communicate with discarnate minds, but calmed fears that living people would be invaded by messages from the dead. "As a rule," he said, "it is possible only to touch in thought those whose minds have a similar attunement." Everyone has his own wavelength, he noted, and can only receive upon that frequency."[24]

Among Russell's subsequent messages was one that described the experience he had following his own death.

> After breathing my last breath in my mortal body, I found myself in some sort of extension of existence that held no parallel as far as I could estimate, in the material dimension I had recently experienced. I observed that I was occupying a body predominantly bearing similarities to the physical one I had vacated forever; but this new body in which I now resided seemed virtually weightless and very volatile, and able to move in any direction with the minimum

of effort. I began to think I was dreaming and would awaken all too soon in that old world, of which I had become somewhat weary to find myself imprisoned once more in that ageing form which incased a brain that had waxed weary also and did not always want to think when *I* wanted to think.

Several times in my life, I had thought I was about to die; several times I had resigned myself with the best will that I could muster to ceasing to be. The idea of B.R. no longer inhabiting the world did not trouble me unduly. Befitting, I thought, to give the chap (myself) a decent burial and let him be. Now here I was, still the same I, with the capacities to think and observe sharpened to an incredible degree. I felt earth-life suddenly seemed very unreal almost as it had never happened. It took me quite a long while to understand that feeling until I realized at last that matter is certainly illusory although it does exist in actuality; the material world seemed now nothing more than a seething, changing, restless sea of indeterminable density and volume.

Jane Sherwood's Account of the After-Death Experience of E.K.

Jane would enter an altered state of consciousness, poise a pencil lightly over paper, and write phrases of which she had no knowledge in her normal state of consciousness. She channeled in this way a message from an entity who identified himself only as E.K.

E.K. reported that, following his death, he found himself awake in what he called the transition state. He rose, feeling marvelously refreshed and happy. He wandered for awhile in the "something-nothing" surroundings of a curious world and was unable to make any sense of it. The brooding silence drugged him into unconsciousness for a long time, but when he next woke his body felt quite different, no longer frail and weak, but vigorous and ready for anything as though he had suddenly stepped back into youth. Then E.K. experienced a panoramic life-review after which he fell asleep. When he awoke from that slumber he found himself on a hillside. He described the view:

> This was no earthly beauty. There was light *on* things and *in* them so that everything proclaimed itself vividly alive. Grass, trees, and flowers were so lighted inwardly by their own beauty that the soul breathed in the miracle of perfection . . . I am almost at a loss to describe the heavens as I saw them from my hillside. The light radiated from no one direction, it was a glowing, universal fact, bathing everything in its soft radiance so that the sharp shadows and dark edges which define objects on earth were missing. Each thing glowed or sparkled with its own light and was lighted as well by the circumambient splendor. The sky, as I looked upward, was like a pearl gleaming with opalescent colors. There was a

> suggestion of unfathomable depth of space as the shimmering colors parted their transparencies to show the infinite abyss. . . .
>
> Above all, I was happy. The lovely import of our journey from cradle to grave and through the valley of the shadow to arrive naked and reborn into this larger life, sang its themes of life triumphant until I was in an ecstasy of love and worship of the whole of which I was a rejoicing part.[25]

Tulku Thondup's Report of the Experience of Tibetan Delogs

The Tibetan master Tulku Thondup gave this account of the experience of delogs, Tibetan deep meditators who seem able to leave their body and return to report on what they experienced. The following is their report of the Blissful Pure Land they experienced when they left their body.

> The terrain of the Blissful Pure Land is soft and even, like the palm of a youthful hand. It is boundless, young, fresh, tender, and comforting to the touch, with no thorns, pebbles, rocks, or slopes. It is quiet, peaceful, joyful, and immaculate. It is made of seven precious materials and adorned with golden designs without any trace of harshness, grossness, roughness, filth, dullness, or decay. It is bright and colorful, emitting rays of light. In this very pure land,

> other immeasurable Buddha pure lands appear as reflections in the face of a clear mirror. . . .
>
> This pure land has no dark or ordinary mountains, but it is adorned with many kinds of smooth mountains of precious gems with high and low peaks. Here and there, the mountains are adorned with heaps of precious gems, mines of precious treasures, caves of precious jewels, and huts made of exquisite vines. . . . This pure land is adorned with chains of wide and deep lakes, ponds, and rivers where many beings are at play with great ease. Comfortable steps of precious gems lead you to the ponds and lakes filled with uncontaminated water. [26]

The above are reports from persons who had lived in widely different cultural settings. They show that basically the same kind of experience appears in different forms for people in different cultures.

There are differences also in the experience of people coming from the same cultural setting but from different socioeconomic strata. This is shown by experiences channeled by the trance medium George Wood. Wood seemed entirely possessed by the entities he channeled, speaking as the entity that possessed him.

George Wood's Account of the Experience of the Farmer George Hopkins

> I just had a stroke, or seizure, or heart attack. Or something of that sort. As a matter of fact I was

> harvesting. I felt a bit peculiar, thought it was the sun and went down the 'edge.' I felt a bit drowsy, a bit peculiar, and must have dozed off. But dear, oh dear, I had such a shock. . . . I must be dreaming I couldn't make head or tail of it. It never struck me at all that I was dead . . . I saw one or two of my old cronies. They all sort of seemed to walk through me. No one seemed to make any comment about me. I thought this a how-de-do.
>
> I stood there for a bit trying to work it out. Then I saw someone hurrying down the road like mad to the doctor's. He rushed in, pushed past me and everybody, and next moment I heard them talking about me. I thought what the hell's wrong? I'm here! I heard them say I was dead!

After the burial Woods, alias Hopkins, saw himself walking behind other people on the path from the cemetery. Directly in front of him and coming towards him was his wife.

> But not my wife as I had known her, in the past few years of her life. But as I knew her when she was a young girl. She looked beautiful, really beautiful. And with her I could see one of my brothers who died when he was about seventeen or eighteen. A nice looking boy who was fair-haired. They were laughing and joking and coming up to me. I thought well here I am and there they are, so I am all right. They're sure to know what to do now.

> My wife and brother made a proper fuss of me, saying how sorry they were that they were late. They said, "We know you hadn't been too well, but we had no idea you were coming as sudden as you were. We got the message but we're sorry we couldn't get here quicker."
>
> I thought that's odd. How the hell do they get about? I knew I'd got about, but as far as I was concerned I seemed to be walking about, same as I did before, except that everything was much lighter. I didn't seem to have any heaviness of the body, and no more aches and pains like I used to have.

Wood also channeled the after-death experience of Robert Hugh Benson, the son of the Archbishop of Canterbury, himself a priest.

> I suddenly felt a great urge to rise up. I had no *physical* feeling whatever, very much in the same way that physical feeling is absent during a dream, but I was mentally alert, however much my body seemed to contradict such a condition. Immediately I had this distinct prompting to rise, I found that I was actually doing so. I then discovered that those around my bed did not seem to perceive what I was doing, since they made no effort to come to my assistance, nor did they try in any way to hinder me.[27]

The frustration of seeing and attempting to communicate with living friends and relatives who do not see the person experiencing them is a frequent feature of the after-death experience. It is reported in the Tibetan Book of the Dead, the *Bardo Thödol* as well. When what the *Bardo Thödol* calls "the consciousness principle"

> getteth outside the body, it sayeth to itself 'Am I dead or am I not dead?' It cannot determine. It seeth its relatives and connexions as it had been used to seeing them before . . . can hear all the weeping and wailing of his friends and relatives, and, although he can see them and can hear them calling upon him, they cannot hear him calling upon them, so he goeth away displeased.[28]

Frustration due to failure of communicating with the living is a frequent feature of after-death experiences, but it is not a strongly negative feature. Strongly negative experiences are rare, as shown by the repertory of reports compiled by the medium Berry Greene with Neville Randall. After fifteen years, with occasional intervals due to illness, Randall and Greene accumulated a library of 500 vivid accounts describing the experience of death and its aftermath. Most of the accounts show that "the dead" took a while to realize that they were dead, as "the moment of death was a dream that changed imperceptibly to a new sense of reality." But none of the accounts speak of a strongly negative experience, such as being frightened or in pain.[29]

Existence Between Lives

Conscious experience beyond death is not uniform; it appears to be a journey with different phases and on different Planes.

Reports of conscious experience on various Planes date back to antiquity. They are conveyed in Hinduism in the *Advaita Vedanta* and are present in Shamanism and Hermeticism, in Neoplatonism and Gnosticism, in the Kabbalah as well as in theosophy and anthroposophy. In more recent times Paramhansa Yogananda described higher Planes in his *Autobiography of a Yogi.*[30] After death, he wrote, individuals first enter the Astral Plane. There they work out the tasks of their karma through astral incarnations, and if they do not succeed, they are reborn to the earthly plane to face the tasks that await them in their next life. But if they attain the meditative state of *samadhi*, they progress to the "Illumined Astral Plane," and from there they may reach the subtler Causal Planes and achieve the supreme state of "final unification."

Most traditions agree that the interlife phase begins on the Astral Plane, and through various intermediary stages progresses to the Causal and then to the Etheric Plane. On the Astral Plane, according to the Canadian psychic Sylvie Ouellet, the vibrations emitted by the emotional body of the deceased can be captured by living people, and information can be exchanged between them.[31]

Quellet claims that the Plane beyond the Astral is the Mental. Living people can communicate with a discarnate consciousness also on this Plane, but to do so they must adjust their level of vibration. This usually calls for mediation by a psychic medium.

On the Mental Plane consciousness leaves behind the issues that occupied the minds of living people in their everyday existence. The focus is on conveying love and compassion, so as to reincarnate in peace and serenity. Communication on this Plane conveys messages of universal relevance rather than of individual interest.

On the Causal Plane only the consciousness of great masters retains distinct awareness; the energy on this Plane is too high—the rate of vibration too different—to allow communication by others. Awareness occurs only as brief flashes, before consciousness lapses into unconsciousness, as in deep sleep.

Ouellet's reports mesh with those of many other mediums. They suggest that existence on the Causal Plane is largely in preparation for rebirth. Feelings and emotions become purified and the sense of separateness is replaced by a genuine form of individuality.

Geraldine Cummins' Report on the Experience of Frederic Myers

Transcendent Planes have been described in remarkable detail by Frederic Myers.[32] Dictating his after-death experiences to the trance medium Geraldine Cummins, Myers said that "the history of consciousness" can be divided into six stages: (1) limitation of consciousness through existence in a material world; (2) expansion of consciousness through existence in the "methereal" world (the immediate station reached by the soul after leaving the body); (3) increased expansion of consciousness on the "Fourth Plane" (a higher plane of beyond-the-body existence) where the soul knows the perfection—or sublimation—of form; (4) cosmic limitation of consciousness in the condition where the soul is again confined within a real-world body (which is a body of flame, a stellar incarnation); (5) cosmic expansion of consciousness (where the soul holds within its awareness the whole of the visible universe and can become one cosmic consciousness); and (6) infinite expansion of consciousness: becoming one with the Creator, holding all universes within the soul's awareness.

According to Myers, the six-phase ascent of consciousness is an evolutionary journey through seven Planes. These are (i) the Plane of Earth; (ii) the Intermediate Plane ("Hades"); (iii) the Plane of Illusion (the plane reached immediately after death); (iv) the Plane of Color ("Eidos"); (v) the Plane of Flame ("Helios"); (vi) the Plane of Light; and (vii) the last Plane Myers called "Out Yonder—Timelessness."

From Hades, the first way station, the soul ascends to the Plane of Illusion. Resting for a while in the Lotus Flower paradise, it can pass to the next way station: the Mental Plane. An ethical soul, he said, will wish to go up the ladder of etheric existence since, with few exceptions, his longing for physical existence has been overcome. The exceptions are those who aspire to a great intellectual feat on earth, or want to "play a major role in the strife of earthly life." They may wish to reincarnate even from the Astral Plane. However, in most cases the soul of ethical individuals is released from Illusion land, "from that nursery in which they merely lived in the old fantasy of Earth."

Myers ascended beyond the Mental Plane to the Plane he called Eidos. Earthly experience is a poor copy of experience in

Eidos: it is a "copy of a masterpiece." In Eidos "we dwell in a world of appearances in some respects similar to the earth. Only all this vast region of appearances is gigantic in conception, terrifying and exquisite according to the manner in which it presents itself. . . . It is far more fluidic, less apparently solid than Earth surroundings."

In *Beyond Human Personality*, the second volume of *Human Personality and Its Survival of Bodily Death*,[33] Myers set forth his account of the stages of the soul's ascent to higher Planes.[34] Eidos, he wrote, is a loftier world:

> magnificent, exquisite, full of strange beauties and forms that may still be, in some respects, reminiscent of earth. These are, however, infinite in variety. They are composed of colors and light unknown to man. There, on this level, will be found a perfection in outward form, in surface appearance; a perfection only occasionally realized in the creation of the greatest of earthly artists. . . . On this lumiferous plane the struggle increases in intensity, the efforts expended are beyond the measure of earthly experience. But the results of such labor, of such intellectualized and spiritualized toil and battle also transcend the most superb emotion in the life of man. In brief, all experience is refined, heightened, intensified, and the actual zest of living is increased immeasurably. The purpose of all the toil and battle is to experience the full possibilities of this plane, so that the soul may pass beyond it, to planes still more removed from earthly existence.

Beyond Eidos is the Plane of Flame (the Causal Plane in many other reports). On this Plane, the soul is

> an artist who lives in his masterpiece, derives from it, in all its features, in the freshness of its evolving, changing creation, that strange exhalation which may, perhaps, at one rare moment, be known to a creative genius—though very faintly—while he still lives upon the earth.
>
> On the Plane of Light, beyond the Plane of Flame, pure reason reign supreme . . . the souls who enter this last kingdom of experience . . . bear with them the wisdom of form, the incalculable secret wisdom, gathered only through limitation, harvested from numberless years, garnered from lives passed in myriad forms . . . they are capable of living now without form, of existing as white light . . . as pure thought.

Beyond the Plane of Light, there is still another Plane, one that, however, baffles description. "It is heartbreaking even to attempt to write of it . . . [entering this state] means the flight from the material universe . . . You dwell not only *outside* of time but outside of the universe on this last Plane of being."

Existence on the transcedental Planes, Myers said, is not existence in the real world: the Planes are "states of mind." By this, he did not intend the mind of individuals in the incarnate state. E.K., the entity channeled by Jane Sherwood, explained:

> When one trespasses on the proper experiences of another plane one can only have them subjectively. They lack their proper environment and have to take place in the part of the self which suits the special plane upon which they are realities. This is equally true for us when we reach above our own plane.[35]

Existence Prior to (Re)Birth

Although most, and perhaps all, people had prenatal experiences, with few exceptions they fail to recall them. Children in certain age groups and in some cultures possess the faculty of recall. They are usually between the age of three, the time when they begin to verbalize their thoughts and memories, and the age of eight, when past-life memories begin to fade and then vanish. In that window in time there are children who recollect encountering, and even selecting, their future parents. Some children also remember the events that preceded conception in their mother's womb.

Reincarnation researchers Jim Tucker and Poonam Sharma collected more than 2,500 memories by children that suggest that they had lived previously at another time and in another body.[36] Some of the children took on the identities of the "foreign personality" to such an extent that instead of their actual parents, they recognized the families of the foreign personality as their own. That personality usually lived in the same geographic region as the child, shared the same culture, was approximately of the same age, and belonged to the same sex. But it may also have been of different age and of the opposite sex. A small girl, for example, could take on the personality of an elderly man and espouse his values, habits, and dietary preferences.

In most cases the time interval between the death of the foreign personality and the birth of the child who remembers being that personality is relatively short. In Tucker's studies the median time is sixteen months. In some cases it is less than nine months, which indicates that the consciousness of the foreign personality did not enter the womb of the mother during or shortly after conception—because at that time the foreign personality was still a person living his or her own life.[37]

These findings refer to standard reincarnation-type recollections. "Experiences of the reincarnation-type with intermission memories" comprise a different category of experience. It could include the recollection of meeting one's parents before being born—in most cases the mother, but sometimes also the father. The recollections typically include episodes of four kinds: memories of one's own funeral, memories of other events from one's previous life, memories of existence in the interlife period, and memories of entering the womb at or after conception.

Recollections that include intermission memories are generally clearer and more verifiable than reincarnation-type experiences. Intermission memories are not dependent on the presence of past-life memories. Only a small fraction of the children who recollected previous lives also had intermission memories, while many children who came up with intermission memories did not recall having lived previous lives.

The Japanese sociologist Masayuki Ohkado carried out a systematic questionnaire- and interview-based survey of the intermission-type recollections of twenty-one children in his country.[38] The median age of the children was 8.16 years, and the median age when memories were verbalized was four years. The memories surfaced most often when the children were in a relaxed state, in the bath or at bedtime. Some mothers noticed that the children became more eloquent while recounting their memories, speaking clearly and with concentration. One mother noticed that her child, who suffered from stutter, became fluent while recalling the memories.

Intermission memories can contain remarkable visual detail. Ohkado reported that a six-year-old boy said, "I was flying in the sky, looking for my mother. Looking down, I could see my mother and chose her. I thought she was the best person. She looked lonely, and I thought, if I come to her, she will not feel lonely anymore." A nine-year old girl described the place where she was before she came into her mother's womb. "There were many children, or souls, and a god, an entity with authority." To the question "Is he like a school teacher?" the girl replied: "No, no, no! He is much more generous. . . . He was looking after us, like a counselor."

Ohkado's research elicited memories of the place where the children had been before they were born. Thirteen children described the place where they were as cloud or sky, and three as light. Four described it as a "wide space where you can see the Earth," "a place like a star," "a place where there are a number of levels," and "up there," and one said that it was "a place in the shape of a long ellipse."

Fifteen of the twenty-one children said they could see "earthly affairs," but could only recall episodes related to their own parents and households. Thirteen described how they felt in their between-lives existence. Eight said they felt peaceful or calm, two said joyful or excited. One admitted feeling lonely, and three said that the feeling was difficult to describe, or that it was not different from what they felt now. Seventeen children reported choosing their parents; nine of them remembered choosing only the mother and eight recalled choosing both mother and father. Of these eight, four chose the mother first, and the other four chose both parents at the same time. Twelve children remembered coming to their mother's womb, and three of them said that an entity—a god, a shining ball, or an angel—helped them.

Three children gave accounts that could be confirmed by their current parents. A girl who was five or six at the time said to her mother "When you were young, I frequently came to you." The mother confirmed that before she got married she often felt that a small child, or child-like entity, was looking at her and bustling around her. Another child said to her mother, "I saw you in a gorgeous white dress. You were holding a dog." The mother recalled that after the wedding ceremony she entered a room where a dog was waiting for her. She specifically remembered holding the dog because she knew that she was not supposed to do that in her wedding dress. The third child made a drawing of a four-story house next to a mountain and said that that was where he had been. The mother confirmed that as a child she had lived in a four-story building from where she could see the mountains.

Not only children, and not even only humans, remember previous lives. The evidence on this score concerns behaviors that suggest subconscious or nonconscious recollections from previous existences. The relevant behaviors show up right after birth. When the fetus leaves the womb, behaviors are exhibited that could not have been acquired in the womb. Such behaviors are said to be "inborn" or "innate" and are ascribed to instinct. They are more likely to be evidence of transgenerational memory: patterns of behavior acquired in a previous lifetime and resurfacing in the newborn. The newborn finds itself continuing the life it has experienced before and, without being aware of its prior lives, applies the skills and behaviors it had acquired previously.

The above cited experiences of existence—and subconscious or nonconscious behaviors based on such experiences—suggest that consciousness survives the body and continues to exist on another Plane. This is affirmed by individuals who have already passed beyond. Sir Donald Trovey, speaking through the medium Rosemary Brown, explained,

> The brain perishes with the physical body, but we have demonstrated our continued powers of thought and imagination and recollection after we have vacated our physical bodies. This shows that immortal Man functions independently of the physical brain, and that he possesses ethereal organs which

> are imperishable and continue to operate after physical death.[39]

E.K., the entity channeled by Jane Sherwood, gave the following account of the survival of consciousness.

> The probability is . . . that life is no mysterious supernatural affair, but the most enduring aspect of matter. You can injure or destroy physical form but you cannot destroy the invisible body which interpenetrates it. Like any form of energy, life changes its form and thus escapes your detection, but no power on earth or heaven can destroy it nor prevent its continuance in form after form. For once matter, itself a form of energy, has produced this higher phase of activity, a new thing has been created which is beyond harm from your plane. It has entered upon an eternity of change and transformation and will go on to recur and develop until the end of time. So life, the delicate, the vulnerable, which appears to be at the mercy of senseless accident or malicious force—this tender thing when seen in its true character, is more enduring than the rocks and less defeated or confined than the ocean. It has achieved immortality having raised itself into a state of implacable continuance.[40]

The Map of Existence

The concept of reality surfacing at the avant-garde of twenty-first century science "re-cognizes" an age-old insight. There is evidence that in regard to the nature of existence, the traditional concept was right. Existence in the world is not linear and finite: it is continuous and cyclic.

Let us recall the principal features of the new map of reality. Self-stabilizing clusters of standing-wave interference composed of in-phase high frequency high amplitude waves create the object-like phenomena that manifest in the universe. Other clusters of wave interference are not object-like but are mind-like: they are composed of low-frequency, low-amplitude waves. The object-like and the mind-like clusters are not fundamentally different. They are both patterns created by interfering standing waves, but they are of different frequency and amplitude and hence appear as different Gestalts.

Human beings, as other organisms at the higher rungs of biological evolution, are hyperclusters of wave interference patterns, oscillating across a broad range of frequencies. They are composed of in-phase, high-frequency, high-amplitude waves as well as waves of low frequency and low amplitude. Their high-frequency, high-amplitude component is less stable and enduring than the low-frequency, low-amplitude component: it is the "body," as contrasted with the "mind." The high-frequency body component persists for relatively brief periods. It degenerates, but is periodically replaced by another high-frequency component—another body. The low-frequency component—the mind or consciousness—survives.

In its body-associated phase the multifrequency "incarnate" entity communicates both with object-like phenomena in the high-frequency domain, and with mind-like phenomena in the low-frequency domain. When the body of the individual dies, he or she does not cease to exist, but shifts from the multifrequency to the uniquely low-frequency mode of vibration.

Communication appears possible between an incarnate multifrequency cluster and a low-frequency discarnate one. It is known as "transcommunication." As the examples cited above indicate, transcommunication can be initiated from either side. Some incarnate human beings—psychic mediums and other sensitive individuals—can contact discarnate entities, and some discarnate entities can send messages to psychic mediums and other sensitive individuals.

In the modern world, unlike in traditional cultures, transcommunication for humans calls for entering an altered state of consciousness. We know that phenomena that transcend the range of everyday experience occur predominantly in altered states, and we also know that in these states the brain functions at the low end of the EEG frequency band. Nonlocal messages are received above all in the range of Alpha, Delta, and low-Theta waves, the frequency domain ranging from just above zero to about five Hertz.

The between-lives phase ends when the surviving low-frequency component encounters a suitable high-frequency template. If this is a fetus in the womb, we have a case of reincarnation;

and if it is a more developed organism, we speak of a case of possession.

Existence, Birth, and Death: The New Definitions

Existence. To exist, *to be*, is to be a cluster of standing-wave interference in a coherence domain of the excited state of the cosmos. The universe is a global cluster comprising all wave clusters in our local coherence domain.

Some clusters appear but briefly and cannot be meaningfully assigned individual identity, while others persist sufficiently to be seen as individual existents.

Birth and Death. Birth and death are phase transitions in the continuous existence of clusters, superclusters, and hyperclusters of interfering waves. In the birth-to-death phase, the high- and the low-frequency components of the hyperclusters conjugate, whereas in the after-death phase the high-frequency component is absent: the physical body is defunct. In rebirth, the high-frequency component is recovered: consciousness is re-associated with a body. Then another phase of multifrequency existence begins.

Death is not the end of existence; it is merely a transition from the multifrequency to the single-frequency mode of vibration and resonant receptivity. Birth is the reverse transition, from the single-frequency to the multifrequency mode. Birth and death are not terminal points but phase transitions in the continuous existence of a particular wave interference hypercluster. The recurrence of birth, death, and then re-birth and "re-death" constitutes the cycle wisdom teachings call the Wheel of Life, or Samsara.

APPENDIX

An Experienced Case of Transcommuniation

The following is an excerpt from this writer's account of his experience of transcommunication. The complete report is in his *Quantum Shift in the Global Brain* (Inner Traditions, 2006).

> I am sitting in a dark room in the Italian town of Grosseto, together with a group of sixty-two other people. It is evening, and there is not a sound, other than the usual static, and the occasional shrill broadcast, of the short-wave band of a radio. It is an ancient radio, the kind that works not with transistors, but with vacuum tubes. I am sitting on a small stool immediately behind an old Italian who wears a hat and is dressed as if it was still winter, although it is warm in the room—and getting warmer by the minute.
>
> The Italian—a renowned psychic who considers himself not a commercial medium but a serious psychic researcher—is Marcello Bacci. For the past forty years he has been hearing voices through his radio, and has become convinced that they are the voices of people who have passed away. Those who come to his regular "dialogues with the dead" are

likewise convinced of this. They are people who have lost a son or a daughter, a father or a mother or a spouse, and hope to have the experience of hearing them talk through Bacci's radio.

We have been sitting in the dark room for a full hour. Bacci is touching with both hands the wooden box that houses the radio, caressing it on the sides, at the bottom and on the top, and speaking to it. "Friends, come, speak to me, don't hesitate, we are here, waiting for you. . ." But nothing happens. As Bacci plays with the dial, the radio emits either the typical short-wave static, or conveys one or another short-wave broadcast. . . . But everyone is waiting. Bacci keeps caressing the radio, turning the dial, and asking for the voices. I sit behind him, and wait for a miracle. . .

And then: there are sounds like heavy breathing or, more exactly, like a rubber tube or pillow pumped with air. Bacci says: *at last*! He continues to move the dial, but there are no longer any short-wave transmissions coming through. Wherever he turns the dial, the radio transmits only the periodic breathing. The entire radio seems to have become tuned to this one frequency—one that an associate of Bacci is carefully monitoring on a device to my right.

Bacci talks to the radio, encouraging whoever or whatever is breathing, or pumping air, to talk back to him. Now voices are coming through on the air. Indistinct, hardly human voices, difficult to understand, but they speak Italian, and Bacci seems to understand. The entire room freezes in concentration. The first voice is that of a man. Bacci talks to him, and it answers. Bacci tells him that there are many people here tonight (the usual group is around twelve), and they are all anxious to get into a conversation. Bacci says that behind him—immediately to my left—sits someone whom they know. "Who is he?" (He is the renowned French psychic-researcher Father Brune, who has written several books on his experiences of talking with deceased people. He has lost his brother about a year ago and has contacted him since, and hopes to do so again.) The voice answers, "Pere Brune" (as Fr. Brune is known in his native France). Fr. Brune asks, "with whom am I speaking?" It turns out that it is not his brother, but a priest, Fr. Ernetti, a close friend and associate of Fr. Brune who died not long ago. They talk for a while, and then Bacci (who continues to lean forward and caress the radio) says, "do you know who else is sitting here, just behind me?" A voice that seems to be different, but is also male, says "Ervin." He pronounces it as one does in Hungarian or in German, with the "E" as in "extraordinary" and not, as in English, with the "E" as in "earth." Bacci asks, do you know who he is, and the voice answers, "*é ungherese*" (he is Hungarian). The voice then gives my family name, but pronounces it as Italians sometimes do: *Latzlo*, and not as Hungarians, with a soft "s" as in *Lasslo*.

Bacci asks for my hand (I am sitting immediately behind him), and places my hand on his. His wife and long-standing associate places her hand on mine. My hand is sandwiched between theirs, and is getting warmer—indeed, quite hot. Bacci tells me, "speak to them in Hungarian." I lean forward and do so. My voice is choked, for I am moved. The unthinkable is happening—just as I hoped but hardly dared to expect. I say how happy I am to speak with them. I do not think I should ask whether they are dead (how do you say to someone you talk to, "are you dead?") but ask instead, "who are you, and how many are you?" The answer that comes is indistinct but I can make it out: it is in Hungarian (a voice adds: "the Holy Spirit knows all languages"): "we are all here." Then I ask, is it difficult for you to talk to me like this (thinking of the seemingly strenuous breathing that preceded the conversation). A woman answers, quite clearly, and in Hungarian: we have some difficulties (or 'obstacles'), but how is it for you, do you have difficulties too? I say, it was not easy for me to find this way of talking with you, but now I could do it and I am delighted.[41]

POSTSCRIPT: REBIRTH AND REINCARNATION IN THE TRADITIONAL CULTURES

Traditional cultures had a firm belief in the survival of what they called Soul or Spirit. In his twelve-volume study *The Golden Bough*, anthropologist Sir James Frazer noted that a person in these cultures,

> arguing apparently from his own sensations . . . conceives of life as an indestructible kind of energy, which when it disappears in one form must necessarily reappear in another, though in the new form it need not be immediately perceptible by us: in other words he infers that death does not destroy the vital principle nor even the conscious personality, but rather it merely transforms them into other shapes, which are not less real because they commonly elude the evidence of our senses.[42]

The pre-Socratic thinkers of classical Greece dressed their belief in survival in the garb of Hellenic mythology. They spoke of Hades, the domain of the dead, traversed by five great rivers, the Styx, the Acheron, the Cocytus, the Phlegethon and the Lethe. A sojourn in Hades was only for a while, after which the surviving Soul (the early Greeks called it "the shade") would return to earthly existence. Before returning, it drank from the waters of Lethe, the river of oblivion. The waters washed away all memories of the past life and allowed it to return to Earth unencumbered by memories from previous lives.

Virgil wrote that at Lethe "the souls who are destined for reincarnation . . . are drinking the waters that quench man's troubles, the deep draught of oblivion. . . . They come in crowds to the river Lethe, so that . . . with memory washed out they may revisit the earth above."[43]

Plato subscribed to the theory of the survival of the soul in his celebrated doctrine of *anamnesis.* In the dialogues *Meno* and *Phaedo* he has Socrates declare that the soul is immortal, repeatedly incarnated, and carrying its knowledge from life to life. However, in the trauma of birth it forgets the knowledge it has accumulated.

Belief in the survival of the soul prevailed in India as well. W.Y. Evans-Wentz, the anthropologist who edited the *Bardo Thödol,* noted that this Tibetan Book of the Dead records the belief of innumerable generations that existence continues after death. Reports that support this belief were handed down for centuries by word of mouth. Later some of the reports were compiled for use in funeral rituals, the purpose for which *Bardo Thödol* was initially compiled.

Buddhist teachings offer a penetrating and detailed account of the various phases of existence after death. There are six major phases (*bardos*) of existence, of which the phase from birth to death is but one (*bardo* means an "intermediate," "transitional," or "in-between" state). The death-to-re-birth "bardo of transmigration" is the most often cited, and it is preceded and followed by five other bardos. These are the Shinay bardo, the bardo of the phase of birth and life; the Milam bardo, the bardo of the dream state; the Samten bardo, the bardo of meditation; the Chikkhai bardo, the bardo of the moment of death; and the Chönyid bardo, the phase of luminosity hallmarked by visions. Then follows the Sidpa bardo, the bardo of transmigration.

The bardo of the incarnate phase of existence begins at conception and continues until death. It includes periods of sleep and wakefulness, ordinary and altered states of consciousness, states of elation and joy, and states of depression and suffering. The complementary bardo is that from death to rebirth. They form a continuous cycle: birth leading to death, and death leading to rebirth. The bardos can be long or brief, harmonious or discordant, fearful or joyous. Their length as well as intensity depends on the state of mind of the individual experiencing them.

According to the Dzogchen branch of Tibetan Buddhism, the six bardos are divided into two major groups: one group embraces the incarnate lifetime of the individual, and the other occurs between the present life of the individual and his or her rebirth to a new lifetime.[44]

The incarnate phases are the natural bardo of this life, the bardo of the dream state, and the bardo of the meditative state. The other three bardos occur during the phase of transmigration from one incarnation to the next. The fourth of the six bardos (the first in the discarnate phase) is the painful bardo of dying, the fifth is the lumonious bardo of dharmata, and the sixth is the karmic bardo of becoming.

The bardo of this life is the interval between the moment of birth and the encounter with the condition that will cause the death of the body. It contains a lifetime of experiences of joy and suffering and is the foundation of the practice known as "the spiritual path." The bardo of the dream state marks the interval between falling asleep and waking. In this interval the appearances of the waking state dissolve, but become perceptible again. The bardo of meditation is the period when consciousness rests in the meditative state of "samadhi."

The painful bardo of death is the follow-up interval between the encounter with the condition that will lead to the death of the body and the actual moment of death. In this interval the coarse and the subtle elements of the person's body dissolve "into space," and the clear light of death becomes manifest.

The phase of transmigration begins with the demise of the body. Tibetan masters speak of the "fatal sickness" that leads to dying, marked by the dissolution of the gross and the subtle attributes of life with the disintegration of the physical, mental, and spiritual elements of existence. The process of dissolution terminates with the cessation of breath and heartbeat.

The luminous bardo of dharmata begins at the moment of death and ends when the person enters the bardo of becoming. Here the "empty yet luminous appearances of the primordial, utterly pure nature of consciousness" become manifest. The bardo of becoming begins when the luminous bardo of dharmata ends. The person enters the womb of his or her future mother. As of this moment the appearances of the natural bardo of life resurface: the incarnate phase begins.

The discarnate after-death phases—the fourth, the fifth and the sixth bardos—mark "the passage of the ultimate nature."

It starts with the emergence of luminous visions that convey light, sound, and images. Some doctrines of Tibetan Buddhism describe the visions in great detail, and others maintain that they last only a moment before the mind falls into unconsciousness. Then the sixth bardo begins, the bardo of transmigration. It ends at the moment of conception.

Rebirth begins about halfway through the bardo of becoming: At that time the individual begins to witness the lights of six realms. These are the realms in which he or she will be reborn. The "wind of karma," the individual's habitual leanings, pulls toward the realm that most closely corresponds to his or her spiritual development.

The six bardos form what Buddhists see as Samsara, the cycle of the soul's existence. The cycle continues through periodic rebirths, or culminates in Nirvana, with the union of the individual soul with the world soul.

PART TWO

Explorations of the New Map

CHAPTER 4

The New Map in Physics

The Physics of Oneness

NASSIM HARAMEIN

As Ervin Laszlo shows in his new map of reality, throughout our intellectual and spiritual history sages and teachers have spoken about a unity underlying and encompassing our world. They professed that there is a great Oneness to existence and creation, and, almost invariably, mainstream scientists have misunderstood or ignored the exact meaning of this profound edict. Yet now more than ever this concept is reemerging at a new level of pellucidity through the science of unified physics. In retrospect, it is no great wonder that the unification of the greatest concepts and theories of twentieth-century science reveals a universe that is intricately and innately interconnected.

One of the most engaging endeavors of modern physics has been the progression towards unification of the two primary, yet seemingly disparate, descriptions of the inner and overall workings of our universe: quantum theory and general relativity. While a great many volumes have been written about this schism at the heart of physical theory, an equally disconcerting dichotomy exists between modern theoretical physics and the complex structures and behaviors of biological systems, notwithstanding the seemingly disparate and oftentimes ignored difficulty of identifying the mechanisms at the base of self-awareness or consciousness.

Central to the difficulty are the fundamental axioms and basic assumptions at the root of physical theories, which presume that evolutionary systems emerge from random interactions initiated by a single "miraculous" event providing all of the appropriate conditions to produce our current observable universe, and our state of existence in it. This event, typically described as a "Big Bang", is astonishingly thought to have produced all of the forces and constants of physical law and eventually biological interactions under random functions.

Yet, a direct observation of the complexity of molecular and biological systems seems to indicate the contrary. We observe highly complex self-organizing systems that eventually exhibit self-awareness capabilities and advanced cognitive capacities, which demand extreme levels of communication and coherency unexpected under entropic, random mechanisms. In fact, statistical analysis demonstrates very clearly that the probabilities for even some of the most fundamental molecular biological functions to occur under random processes is improbable if not completely implausible.

The resistance of the scientific community to address these issues comes from the cultural tendency to associate the remarkable self-organizing and self-ordering dynamics of our environment to religious and theistic beliefs, resulting in the hold-fast in academia to the concept that all physical processes *must* occur from random functions. However, as we have seen, the probability that even some of the most fundamental mechanisms of biological evolution to follow from random behavior in the (cosmologically speaking) relatively short span of time of the formation of the earth is extremely unlikely even if it were to only produce a monocellular structure. The statistics just do not add up. Yet, there are other options beyond "the universe is random" or "the universe is organized and ruled by some deity or supernatural principles that cannot be understood." There are simple and elegant feedback mechanisms that can dramatically elucidate not only the coherent and self-organizing behavior of our biosphere but also the scale relationships that define structures in our universe and the physical laws that unifies them from the cosmological to the quantum scale.

A good example of the difference in probabilities for a system to self-organize under random processes versus feedback mechanisms is the one given by the English astronomer Sir Fred Hoyle. Hoyle calculated the probabilities of a blind person ordering the scrambled faces of a Rubik's Cube.[45] The calculations demonstrated that, because the blind person does not know if he or she is getting closer or further to the objective on each move, the probabilities of matching the six colors on each face of the cube are on the order of 1:1 to 1: 5×10^{18}. Thus, if that person was to labor at a rate of one move per second, it would take 5×10^{18} seconds to complete all possibilities. That is to say that it will take up to 126 billion years for that person to go through the probabilities of ordering the cube (it should be mentioned that the complexity is nowhere close to 10^{8896} permutations of nucleotide configurations).

Clearly that time period not only grossly exceeds the life expectancy of the Rubik's Cube player, but it exceeds the lifetime of the earth or, for that matter, the existence of our universe since its estimated inception of 13.7 billion years. However, if the blind person is given a simple piece of information, something like a "yes" or "no" prompt every time a move is made, which is every second, the time needed to complete the Rubik's Cube equation is drastically reduced to approximately two minutes. Could feedback mechanisms and information network processing be the key to a deeper understanding of the dynamics that have created our world and unified physics?

The resolving of unification extends equitably from the description of quantum and classical mechanics to the supposedly subjective phenomenology of conscious processes. Remarkably, some of my recent findings demonstrate that the same equations that have the capacity to unify the ultra-small discrete world of quantum theory with the ultra-large continuous world of classical physics may also describe the information structure that is central to the great scientific enigma we refer to as self-awareness. These approaches reveal that the *structure of space*, whose dynamics are matter and energy, and the memory of their interaction, which we call time, all emerge as expressions of a fundamental domain of information present at the Planck scale, making classical spacetime an emergent property of the dynamics of that information domain.

In simple terms, these findings demonstrate that there is a fundamental field of information at the base of reality—what Laszlo calls the "deep dimension"—that everything emerges from and returns to. The dynamical feedback/feedforward information flow of that field may be the source of matter creation and the mechanism at the root of biological organization which ultimately expresses itself as a self-aware or conscious entity. As such self-awareness, or consciousness, may be an intrinsic property of the feedback dynamics of this fundamental creation field.

It is important for the reader to understand that these approaches are no longer in the realm of complex theoretical and philosophical speculation, but that they are now the source of some of the most accurate experimentally verified predictions. What will come to light as we take this brief journey into the discovery of the holographic information structure engendering the properties of space through quantum gravity, and hence realizing a science of Unified Physics, is that there is indeed a Oneness to reality—a fundamental field of information that connects us all. As a result, the concepts and mechanisms of universal unity are no longer left to esoteric beliefs, but are fundamental mechanics at the root of the structure of creation.

The Natural Units of the Planck Scale and the Rise of Quantum Mechanics

Through the work that my colleagues and I have been doing, as well as the general evolution of other models, specifically quantum field theory, quantum gravity, and quantum cosmology, more and more evidence is emerging which demonstrates that at the foundation of physical reality there is a fundamental field from which particles and forces emerge. This beyond-spacetime fundamental field, called in this book the "deep dimension," can now be understood in terms of discrete bits of information interacting to generate mass and energy, whether at the cosmological scale or at the quantum scale.

Quantum mechanics provided a foundation for a quantitative theory of matter, where the spin of subatomic particles is quantized within the angular quantum of action of Planck's constant. This was a great revolution in physics, yet as physicists looked deeper, more of the mystery began to unfold. For example, it was soon realized that the spontaneous emission of photons by atoms could not be explained in the parameters of quantum mechanics. Spontaneous emission is when an atom emits a photon in a spontaneous transition from a higher energy state to a lower state, or the ground state. Quantum mechanics alone was unable to account for this behavior in the context of a theory where the dynamics of the atom is quantized but the electromagnetic field is not. Zero probabilities were found for spontaneous emissions when calculations were made with the initial approach. In order to account for these behaviors and other observed dynamics of the quantum world, and in an effort to find a way to relate special relativity to the quantum scale, quantum mechanics had to be generalized or extend its framework to express the electromagnetic field as quantized modes of oscillations at every point in space. This lead to the development of quantum field theory (QFT) which was initiated by Paul Dirac in the early 1920s in his now famous Dirac equation.

In other words, QFT eventually described space as if it was filled with interconnected discrete packets of energy and waveforms, like little balls connected by springs. Therefore, a spontaneous emission occurs when an electron, for example, transitions from an excited state to the ground state, resulting in the ground state of the electromagnetic field emitting a photon that is equal to the difference between the initial state and the final state. The interaction of an excited atom with the lowest quantum state of the electromagnetic field (the ground state) is what leads to spontaneous emission even when no external perturbation of the atom is present. Therefore, to describe the electromagnetic field as quantized, the ground state of that field is critical. The electromagnetic ground state is known as the quantum vacuum energy, which is pervasive throughout all space, and spontaneous emissions are therefore dependent upon these vacuum fluctuations.

However, a difficulty arose when quantum field theory, which applies to the vacuum itself, attempted to sum all the oscillation modes of excitations for this quantum vacuum energy. In 1913 Albert Einstein and Otto Stern established that the quantum vacuum (the structure of spacetime at the quantum scale) undergoes significant excitations even at absolute temperatures such as zero Kelvin, which earned it the name "zero-point energy." The vacuum expectation value when all modes of excitations were considered resulted in an infinite amount of oscillations—an infinite amount of energy in each point. This problem was dealt with by the utilization of a cutoff value, a so-called "renormalization." The cutoff value would naturally be the Planck wavelength as it is the smallest possible oscillation of the electromagnetic field. Yet, the resulting vacuum energy density is still extremely large.

The Planck density, as it is known, can be calculated for the value of the vacuum energy density by simply counting the number of Planck oscillations in a centimeter cube of space. This would correspond to the oscillation mode present in the vacuum of that volume. The resulting value of the vacuum energy density within a centimeter cube of space exceeds the mass energy of the known universe by a significant amount, and although most of that energy is thought to cancel out, many physical phenomena are attributed to the vacuum energy fluctuations. In the words of physicist John Archibald Wheeler, "spacetime in small enough regions should not be merely 'bumpy,' not merely erratic in its curvature; it should fractionate into ever-changing, multiply-connected geometries. For the very small and the very quick, wormholes should be as much a part of the landscape as those dancing virtual particles that give to the electron its slightly altered energy and magnetism [lamb shift]."[46]

As described by Wheeler a half-century ago, the energetic dynamics at the Planck scale are so great that the very concepts of space and time are no longer applicable—within this fluctuating and vortexing field of microwormholes, nonlinear (nonlocal) interactions dominate. As such, space and time are derived, secondary characteristics of this extremely high-energy field and only become emergent at scales much larger than the Planck length in sufficiently complex systems. This is a direct result of the merger of quantum field theory with the general theory of relativity.

Quantum field theory demonstrates that the vacuum is diversely complex in both mechanism and structure, and all calculations in the theory are made in consideration of these multiple processes in the vacuum. As seen above, this is critical to the theoretical constructs of quantum theory starting with the explanation of phenomena such as spontaneous emission, to the slight excitation of the electron (known as the lamb shift attributed to vacuum fluctuations interacting with the electron field). Furthermore, the vacuum energy fluctuations have been confirmed experimentally for decades. Initially, the first experimental validation of their existence came from the so-called Casimir effect, where two plates are pushed together due to a slight difference in vacuum energy density created by the close proximity of the plates, and more recently the dynamical Casimir effect, where the plates are reproduced electronically, literally resulting in the extraction of microwave photons from the vacuum energy fluctuations.

Vacuum fluctuations are also expressed in quantum electrodynamics (QED) as a sea of so-called "virtual particles," producing short-lived particle-antiparticle pairs. This interpretation of the vacuum energy was initiated by Dirac as a result of his equations and was dubbed the Dirac sea. This eventually led to the discovery of the first antiparticle, the positron. These virtual particle-antiparticle pairs emerge from the vacuum and annihilate each other very rapidly except in the presence of a very large gravitational field, such as that near the event-horizon of a black hole. Here quantum theory reaches to cosmological scales (quantum cosmology) as the classical gravitational equations of general relativity define a "gravitational well" called a black hole. In this case, one "virtual" particle from the quantum vacuum fluctuations may fall into the black hole while the other becomes a "real" particle producing what is known as Hawking radiation (from Stephen Hawking's description of this mechanism, which is known as the Hawking temperature or Hawking entropy of a black hole). This behavior, however, led to one of the largest difficulties to plague contemporary physics—the information paradox—namely the question of whether the quantum information that falls into a black hole is conserved or vanishes completely, which would violate the quantum parameter that no information can be destroyed.

The information paradox has been resolved by the holographic principle. Where, generally speaking, Nobel laureate and physicist Gerard 't Hooft, utilizing the Bekenstein bound, demonstrated that all the information contained in the volume of a black hole can be expressed in terms of Planck information-bits on the surface horizon of the black hole, thus conserving the information as a "holographic imprint."

The Path to Unification

The goal was to find a solution to mass and energy in which the gravitational component could be applied at the quantum level, accounting for quantum gravity. Finding such a solution would unify Einstein's relativistic equations with the quantum scale where gravity seemed to be the odd man out. Over the years, when I looked deeply at both theories (general relativity and quantum field theory) I realized that in both cases at the very fine scale infinities would emerge that had to be cut off by a fundamental value—typically the Planck scale. In the case of general relativity, a singularity inevitably develops at the center of a black hole, and produces an infinite well of energy potential that is thought to terminate near or at the Planck scale.

On the other hand, in quantum field theory, the electromagnetic fluctuations of the structure of spacetime itself (the vacuum, identified in this book as a beyond-spacetime holofield), at the atomic level, were found to be so violent that an infinite amount of energy could be present in each point of space (the quantum vacuum fluctuation) and thus had to be renormalized using the cutoff value of the Planck length oscillator. To me, this was a hint that the Planck entity may be a fundamental scale—a fundamental universal pixel—of an electromagnetic field at the source of mass which had the potential to unify the cosmological Einsteinian gravitation and the quantum dynamics of an atom.

Already, efforts of some of the most respected theorists had resulted in a holographic principle describing the entropy, or temperature, of a black hole by tiling the two-dimensional surface event horizon with information bits of the Planck area to generate a solution to the information paradox. Yet this seemed unnatural to me, as a two-dimensional surface is a mathematical concept, not a fundamental principle of creation. Clearly, the surface may be thought of as two-dimensional when it is of the thickness of a Planck length, which is many billions of times smaller than an atom. However, it would still have a volume (a thickness) of the Planck dimension.

I started to investigate not only the surface event horizon but as well the volume information bits of the system (the black hole) in terms of Planck lengths cubed; yet none of my results made any sense. Somehow, if the fundamental Planck field was at the source of mass and energy for any system, then by some means the relationships of the Planck information bits must have been the source of the energy event that we experience as mass or gravitational curvature. Realizing that what we do casually in calculating volumes by "cubing" lengths may be as unnatural as a two-dimensional surface, I modified my approach to represent more of the spherical dynamics we observe at the cosmological scale of planets and stars. Clearly, it is doubtful that the universe would utilize a little Planck electromagnetic oscillator in the shape of a cube pixel (more accurately voxel since it has volume) to tile the universe. I changed my equations to represent a triangulation of sphere packing and that's when the solutions emerged naturally.

All of a sudden, a simple surface to volume ratio of Planck spherical units (PSU) generated the precise mass of any black hole, giving an exact analogue to Einstein field equations, but in this case describing spacetime as discrete Planck quanta of information instead of a smooth curvature. Applying the same Planck spherical unit approach to the heart of an atom—the proton—yielded the correct value for its mass, and eventually allowed me to predict the exact charge radius of the proton, which has now been confirmed by experiments. These experimental results are inconsistent with the predictions of the Standard Model and thus challenge some of the most fundamental values of the current approach.

In my *Quantum Gravity and the Holographic Mass* (2013), I used a generalized holographic approach to describe the fundamental information structure comprising the architecture of spacetime and the solution to quantum gravity. Realizing that the Planck electromagnetic pixel of the vacuum structure can be thought of as a unit bit of information (in the spirit of the holographic principle already present in the standard model of physics to describe the entropy, or temperature, of a black hole and resolve the information paradox), it became apparent that the information present in terms of Planck bits within the boundary of a system must be in relationship with its surface horizon, and that this ratio may be the source of its mass.

The first step in doing the computation was to calculate the exact volume of a teeny Planck spherical unit, or PSU. A PSU with a diameter of the Planck length has a volume of 2.21×10^{-99} cm^3 and an equatorial area of 2.0×10^{-66} cm^2.[47] The Planck entity being so small, one would expect that an unmanageable amount of them would pack in the volume of a black hole and that a computation of their relationship to the surface horizon would have little meaning due to the enormous quantities involved. On the other hand, if the Planck spherical information unit is truly a fundamental building block of universal architecture, then the value obtained by utilizing it would be extremely precise due to the high-resolution of the unit of measurement.

As I have found, if one calculates the amount of PSUs inside the volume of a well-known black hole such as Cygnus x-1, one finds that there are 2.96×10^{118} of them in there, and 3.82×10^{79} on the surface. Remarkably, if one computes the volume-to-surface ratio of PSUs and multiplies it by the energy or mass of a PSU (2.17×10^{-5} grams) to obtain the mass energy, one finds the exact value for the mass of that black hole (1.68×10^{34} grams).

Astonishingly, this is the same value given by the Schwarzschild solution to Einstein's gravitational field equations in general relativity.

However, in this solution, gravity is discrete and no concepts of spacetime manifold are necessary! That is, all that is required is the relationship of the Planck information field between the volume and the surface of the system in terms of quantized bits of information. This demonstrates that space is actually granular at the very fine scale and can be conceptualized in terms of information bits on the structure of the vacuum, from which mass-gravity emerges. This eventually leads to the concept of "spacememory" beyond spacetime, where every consecutive Planck bit of information constitutes the continuum that appears to us as time, somewhat like the frames of a movie: consecutive relationships seem to produce an evolution in time seen as movement. If there is no spacememory, there is no time.

This gravitational solution has many deep implications for our understanding of physics, from the formation of stars and galaxies to the structure and dynamics of the universe as a whole—cosmogenesis. Of course, we will not be able to explore all of these results here but we can construct an analogy that we will see holds at the quantum level. If Einstein described spacetime as a surface curving to produce gravity then what we have done here is describe what actually makes up the surface, demonstrating that the "spacetime manifold or matrix" is made up of what could be called a quantum Planck fluid producing gravity or mass.[48] Thus, spacetime is an emergent property of a more fundamental dynamic occurring at the quantum scale of the Planck field, as demonstrated by our results.

In order to achieve a quantum scale solution for gravity, after five years of calculations I realized that the volume-to-surface ratio of Plancks in the holographic cosmological (large-scale) gravitational solution must be inverted at the quantum scale, so that the surface information content is divided by the amount of Planck information within the volume (in terms of PSUs) to define the standard mass of the proton. The first order approximation result was extremely compelling.[49]

This was a remarkable result due to the fact that incredibly large numbers, like the mass of the universe at 10^{55} g, were utilized for the calculation and yielded a significantly accurate value for a tiny proton. Indeed, when the calculation is made for the number of Plancks within a proton volume, which is extremely small, one finds that there are 10^{60} protons in there and if we multiply that by the Planck mass (10^{-5} g) we obtain 10^{55} g for the total mass of all the Plancks inside the proton. This is equivalent to the mass of all the other protons in the universe, or if you like, the mass of the universe. This is truly representative of a holographic unified field since the mass energy or information present inside one proton volume is equivalent to the information of all the other protons in the universe holographically represented in the Planck field within one proton volume. Therefore, the relationship of the information of all other protons to the surface event horizon of that one proton is equivalent to the mass we observe when we measure that individual proton. The fact that the tiny value for the mass of the proton came out so accurately when utilizing numbers of such large magnitude, such as the mass of all the other protons in the universe, indicates that this is not a coincidence.

I spent some time, however, wondering why the solution was not exact. Why a small discrepancy when the solution for cosmological objects was precise? I eventually realized that the radius of the proton (or what is technically called the charge radius of the proton) that I was utilizing to yield the mass was inaccurate. Indeed, for decades we have been struggling in obtaining an accurate measurement for an object as small as the proton, yet we have been able to measure very accurately its mass. Therefore, by manipulating the algebra, I was then able to utilize the measured mass of the proton to predict the exact charge radius of the proton should be according to my new quantum gravity solution.

I included the prediction in a paper published in November 2012, thinking that it may be years if not decades before a more accurate measurement of the radius could be made and refute or confirm the prediction. Yet, within two months of the prediction, the result of the most precise measurement ever made of the charge radius of the proton was published by a team at the Paul Scherrer Institute's proton accelerator.[50] This time the result was extremely compelling as the new measurement was within 0.00036×10^{-13} cm of the predicted value generated by my theory. To this day, this is the most precise prediction for the charge radius of the proton, since the Standard Model prediction is now off by four percent. In fact, the prediction may be exact, as the discrepancy is now so small that it is within one standard deviation (or within the margin of error) of the experiment. Therefore, the prediction may be the exact value and the experiments are slowly approaching it.

Let us look at this from another perspective. In the cosmological (large-scale) quantized Schwarzschild solution, the internal volume Planck information for an object like a black hole is divided by the information present on the surface of the event horizon in terms of the number of PSUs, or "Plancks" (as I call the Planck Spherical Units). Then in order to achieve the standard mass solution for the proton at the quantum level, the surface area (from the charge radius) is divided into the internal information (or volume of the proton).

However, as we discussed earlier, the internal mass information value for the Plancks present inside the proton is equivalent to the mass of the entire observable universe (all other protons combined), that is $\sim 10^{55}$ g. Therefore, since the information outside the proton (all other protons that make up 10^{55} g) is holographically present inside the proton, the equation is inverted, reflecting the influence of one proton on all other protons in the universe, which is really small and manifests itself as the rest mass of the proton. This has very deep philosophical implications that extend beyond physics. The fact that every point seems to contain the information of all other points in a holographic network field of information tells us something very fundamental about the universe. *The universe is entangled in all of its relationships and acts as* ONE.

But how can the information for all of the protons in the universe be present in one proton? While the idea of wormholes, and certainly ubiquitous quantum wormholes, giving rise to the fundamental architecture of space and time may seem outlandish, the idea is firmly rooted in modern physics and goes back to the earliest days of the general theory of relativity. Physicists such as Einstein and Podolsky explored the idea of particles interacting via quantum wormholes when attempting to remove singularities (infinities) that arose from point particles. Particle pairs were modeled by John Wheeler in his geometrodynamic approach. Incidentally, this approach has seen a modern revival as Julian Sonner has shown that entangled quark-antiquark pairs are accurately described as forming a quantum wormhole through the holographic Schwinger effect, which is very reminiscent of the Wheeler quantum vacuum wormhole field (recall that Wheeler describes the quantum vacuum as filled by Planckian wormholes).

One of the key ideas developed recently by physicists Leonard Susskind and Juan Maldacena is the equivalence of the nonlocal behavior of particles, such as "entanglement," with wormholes. Considering a quantum wormhole architecture of spacetime at the Planck scale, it has even been suggested by Mark Van Raamsdonk that spacetime is constructed from an architecture based on quantum entanglement. On my part I have described the surface horizon of the proton as containing an unimaginably large amount of Planckian discrete entities. These can be thought of as the termination of vacuum fluctuation wormholes connecting protons to protons in a wormhole network structure of the Planckian field (the "deep dimension"), thus generating the proton's exact mass and radii.

The Planck scale wormhole solution of spacetime (where spacetime is an emergent property of the wormhole network information structure of the so-called quantum vacuum), becomes pertinent in the consideration of superluminal, or quasi-instantaneous interactions, as classical signals traveling through the wormhole network may appear to be transmitting instantaneously even though they are traveling at or below the speed of light. Therefore, this universal network plays an essential role in the nonlocal, or holographic processing and integration of information. As we will see, this is highly salient to understanding the emergence of space, time, and awareness.

Spacememory and Brain-Body Awareness

In our latest publication, *The Unified Spacememory Network: from Cosmogenesis to Consciousness*,[51] molecular biologist William Brown, astrophysicist Dr. Amira Val Baker, and I describe the mechanisms and dynamics of memory and awareness of the fundamental field of information that are integral to the ordering and evolution of the universe. It is a unified mechanism (hence the appellation Unified Spacememory Network) and as such applies to all scales, from the genesis and evolution of the universe itself to the development and increase in complexity and ordering of matter—leading all the way to the emergence of the order defining biological organisms and systems expressing self-awareness, by which the universe is ultimately aware of itself.

As a primary mechanism for the nonlocal intercommunication and ordering of information, the holographic and fractal architecture of nature explains the general and basic information structure and patterns of the universe. As such, the Planckian wormhole network manifold intimating signals quasi-instantaneously is a key structural component of this information architecture. And as we have seen, it is integral in generating the properties of space, and structures of space, such as protons and all the matter comprised of protons. What about time? As quanta and conduits of information, the fundamental units engendering the properties of space we are so familiar with also process, integrate, record, and transmit information—processes that form the definition of memory. Time is a result of the memory capabilities of space, which is to say if there is no memory, there is no time—making spacetime more appropriately called spacememory. Consequently, the fundamental information processes and structures engendering space and time naturally generate an innate awareness through the concordant action of information processing and memory in the quantized Planck structures of the Universal Unified Field—in Laszlo's cosmology, the beyond-spacetime holofield.

However, it is not just a one-way flow of information. It is incumbent upon us to remember that the seemingly emergent properties and structures of this fundamental information and awareness field are constantly feeding information back into the system, thus engendering evolution through a constitutive interplay. Perhaps instead of the suspicion that it is all an illusion, it should be regarded that it is all real, from the fundamental information and awareness field to the phenomenal world. The paramount example of this intercommunication with the fundamental field of awareness, especially in producing processes of natural evolution, is the biological system.

As a complex component of the spacememory field, the biological system is innately "plugged" into the universal wormhole information network. Following this paradigm, the intercommunication of information through the universal network is occurring constitutively during the normal functioning of every biomolecule and cell of the biological organism—an intrinsic awareness and ordering mechanism. From the research I have done, similar to what is discussed in Part Two, I have found, as did Laszlo, that from the smallest to the largest scales the components of the biological system are fundamentally transceivers, transmitter/receivers like antennae. This signal transmission of the biological system occurs locally via mechanical and electromagnetic resonances (orbital rearrangements during chemical bonding change the electronic resonant structure of biomolecules, a primary signaling mechanism), and nonlocally through the quantized spacememory wormhole network.

Under this model, the macromolecular and cytoarchitectonic structures of the brain are not so much involved in producing a virtual re-creation of the "external" environment, but receiving the information and recording it, as well as orchestrating responses. In this sense, the brain-body system operates as receiver and transmitter antennae with reply-back operations, recording the information in spatial configurations of myriad neuronal synaptic, subsynaptic, and supramolecular assemblies. However, as indicated in part two of this book, this type of behavior may not be restricted only to the brain, all the more so that the brain arises from this process in physical systems in general. These developments generating bio-oscillator antennae (the body) are a highly refined and paramount example of such intrinsic spacememory mechanisms present at the more basal level where there is a continuum formed by the "external" interpretations of the field fed back through the "internal" nonlocal spacememory network in a continuous feedback/feedforward process.

Underlying the material and cellular structure that comprises the living systems, there may be memory imprinting into the Planckian wormhole-spacetime structure, in which time is a function of information on the structure of space during evolution. Memory and recursive information feedback/feed-forward processes of the quantum vacuum (or holofield) allow for learning and evolutionary behavior. This applies not only to the mesoscale of the biological organism, but to physical systems ranging from the Planckian to the cosmological scale, and to the universe as a whole. As such, the process of cosmogenesis can be equated with a biological process of iterative evolutionary development—*biological cosmogenesis.* In this sense, there are living processes occurring at all scales of the universe, and with memory and learning being functions of awareness—life and consciousness are intrinsic ubiquitous characteristics, embedded in the very dynamics and mechanics of physical processes of the basic quantum vacuum or Holofield structure, and thus in the universe itself.

At the base level of the biological organism, the cellular membrane is the primary receiver, integration, and communication structure of information. Within the cell, organelle systems such as the cytoskeleton—the most well-known structure of this cellular organelle system being microtubules—may be involved through their high-energy interaction with the structure of the vacuum in recording information, and hence memory.

Note that the cytoskeleton and plasma membrane are present in every cell of the body, and hence the body itself is involved in information processing and consciousness. It is clear that, as noted in this book, not just the brain is involved in consciousness. Indeed, the connective tissue network of the body (which includes such structures as the meninges, dura mater, and tunica adventitia of blood vessels) is perhaps the largest continuous system integrating and transmitting information from every tissue and organ. It is the omnipresent surface structure, and as we know from holofractographic physics, this surface boundary condition is directly involved in information dynamics.

Other subcellular organelles, such as mitochondria, may further process information and generate signals internally. It almost goes without saying that in multicellular organisms single cells cannot be regarded as functioning independently of the whole system.

The reception, integration, processing, and transmission of information naturally leads to awareness: to the fundamental phenomenon we call consciousness. Although awareness is often portrayed as some mysterious and unexplainable process, in this light we can see that the natural processes of the cell would result in awareness, even in self-awareness at the level of complex organisms such as the human being where there are up to a thousand trillion connections in the brain signaling five to fifty times a second, and up to 60,000 miles of vessels and several orders of magnitude more surface area compacted into highly intricate fractally-branching and folded domains.

Our consciousness (self-awareness) is built of multiple layers of spacememory—it is not localized to any one particular spatial or temporal frame. Through the ultimate connectivity of the holographic information network, it functions in part beyond the domain of spacetime. Clearly the brain and body are important in transmitting and facilitating the functions of consciousness. For instance, it is because of the specific and unique structural and functional characteristics of the human biological system, from the molecular organization within the cell to neuronal patterning and the connective tissue matrix, that our awareness is so much more highly capable of conceptualization than most other organisms (as far as we can ascertain). As described, the nonlocal intercommunication, beyond any one frame of space and time, is made possible by the microwormhole network information of the Planck-level basic *holographic field of information.*

For instance, the body receives information about the immediate environment that is processed in part by the brain—this is local information processing. If consciousness were just the epiphenomenon of neurocomputation, this information would simply produce our next conscious experience and the behavioral responses associated with it in a largely automatic function. Instead, however, the information processing of the brain-body system may occur as well through the spacememory wormhole network, where it is compared with past experiences or even influenced by potential future ones of the whole evolutionary structure (all the other points in the universe) that are recorded on the structure of space and generate a coordinated relationship between the individual and the field as a whole. Because this level of awareness is beyond the brain, beyond any one particular frame of space and time, the subsequent actions of the system, down to the molecular level, will be nonlocal, beyond the computational generation of consciousness in the brain.

Just as the recurrent information feedback/feedforward processes of the Planckian microwormhole network are integral in the general formation and organization of matter, so too in the dynamical interaction within the biological system, which involves tens of millions of chemical changes every second, the unified spacememory network may be an integral component and ordering influence. As such, the intrinsic awareness of this universal system is present at the most basal level of function in the biological system, from the atomic and subatomic Planck network, and it is not merely an emergent result of it. From that perspective, the biological structures are an extension of the fundamental field of awareness defined by the feedback structure of the network. (Einstein said, "Physical objects are not *in space*, but these objects are *spatially extended*. In this way the concept empty space loses its meaning."[52])

Considering the cytoskeleton (a highly fractal and intricate system, also referred to as a reticular matrix) there are protein subunits called tubulin that form long helical tubes known as microtubules. The tubes, or luminal interior, are filled with atomically ordered water as well as ionic molecules. The tubulin subunits forming the microtubule channels have two distinct states, or conformations. These can be switched (like computational bits) by the oscillation of electrical dipoles within the tubulin. The overall configuration of the tubulin subunits can thus potentially serve as an information processing mechanism interacting with the quantum polarized vacuum to produce memory storage.

Therefore, the oscillations of the tubulin dipoles are not random, or chaotic, but instead influenced by local events (such as ionic fluxes within the cell) as well as by nonlocal mechanisms. For example, the spacememory wormhole network may influence the oscillatory characteristics of the electrical and magnetic dipoles within the tubulin residues of the microtubule reticular matrix, stimulating a resonant and coherent oscillation of molecular dipoles of atomic water ordered within the microtubule channel. This oscillation of the water molecule's electromagnetic dipole interaction with the vacuum may be the source of the 'laser-like" photon emission observed in microtubules, DNA, and mitochondria (a phenomena referred to as superradiance by Stuart Hameroff, et al.).[53] The stimulated emission is similar to that which produces laser light (used in holography and optical information transmission), and indeed the microtubule channels have been shown to function as an optical waveguide. The coherent biophoton emission (stimulated laserlike EM emission) being generated within the cellular information system of microtubules, mitochondria, cellular water, and DNA will affect the electronic chemical binding properties of specifically resonant biomolecules. This directly links the behavior of components of the cell, and hence the cell and cellular assemblies, with the orchestrating influence of the microwormhole network. The ultrafast information transmission of biophotons (at the speed of light) and nonlocal quantum effects mediated through the microwormhole network clearly explain how such an incredibly large and diverse assembly of chemical reactions and molecular interactions can be orchestrated to produce a seamless, whole organism.

Furthermore, given how the nonlocal mechanism of awareness and information intercommunication through the microwormhole network can direct responses, and even generate thoughts, from the molecular to the organismal level, we see the link between the awareness inherent in the unified space-memory network and that expressed by the biological system. The awareness exhibited by the biological system is not merely the result of neurocomputation driving automatic responses under the illusion of conscious free will, but the result of a much deeper, more intrinsic awareness that is built up across multiple frames of space and time.

Of course, processes involved with biological consciousness and information exchange through the vacuum structure are not just occurring within the cellular and molecular domain, but at the tissue and even entire organism level. The idea is similar to that of a fractal antenna, in which information processed at microscopic and quantum scales can be transduced up to the whole organism (and "broadcasted" into the field to larger domains, even at the cosmological scale) and vice versa. Consider the architectural arrangement of the brain, skull, and spine—an antenna in and of itself. At the center of the brain and running down the core of the spine is a water-filled chamber, known as cerebrospinal fluid. The cerebrospinal fluid is pumped through the entire system in a rhythmic, cyclic fashion, similar to the pumping of blood, but with a separate, independent rhythm. As with the plasma of the circulatory system, this is a highly important aspect animating the system and continually potentiating it for information transmission processes, local as well as nonlocal.

Each tissue system of the body is receptive to a particular domain of information of the holofield due to its specific structure, and will process information in a unique fashion. This body consciousness, although often marginalized in theories which focus only on the brain, is an integral component of biological awareness, as well as information exchange processes with the quantum vacuum and its microwormhole network. As such, in vertebrates the heart, the gut, and the connective tissue matrix connecting them with the brain are highly relevant in the reception and processing of information.

As argued in this book, interaction with the vacuum, herein called the deep dimension, elucidates many documented phenomena such as remote viewing capabilities, remote healing, and other instances of nonlocal information accession/exchange that cannot be explained by conventionally understood sensory inputs.[54] Other evidence of the nonlocal capabilities of biological systems includes recent experimental results wherein cells in an isolated medium mutate in response to daughter cells exposed to toxins in a separate culture.[55] All of these phenomena are elucidated when a nonlocal quantum field network is considered as the source of mass energy or information, as demonstrated in our generalized holographic mass solution.

The extension of the memory imprint on the structure of space is highly pertinent, as this suggests that there is a physical mechanism by which the unique consciousness of each individual can exist and survive beyond the dissolution of the body, given that it is recorded and continues to interact with the unified universal field of information—the deep dimension of Laszlo.

As we have seen from the results of the research carried out by my colleagues and myself, as well as in the research reported in this book, we live in a highly entangled, interconnected universe where a fundamental information field is shared across all scales to generate organized matter and eventually self-organizing systems, leading to organisms reflecting back on themselves and asking fundamental questions about existence. This process drives evolutionary mechanisms in which the environment influences the individual and the individual influences the environment, in a nonlocal interconnected wholeness—a universe that is ultimately ONE.[56]

The In-formed Cosmos

JUDE CURRIVAN

THE CHALLENGE OF ANSWERING philosopher David Chalmers' famous "hard" question about the nature of consciousness—how something immaterial can arise from something material (i.e., the brain)—is not real, because this is not a real question. Its fallacy is the assumed duality between the apparent immateriality of mind and the seeming materialism of the physical world. As leading-edge science is coming to realize, this is not the case.

The difficulty begins with the physical appearance of what we thought of as reality. Already a century ago, physicists were coming to understand that instead of the deterministic interactions of solid billiard ball–type atoms, they needed to reconsider energy and matter as two sides of the same coin, with energy being the more fundamental of the two. Matter has been relegated to the intersections and influence of energy fields and its manifestation responsive to the influence of an "observer." The absolute nature of space and time, hitherto seen as a passive backdrop to the reality of "matter," was discovered to be dynamically relative to the location of the observer and was related to the concept of spacetime.

With such advances, physical reality was recognized as being less "physical" and "objective" than previously thought. The gap between matter and consciousness began to narrow inexorably. Whereas much of mainstream science has been manning the barricades against such encroachment, leading-edge physics and its new ally, information theory, started the inevitable rapprochement that would ultimately lead to the map of reality presented in this book.

To paraphrase mathematician Hermann Minkowski, who pioneered the geometrical understanding of spacetime in the early twentieth century, and to update his insights for our own era of groundbreaking discovery, henceforth spacetime by itself, and energy-matter by itself, are doomed to fade into mere shadows; only a kind of union of the two will preserve an independent reality. The perspective now emerging is that it is information that underpins this union; it pervades all of physical reality.

The first indication of the rise of the unitary paradigm came not long after World War II, when IBM scientist Claude Shannon showed that the information content of a system is *exactly* the same as the energetic entropy of a hot gas described in the Boltzmann equation of thermodynamics. Further support that information is an innate feature of all physical systems was proposed by physicist Leo Szilard, who showed that a definite amount of work is needed to store one piece of digital information, or one "bit." In 1991 information theorist Rolf Landauer mathematically demonstrated that the erasure of one bit of information increases entropy precisely in accordance with the Shannon and Boltzmann equations. Then in 2012, physicists Antoine Bérut, Eric Lutz, and collaborators were able to experimentally prove Szilard and Landauer's predictions by measuring the dissipation of heat from the erasure of one bit of information. Reporting in the journal *Nature*, they succeeded in verifying the link between the role of heat and temperature in the relationship between energy and information, thereby confirming the physical reality of the latter.[57]

As physicality is being progressively shown to be immaterial and information to be physical, their congruence is leading to an increasing awareness that to understand the essential wholeness of reality requires restating the principles and laws of physics in informational terms. Two of the most fundamental laws are the First and the Second Law of Thermodynamics, which describe the conservation of energy and the flow of entropy, respectively. The emerging insight is that information is expressed *both* as universally conserved energy and as embodying entropy. From the first moment of spacetime, the incredibly fine-tuned information underpinning the totality of energy-matter and the interactions of the fundamental forces from which physical reality is manifest, is universally conserved. By also being encoded entropically, from its minimum level at the beginning of our universe, it is inexorably increasing through time.

In the 1990s along with the growing recognition of the primacy of information, two further propositions have led to a radically new perception of the nature of physical reality. These arose from the study of black holes.

The first proposition was the recognition that the informational entropy of a black hole is proportional to its two-dimensional surface rather than, as would be expected, its ostensibly three-dimensional volume. The second proposition was that all such 2D information can be considered as pixelated bits at the Planck scale, the primordial unit of physical reality. Equivalent to the way in which a hologram projects a 3D image from a 2D informational pattern of an original object, these two pioneering propositions form the basis of the holographic theory of the universe.

Extending these propositions to all the information in spacetime suggests that information is encoded in the universe on a two-dimensional spacetime boundary. This hypothesis is supported by a number of independently formulated theories of quantum gravity—theories seeking to integrate relativity and quantum theories. This points to the holographic nature of spacetime, and to gravity as an emergent, informationally entropic phenomenon.

Central to the new whole-system understanding is the phenomenon of nonlocality. Initially a prediction that quantum entities could behave as a single unit despite their apparent separation in space and time, the reality of nonlocality has been proven in numerous experiments, even at scales far beyond the quantum. Experiment and theory show that nonlocality is an inherent feature of the universe, crucial to its evolution as a coherent whole entity. The universe was born in a Big Bang, that, contrary to its denomination, was neither big nor a bang. It was initially minuscule and it embodied immaculate order. It then expanded at incredible speed and with incredible precision. Lee Smolin estimated that if the strength of the fundamental forces generated by this event had varied by only one part in a thousand trillion trillion, a universe of atoms, stars, planets, and people could not have come into being.

The embracing coherence of the universe is expressed by the geometric flatness of spacetime, the conservation and overall zero balance of its positive and negative energies, and the encoded fine-tuning of its physical parameters. Its extraordinarily ordered state is embodied in the minimum informational entropy that has increased ever since, causing the arrow of time to flow and the principle of causality to be preserved. The flow of informational entropy, increasing from the past to the present and to the future, is the flow of time itself.

Given that everything within spacetime is finite and that our universe had a finite beginning, this entropic process suggests a finite ending as well. Evidence for this case is accumulating. One clue came in a 2003 analysis of the CMB, the residual cosmic microwave background from the initial birthing event, which revealed that the wavelengths of the tiny variations that appear have a cutoff point. An infinite universe would include wavelengths of all sizes.

A finite universe can embody only finite information. Quantization, with its introduction of discrete units, is the perfect mechanism to enable the essentially unlimited wave functions of quantum potentialities to become finitely realized. Information expressed as digitized bits, with each bit encoded at the Planck scale on the spacetime boundary, is the simplest and most efficient method for communicating and processing information.

The finite speed of light, ensuring that information is transferred at a maximum rate in spacetime, enables holographically scaled causal relations to be universally maintained. The universe evolves as a whole system, whose macrocosmic intelligence is experienced, explored, and evolved at all scales of existence.

The holographic manifestation of the physical world is also revealed at scales nearer to home. Following pioneering work of mathematician Benoit Mandelbrot, computer analysis has demonstrated that the fragmented dimensions of self-similar fractal geometrical patterns holographically underpin and pervade the universe at all scales. Their presence is encoded not only throughout "natural" phenomena, such as coastlines, weather patterns, and earthquakes, but in the human world as well. The recurring geometric and informational relationships, as all features of physical reality, are expressed in the language of mathematics. They manifest from a fundamental domain of the cosmos beyond spacetime.

The quantum-physics concept of the "complex plane"—defined in this book as the deep dimension—is far more than a mathematical tool to describe phenomena. It is the essential underpinning of the reality of the physical world, including the dynamic informational patterns of fractal attractors that guide the development of complexity and diversity in the universe.

At this momentous time we are coming to recognize that everything we call physical reality is expressed as a cosmic hologram, and that each of us is a holographic microcosm. Our new science-based understanding tells us that there is no real separation between cosmos and consciousness, and that the appearance of this separation is merely the perspective from which consciousness in the cosmos views its own projection.

The apparent duality of mind and matter questioned by David Chalmers is an illusion. The wholeness of consciousness, of what Einstein referred to as the cosmic mind, is being progressively revealed in the context of the wholeness of the cosmos.

The Holographic Theory of Reality

ALLAN COMBS AND STANLEY KRIPPNER

IF WE LOOK DEEPLY AT THE implications of many holographic and informational theories of the cosmos, an extraordinary prospect presents itself. This is the possibility of the existence of entire worlds that are not simply distant in space, but which lie entirely outside the "material" universe of physical events as we know them, though still resting in the same holographic informational plenum as ordinary reality. Informational fields of the holographic variety are of special interest in this regard because they store dense quantities of information, and because entire nonoverlapping fields of information can be activated in them by modulating the wavelength of an eliciting signal such as a coherent beam of light.[58]

The idea of alternative realms of reality is not new. It may, in fact, be as old as humanity itself. For instance, some scholars believe the images on the walls and ceilings of the ancient cave sanctuaries of southern Europe, drawn as far back as thirty to forty thousand years ago, are outward depictions of inner shamanic trance experiences of other realms.[59] It is likely that those who actually experienced these realms believed, as do current-day shamans, that they were valid encounters with alternative realms of existence. In fact, shamanic overworlds and underworlds are reported in remarkably similar terms in shamanic traditions throughout the world.[60] In a related vein, the contents of visual imagery reported by people ingesting the shamanic brew ayahuasca often contain common elements such as "serpents, large cats (jaguars, tigers, and pumas, but not lions), birds, and palaces."[61] Shamanic traditions often use psychoactive substances (e.g., ayahuasca, peyote, certain varieties of mushrooms) to experience alternative realities, though many rely more on dance, chants, and similar activities. From this it is clear that experiences of alternative realities do not require the brain to be under the influence of psychoactive drugs, or to be injured or compromised.

Indigenous cultures around the world have created rich mythologies that point to alternative and postmortem realities.[62] Along these lines, it goes almost without saying that virtually all ancient and modern religions have belief systems that include the existence of experiential postmortem realms. As noted in this book, many of these involve challenging journeys for the soul, experienced for instance while passing through the Egyptian underworld on the barge of Osiris, or facing the trials and tests that determine the final postmortem status of the soul in Huichol Indian mythology.[63] Many such beliefs involve themes of heavens and hells that exhibit striking similarities whether depicted in Eastern or Western religious traditions, or in stories told in indigenous cultures.[64] Descriptions of leaving the earthly world often include traveling through a tunnel or aperture followed by the appearance of beings of light and darkness. As noted by Laszlo, judgment scenarios are common. They include viewing oneself in the clear Tibetan mirror of truth; testing the deceased's heart on the scales of Osiris; balancing on the narrow bridge to the Zoroastrian paradise; or facing the last judgment of Christian tradition. Though these scenarios may seem more symbolic than real, they point to universal themes and stages of postmortem experience and have been identified in the reports of near-death experiences as well.[65]

Near-death experiences have "face validity" in the sense that they represent dramatic episodes in the lives of those who have undergone them. As we have seen, these experiences can occur under the influence of general anesthetics during heart surgery,[66] but they were first scientifically described in an 1892 report by the Swiss Alpine Club in association with precipitous falls and other near escapes from death.[67] It is worth noting that some traditional religions' belief systems claim the authenticity of nonordinary realms to be based on the actual reports of those who have experience them; one is reminded of Muhammad's celebrated Night Journey through the seven heavens. Shamans frequently report dreams in which spiritual entities transport them to alternate realities and otherworldly realms.[68]

We may question whether a dream experience involving alternative realities can be considered valid beyond the sleeping imagination of the person who has it, but there are other entrances into such realms. For instance, in the Sufi tradition certain contemplative states open out into extensive "imaginal" landscapes. Sufi scholar Henry Corbin reflects on the difficulty many scholars have in distinguishing between the imagination and imaginal reality. He writes, "We are not dealing with unreality when we talk about the imaginal. The *mundus imaginalis* is a world of autonomous forms and images. It is a perfectly real world preserving all the riches and diversity of the sensible world."[69] This world is reminiscent of the *imaginario,* as exemplified in the prose of science fiction and "fantastic realism" and the motifs of surrealism and "visionary art" motifs (e.g., Piper & Piper, 1975).[70]

The cosmos as we understand it today is nothing if it is not abundant. We see this everywhere in biology, from the evolutionary efflorescence of species to the flowering of the neonate nervous system in teeming multitudes of nerve cells. We find a similar motif in cosmology, with vast collections of stars, galaxies, and clusters of galaxies stretching in every direction nearly to infinity—and some writers[71] (e.g., Leslie, 1989) speak of numerous, perhaps infinite universes as real as our own.

Surely, such a profusion, taken seriously also by conventional scientists, has room for the possibility of multiple experiential realities. All that is needed is a way to conceptualize them in a manner that allows for the fact that they are experienced in different ways by different people. Holographic models, such as Laszlo's and Bohm's holographic theory, seem well-suited for this task. Holographs can encode large quantities of information that can be activated selectively by distinct eliciting stimuli. It would seem that human consciousness is just such a stimulus. Different for each of us, but also with much in common, its numerous individual aspects might potentially activate many inflections of the cosmic in-formation–conveying deep dimension. In so much as human beings share common beliefs, perceptions, expectations, emotions, memories, and physiological states, our angles of activation have much in common and our individual experiences will converge, as Laszlo describes here, not only in the material world, but also in the realms beyond space and time.

CHAPTER 5

The New Map in the Study of Consciousness

A New Map of Reality Based on Consciousness

STEPHAN A. SCHWARTZ

I AM ENDLESSLY FASCINATED by the Hubble Telescope Deep Field images, and have different ones as screensavers on my computer's two monitors. I look at them and always marvel that what might be taken for stars in the sky are, in fact, galaxies, each containing billions of stars. The European Space Agency estimates there are "something like 10^{22} to 10^{24} stars in the Universe"—that's ten followed by 22 to 24 zeroes.[72] I have no idea what that number would be called, but it is very vast. The astronomers at ESA note, "This is only a rough number, as obviously not all galaxies are the same." And of course many of those stars have a system of planets. Stars plus planets—that's a number too large to conceptualize. One might as well ask how many grains of sand make up the dunes of the Sahara. And whatever the number named it would probably be smaller than the true number.

Now imagine that the astronomical vastness of that space is undergirded by consciousness. Can this be possible? The physicalist worldview says no; consciousness arises from physiology. Yet thousands of well-conducted experiments and case studies insist there is an aspect of consciousness that is not physiologically based, and that is not limited by spacetime. More than that they propose consciousness itself is the foundation of all that is. Journals in fields as disparate as physics, biology, and medicine publish papers on this research. There are so many that each discipline has its own literature.

On PubMed, index of the National Library of Medicine of the National Institutes of Health, the search term "meditation" will return 3,257 results, "quantum biology" 3,367. This is not yet the dominant view in science but that is the direction of the trend. Increasingly this nonphysiological aspect of consciousness is being called nonlocal consciousness, a term of art coined by Integrative Therapy pioneering physician and author Larry Dossey, who used it for the first time in 1987.[73] This aspect is a basic premise of the integral map of cosmos and consciousness described in this book.

The collorary to the idea of nonlocal consciousness is that all life is interconnected and interdependent, that we are part of a matrix of life, but even more fundamentally that spacetime itself arises from consciousness, not consciousness from spacetime. It is not a new idea. The excavation of burials dating to the Neolithic (≈ 10,200–2,000 BCE) have revealed that early humans had a sense of spirituality and some concept about the nature of human consciousness.[74,75]

In recorded history it dates back at least two millennia. To cite just a few from a much larger list, Patanjali (~500–200 BCE) clearly expounds upon the concept. Empedocles (~490–430 BCE), considered one of the greatest pre-Socratic philosophers, put it this way, "The nature of God is a circle of which the center is everywhere and the circumference is nowhere." Plato (427–347 BCE) explicitly had a concept of the relationship of materiality and the nonlocal information architectures now being studied, saying, "And do you not know also that although they make use of the visible forms and reason about them, they are thinking not of these, but of the ideals which they resemble; not of the figures which they draw, but of the absolute square and the absolute diameter, and so on—the forms which they draw or make, and which have shadows and reflections in water of their own, are converted by them into images, but they are really seeking to behold the things themselves, which can only be seen with the eye of the mind?"[76]

Plotinus (~204 CE) is generally recognized as the first person in the West to attempt a formal study of consciousness. George Sidney Brett, an English-Canadian psychology pioneer whose three volume *History of Psychology* is recognized as the earliest history of psychology written in the English language, speaks of Plotinus's work this way: "for the first time in its history, psychology becomes the science of the phenomena of consciousness, conceived as self-consciousness."[77]

I cite these ancient thinkers to make two points. First, that the idea of nonlocal consciousness is universal across time, culture, and geography; probably because it is so often based on personal experiences. For as long as we have had records some in each society have recognized consciousness as fundamental and in part nonlocal. Second, I cite them to remind us that they were as smart as we are today, anatomically equal, capable of close observation, and just as concerned with cause and effect as we are. But they lived in a time when there was a different paradigm, a different reality.

Premodern science writers and thinkers had no other way to describe what they were experiencing and witnessing in others than in religious terms. They speak of it as contact with a god, or a spirit, or a genii, or the many other terms human culture has devised across the ages to explain the experience of oneness—"timeless time" and "spaceless space," and a sense of connection with "a great unity." But all this would change.

In the bargain made between the Roman Church, and the emerging discipline of science in the 16th century, one taking consciousness (packaged as "spirit"), the other spacetime, physicalism took root as a worldview and became the prevailing paradigm. One effect was the severing of a feeling almost all humans had had up until then; a sense of being embedded within a great universe of life and in an interactive relationship with this whole.

Yet paradoxically as science, particularly physics, proclaimed materialism, many of its greatest thinkers, particularly those who created modern physics, expressed a different view. Consider the observations of the Olympiad of German physicists in the early 20th century: Max Planck, Wolfgang Pauli, Werner Heisenberg, Erwin Schrodinger, Albert Einstein and others.

Planck, the father of Quantum Mechanics, framed his thinking clearly in an interview with the respected British newspaper, *The Observer,* in its January 25, 1931 edition: "I regard consciousness as fundamental. I regard matter as derivative from consciousness. We cannot get behind consciousness. Everything that we talk about, everything that we regard as existing, postulates consciousness."[78] After more that a decade of additional research, in 1944 in a lecture in Florence, Italy, Planck doubled down on his point. As quoted by Laszlo at the beginning of this book, he said that there is no matter as such—all matter originates and exists only by virtue of a force. . . . We must assume behind this force the existence of a conscious and intelligence mind. This mind is the matrix of all matter.[79]

Einstein explained it this way, "A human being is a part of the whole, called by us 'Universe,' a part limited in time and space. He experiences himself, his thoughts and feelings as something separated from the rest, a kind of *optical delusion of his consciousness.* [italics added] This delusion is a kind of prison for us, restricting us to our personal desires and to affection for a few persons nearest to us."[80]

Schrödinger, whose famous cat thought experiment is one of physics' best known stories said, "If we have to decide to have only one sphere, it has got to be the psychic one, since that exists anyway."[81] And he was in agreement with his fellow physicist, friend and colleague, Wolfgang Pauli, who was equally straightforward: "It is my personal opinion that in the science of the future reality will neither be 'psychic' nor 'physical' but somehow both and somehow neither."[82]

In the next generation, physicist Oliver Costa de Beauregard observed, "Today's physics allows for the existence of so-called 'paranormal' phenomena. . . . The whole concept of 'nonlocality' in contemporary physics requires this possibility."[83] It was not just physicists, however, who saw that what had formerly been conceived of as religious could, with science, be approached through objective measurement. Consciousness could be explored. Nineteenth-century German polymath Adolf Bastian described what he called *Elementargedanke*—literally 'elementary thoughts of humankind." It was an early attempt to recognize and try to study the nonlocal informational matrix, and it was enormously influential. It made a particularly significant impression on all the German physicists I have just mentioned. Carl Jung and Franz Boas, the founder of American anthropology, were both also strongly affected by the idea of a matrix of consciousness. It is from these roots that Jung developed the concept of the Collective Unconscious.

William James said,

> The whole drift of my education goes to persuade me that the world of our present consciousness is only one out of many worlds of consciousness that exist, and that those other worlds must contain experiences which have a meaning for our life also; and that although in the main their experiences and those of this world keep discrete, yet the two become continuous as certain points. . . . By

> being faithful in my poor measure of this over-belief, I seem to myself to keep more sane and true.[84]

I understand that quoting famous scientists is not practicing science. But I go into this at some length because I think it is notable that while materialism dominates and consciousness is thought to be the result of physiological processes, all of these individuals who rank amongst humanity's great minds and who created modern physics seem to have come to a different conclusion regarding the foundational nature of consciousness, and felt it was important enough to talk about on the record.

And I think they were right. I think the evidence is sufficiently strong that we can say that they are. After decades in which the research into the nature of consciousness has been dismissed as "The Ghost in the Machine," a fundamental change is going on in science. Whole new sub-disciplines have emerged driven by the results of this experimentation.

One such is quantum biology which posits: Life is a molecular process; molecular processes operate under quantum rules. Thus, life must be a quantum process. Experimental evidence is beginning to accumulate that this quantum view of life processes is correct. UC Berkeley chemist, Gregory S. Engel, led a team that ingeniously found a way to directly detect and observe quantum-level processes within a cell using high-speed lasers.[85]

Another of the new subdisciplines is neurotheology. Radiologist Andrew Newberg at the University of Pennsylvania, using standard imaging technologies, has focused on monitoring the brain activity of spiritual practitioners as they exercise their practice. His data has led him to conclude, "It is important to infuse throughout the principles of neurotheology the notion that neurotheology requires an openness to both the scientific as well as the spiritual perspectives."[86]

And there is research data showing collective effects as well. Johanna Sänger, leading a team at the Max Planck Institute for Human Development in Berlin, reports that when musicians play duets their brains synchronize. The detail in the data is so fine that they can distinguish which musician is playing lead, and which is backup. "When people coordinate actions with one another, small networks within the brain and, remarkably, between the brains are formed, especially when the activities need to be precisely aligned in time, for example at the joint play onset of a piece," says Sänger.[87]

Threaded through all of this work is a growing awareness of a new reality based on consciousness as Planck stipulated.

One of the most interesting aspects of this process validating Planck's truth is that this transition is being driven not by a discipline like parapsychology which explicitly explores nonlocal consciousness but, as I have said by physicists, neuroscientists, physicians, and biologists. Researchers who did not set out to explore the new reality but whose data compelled them to do so.

And their work has begun to suggest how nonlocal consciousness through quantum processes projects itself into the physiology of consciousness. One example of this can seen in the insight studies of Mark Jung-Beeman. Beginning in 2003 and continuing with a shifting list of collaborators, he has steadily sought to understand the neurobiological process of insight: that aspect of consciousness that solves problems that cannot be worked with the intellect alone.[88] This work has yielded many insights, most notably: "We observed two objective neural correlates of insight. Functional magnetic resonance imaging revealed increased activity in the right hemisphere anterior superior temporal gyrus for insight relative to non-insight solutions."[89]

Contemporaneously, Jeanne Achterberg's studies in Hawaii showed changes in the brain of the recipients towards whom a healer has expressed therapeutic intention.

> Each healer selected a person with whom they felt a special connection as a recipient for Therapeutic Intention. Each recipient was placed in the MRI scanner and isolated from all forms of sensory contact from the healer. The healers sent forms of (TI) that related to their own healing practices at random 2-minute intervals that were unknown to the recipient. Significant differences between experimental (send) and control (no send) procedures were found ($p = 0.000127$). Areas activated during the experimental procedures included the anterior and middle cingulate area, precuneus, and frontal area. It was concluded that instructions to a healer to make an intentional connection with a sensory

isolated person can be correlated to changes in brain function of that individual.[90]

Let me stress these are but two series of studies chosen from a large and growing corpus of peer-reviewed research, these chosen because they clearly illustrate the point.

What Is the Standard of Proof?

Today there are eight stabilized parapsychological protocols used in laboratories around the world. Each of them has independently produced 6-sigma results. Six sigma is one in 1,009,976,678 or the 99.9999990699 percentile.[91,92]

Those that have been analyzed in detail are:

Nonlocal Perception:

RV: Remote viewing Presentiment
The Bem Future Feeling Protocol
Retrocognition/precognition

Nonlocal Perturbation:

REG: Random event generator
GCP: Global consciousness project

And then there are other experimentally studied phenomena that may involve both, or there may be only one category:

- Staring
- Therapeutic Intention

In addition to these laboratory protocols, recent well-conducted studies reveal that 4.2 percent of the American public has reported a Near Death Experience.[93] The population in the US is a bit more than 321 million. So 4.2 percent is 13.5 million people in the reported NDE population. That is equivalent to all the Jewish people, all the Mormons, and Muslims as well, and most of the Buddhists.

The NDE population though is almost certainly larger, since research has also revealed many people do not immediately report experiences. Often they don't speak of it until years later, which was what initially laid the research open to criticism. That criticism fell away in 2001, however, when Dutch cardiologist Pim Van Lommel published in *Lancet* a landmark large *n* prospective study of Dutch patients.[94] But perhaps most important of all is the emergence of the new medical sub-speciality Resuscitation Medicine. This new work has taken the monitoring of the body's processes to a much more sophisticated level providing new insights into when death occurs, and made hallucinating dying brain scenarios and similar criticism impossible to sustain.[95]

And as argued and illustrated in Chapter 3 of this book, there are studies of both post-death communications[96] and reincarnation[97] that have also withstood aggressive criticism. The implications of all this are clear: Some aspect of nonlocal consciousness exists before corporeal birth, and exists after physical death, and episodically manifests another incarnated personality. As Laszlo says, accepting that this is so is part of the new map of reality.

The fact is nonlocal consciousness events are, perhaps, the most broadly experienced mystery for which the culture seeks an explanation because, at sometime in their lives, almost everyone has experienced deja vu, had a precognitive dream, or a premonition that came true. And consider the role of nonlocal awareness in religion.

Consider all the religious services across human history; they have certain elements in common. There is a designated place to gather, appointed times for gathering; a statement of shared belief and intention; a period for music, dance, chant, or choir; and then a time when some but not all of the group may have a nonlocal experience that is witnessed by the other members of the group. Whether it is Christian Charismatic speaking in tongues, or the pronouncements of Voodoo possession, the point is to affirm the validity of the faith and manifest evidence of the living connection the faith has with divine (read nonlocal) consciousness.

Although Western society rarely speaks of it, altered state-of-consciousness experiences are woven through the culture, and it is this larger cultural context which gives these issues their importance. The mysteries of subatomic particles are of great interest to scientists, and of enormous importance, but average men and women are not confronted with them in their normal lives, as they are with altered states of consciousness and the forward phenomena of nonlocal consciousness. That is why it is so much a part of myth and art.

The Role of Denierism and the Emergence of Paradigms

But there is also enormous resistance to this new reality, this new paradigm in which consciousness is fundamental. I mean here something different than skepticism. All good experimentalists are skeptics; that's why they do experiments. And when skeptics do experiments or read compelling rigorous research studies they change their worldview. Consider Carl Sagan. In 1977 in his classic *Dragons of Eden* he wrote, "[The brain's] workings—what we sometimes call mind—are a consequence of its anatomy and physiology, and nothing more."[98] Then, in 1996, in his last book, *The Demon Haunted World*, he said,

> . . . there are three claims in the ESP field which, in my opinion, deserve serious study: (1) that by thought alone humans can (barely) affect random number generators in computers; (2) that people under mild sensory deprivation can receive thoughts or images projected at them; and (3) that young children sometimes report the details of a previous life, which upon checking turn out to be accurate and which they could not have known about in any other way than reincarnation.[99]

What had changed? In the interim Sagan had met his Cornell faculty colleague, psychologist Daryl Bem. When Sagan made the usual skeptic assertions about poor research quality Bem asked him whether he had actually read any recent research. Sagan admitted he had not and asked Bem to send him a copy of a paper Bem had recently written. After reading this research Sagan, a true scientist, bowed to the evidence.[100]

Deniers are something different. Whether their denial is of consciousness, evolution, or climate change, their position is marked by a kind of willful ignorance completely impervious to data. I was once in a debate at a university in Virginia as a kind of midpoint between a creationist and a materialist, both equally fervent. I was "nonlocal consciousness but not religious." I asked the creationist, "What is wrong with the speed of light?" He replied, "Nothing." Then how, I asked, "can I be looking at light from half a million years ago or more if the earth is less than 10,000 years old?" His response was: "It is one of God's mysteries."

In the case of the physicalist who asserted that all consciousness was physiologically based, I asked him what he found wrong with the remote viewing data from thousands of rigorously controlled double-blind and triple-blind remote viewing sessions demonstrating nonlocal consciousness. This was data I was particularly familiar with, having been one the creators of the remote viewing protocols. He hadn't read any of it, but he felt very strongly it must be impossible.

It is important to understand this kind of resistance because Denierism is a powerful force in both science and society. Science in the twenty-first century is the arbiter of what is real, and the transition to this new map of reality is a process that will in large measure be controlled by the science community's acceptance. If we are to understand how the integration of consciousness into science is going to happen we must comprehend not the mythology but the authenticity of how science works.

Thomas Kuhn is generally acknowledged to be the most influential historian and philosopher of science in the twentieth century. As he explains it, scientists are a special self-selected community dedicated to solving certain very restricted and self-defined problems whose relevance is delineated by a worldview or paradigm. Kuhn, who is the father of the concept, explains it, thus: "universally recognized scientific achievements [in a given field] that *for a time* provide model *problems and solutions* to a community of practitioners. . . [101] For scientists who are immersed in it, a paradigm is their worldview. Its boundaries outline for them both what the universe contains and, equally important, what it does not contain. Its theories explain how this universe operates.

Paradigms are absolutely essential to science, although ultimately they become self-limiting. Without the set boundaries provided by the paradigm, no observation has any greater importance or weight than any other. Without this differentiation, Western science is impossible. The benefit it confers is that with boundaries comes depth, and with depth comes detail. The narrowness of this definition increases as a science matures, and manifests itself in increased subspecialization; one is not simply a chemist but an *organic* chemist. It should be obvious then, to quote Kuhn again, that "one of the reasons why normal science seems to progress so rapidly is that its practitioners concentrate on problems that only their own lack of ingenuity should keep them from solving. . . . though intrinsic value is no criterion for a puzzle, the assured existence of a solution is."[102] This efficiency in puzzle solving collectively is "normal science." Obviously, this normal science is accumulative, but does it also seek the Copernican leaps, the insights that will change the course of history? No, it specifically does not. Normal science, in fact, is specifically not interested in the very thing it is popularly supposed to be obsessed with doing. It is this which is the source of denierism. It threatens the paradigm.

"The scientific enterprise as a whole does from time to time produce anomalies that open new territory, and test long-accepted beliefs. But the *individual* engaged on a normal research problem is almost never doing any one of these things [emphasis by Kuhn].[103] He finds himself instead working from a different motivation, the desire to demonstrate that he is capable of solving a problem within the paradigm that no one has ever solved before, or has not solved as elegantly. "On most occasions any particular field of specialization offers nothing else to do, a fact that makes it no less fascinating to the proper sort of addict. . . . Scientists normally [do not] aim to invent new theories, and they are often intolerant of those invented by others."[104] In fact, most deniers of nonlocal consciousness are nearly illiterate concerning the actual research. It's outside of the paradigm; it can't be any good. QED.

The great irony is: where does an Einstein, a Newton, a Planck, a Ramanujan, a Jung, a Salk come from? The answer, as each of them has said quite clearly, is that their great insight came in a special state of consciousness, when all things seemed interconnected and interdependent, and out of space and time.[105, 106]

Science is by nature narrow and rigid—and this should not be construed as a pejorative description because the vast bulk of research could be practiced in no other way—normal science always produces anomalies in the course of its work, and as it proceeds inevitably to reach its boundaries the encounters with anomalies increase. The reason is simple: Before paradigm is achieved, clearly nothing can be anomalous; after paradigm, a great deal will be, and as the limits of paradigm are reached, what lies beyond is that much closer.

Normal science, however, abhors anomalies since they are not tailored to the scheme by which it defines the universe. At first, then, anomalies are ignored on the assumption that subsequent normal science research will deal with them when either instrumentation or theory articulation or both are improved. If this does not happen, an attempt is made to extend the endangered theory in the hope that an extension of the paradigm's accepted propositions will bring the anomalies back into the fold.

In the beginning of a paradigm's lifespan, better instrumentation or theory extension does eliminate most of the anomalies by making them conform; some, though, will not conform, no matter how artful the experiment or ingenious the development of the original premise. Most scientists are happy to leave these anomalies in a state of limbo, which is why parapsychology is both science and non-science at one and the same time. Everyone knows anomalies are out there, lurking on the edges of the paradigm like hungry beasts around a campfire. But scientists assume, mostly correctly, that the majority of problems can still be contained within the paradigm, and so for a time, at least, normal science continues, and the paradigm provides a reasonably secure framework.

However, as normal-science research continues to get closer to the edge of the "known" it pushes so intensely, and with such specific focus that its explorations produce just the opposite effect from that desired. Not only does such research fail to strengthen the paradigm, which was its original purpose, but it produces still more anomalies. Ironically, at the end of the paradigm's lifespan, the better the instrumentation the more intractable the challenge presented by anomalies. These begin to cluster until so many exist that not only theory but the paradigm itself is called into question. When this happens, the science enters a state of crisis from which there is no turning back. This is the phase we are now entering.

There is extraordinary resistance in the scientific trenches to this final phase—in an individual it might be called denial. Scientists hate crisis even more than anomalies. Researchers delay retooling as long as they can, since it is expensive, involves much aggravation, and threatens careers and hard-won status. Paradigm crisis is the last stage in a process of scientific death.

When it becomes irresistible, and the limits of the paradigm's lifespan are acknowledged by a critical consensus of its practitioners, several significant events take place. This is what is happening now.

The assumptions of normal science include: (1) the researcher and the experiment can be isolated from affecting each other except in controlled and understood ways; and, (2) since the experiment exists in a time-space continuum, the conditions under which it is carried out can be duplicated and the experiment replicated by any other researcher if it is valid.

All of this, the common techniques, the various levels of the collective fundamental assumptions that often go unspoken seem to irresistibly argue for the conception with what I will call the Myth of Gradualism. Yet both that myth, and the materialism its supports are refuted by the undeniable reality of scientific change, and how it actually comes about. Those individuals who produce extraordinary research do so not by force of intellect or will alone, although these are important, but because they have had nonlocal intuitional insights *at the same time that there was a crisis.*

It is on this point that most commentators describing the development of scientific breakthroughs are uncomfortably silent. One who has tried was John Mihalasky who invoked intuition as an overt explanation, but tentatively.[107] He echoes Kuhn, who notes that it represents a change in Gestalt, a change in "beingness." "Normal science," he says, "ultimately leads only to the recognition of anomalies and to crises. And these are terminated not by deliberation and interpretation, but by a relatively sudden and unstructured event like a Gestalt switch. He notes that scientists then often speak of the "scales falling from the eyes" or of the "lightning flash" that "inundates" a previously obscure puzzle, enabling its components to be seen in a new way that for the first time permits its solution." To someone interested in the field of nonlocal informational interactions this wording is virtually identical to that used by healers, remote viewers, spiritual pilgrims, and great artists.

Kuhn is willing—since the evidence is so great that it cannot be denied—to invoke the inspiration of dreams, although how this actually works he does not venture to say. He makes one speculation on the nonintellectual aspect of puzzle solving. He notes, "No ordinary sense of the term 'interpretation' fits these flashes of intuition through which a new paradigm is born. *Though such intuitions depend upon the experience, both anomalous and congruent, gained with the old paradigm, they are not logically or piecemeal linked to particular items of that experience as an interpretation would be* [emphasis added.][108] What makes these key figures revolutionaries, then, is not just the quality of their work. They are also revolutionaries because of the source, mechanism unknown, from which their information derives. At the deepest level the process by which the information is obtained is as revolutionary as the information itself.

Intellectual excellence and intuitive insight, however, are not the only criteria for success as a "paradigm shifter." A careful analysis of the process also suggests that some kind of inter-connectedness between breakthrough researchers and their peer communities is involved. A kind of interactive collective awareness must coalesce until it comprises a critical consensus. How many people is that? A study done by the Social Cognitive Networks Academic Research Center at Rensselaer Polytechnic Institute provides data-based guidance: "To change the beliefs of an entire community, only ten percent of the population needs to become convinced of a new or different opinion. At that tipping point, the idea can spread through social networks and alter behaviors on a large scale."[109]

As Gunther Stent demonstrates, if an intuitive researcher is premature, no matter how great the insight, the response of peers is indifference at best, and martyrdom at worst.[110] We all know the story of Galileo. Not as well known is that in 1499 Leonardo da Vinci figured out what fossils were when they were turned up as he oversaw the dredging and repair of Milan's St. Marco Canal, critical to both defense and commerce. At the time the paradigm held they were anything but the mineralized casts of ancient plants, animals, and sealife. Some thought that fossils were the products of "a cosmic force, *vis plastica.* Others felt that they were the result of mysterious emanations from the sun, moon, and stars. Still others held they were the remains of giants, elves, and fairies."[111] A middle-aged Leonardo with nearly a lifetime of close observation of the world around him recognized them as fossilized life forms, some of which he could identify. But that was outside the paradigm and no one could absorb what he was saying.[112] Only when intuition and crisis are correctly juxtaposed can the necessary change in Gestalt occur. Genius is an individual experience, but its acceptance is a social phenomenon. We are getting there.

Larry Dossey puts it well: "If nonlocal mind is a reality, the world becomes a place of interaction and connection, not one of isolation and disjunction. . . .[113]

Rumi, a thirteenth-century Persian poet, jurist, Islamic scholar, theologian, and Sufi mystic says much the same:

> *Out beyond ideas of wrongdoing and rightdoing,*
> *there is a field. I will meet you there.*
> *When the soul lies down in that grass,*
> *the world is too full to talk about*
> *language, ideas, even the phrase each other*
> *doesn't make any sense.*"[114]

The prudent question I propose is: What happens when a cultural Gestalt change of this magnitude happens? Even the most superficial assessment makes it clear this new reality will be a much greater transformation than anything produced just by technology. As profound as the Internet or the iPhone have been, a paradigm change of this existential magnitude is greater. How do we know? Because this kind of transformation has happened before.

As I wrote in an earlier book:

> Consider what German psychiatrist and philosopher Karl Jaspers (1883–1969) called the axial

> period, roughly the eighth to the second century BCE, and mostly centered in the two centuries from 800 to 600 BCE. In that historically small time period, most of the world's great pre-Christian religious movements and philosophical lines developed. Confucius (555–478 BCE) and Buddha (567–487 BCE) were almost exact contemporaries, as was Zoroaster, according to the best approximation, as well as Lao Tzu, the founder of Taosim, and Mahavira, who is the most probable founder of Jainism.
>
> In the Middle East, the line of monotheistic prophets, which began with Amos of Tekoa midway through the eighth century, reached its culmination near the end of the sixth century with Deutero-Isaiac Judaism. At this same time, in the northern Mediterranean area the Greeks were experiencing the birth of philosophical speculation with the work of Thales and his successors. And in Athens democracy was established.[115]

In my view we are now in the beginning of the third century—I date this from the founding in 1882 of the Society for Psychical Research—in the emergence of a scientifically grounded consciousness-based reality. And I think it will ultimately be seen as a change of a similar magnitude to its BCE predecessor. As Laszlo does in this book, we should start thinking about what this new reality entails.

But even accepting both the unity and individuality of nonlocal consciousness, and Earth's matrix of life and consciousness, how is one to reconcile that consciousness with what is seen looking at a Hubble Deep Field image? Because if consciousness is causal then the unnumbered vastness of galaxies, stars, solar systems, and planets spread across millions of light years of distance are its creation. It is consciousness at an unthinkable scale, and yet the research suggests, no scale at all. Are we ready to accept that? Not yet. But it is coming.

As I look at the Hubble distant galaxy images on my screen millions of light years away, I try to imagine that unity of consciousness in what I see. It is very humbling.

The Deep Roots of Consciousness

EDE FRECSKA

A GOOD NUMBER OF scientific essays and entire volumes have been written to elucidate the quantum aspects of consciousness. Only a few among them have addressed the issue of the biological interface, namely, how the quantized spacetime world interfaces with the nervous system. My expertise is in biophysics and neuroscience, and, like Ervin Laszlo, I do not find it possible that the neuroaxonal network of the brain could perform this interface function. The principal fallacy of neuroscience is the assumption that every human experience—most of all consciousness—can be reduced to the function of a single system: the neuroaxonal network. Such a reduction cannot solve one of the most puzzling enigmas of modern physics, the quantum measurement problem, since it cannot answer the basic question: how can an electrochemical system produce quantum phenomena? Interface function by the neuroaxonal network of the brain cannot account for the thoroughly researched findings in parapsychology, nor can it explain the documented results of alternative healing, data from near-death experiences (NDEs), insights from nonordinary states of consciousness, and other phenomena that Stanley Grof denotes collectively as "anomalies." Attempting to defend the dominant paradigm, the one-network theory of neuroscience bluntly refuses to address these anomalies.

In an effort to break out of the obsolete framework of the mainstream, I concluded that networks other than the neuroaxonal are involved in the processes of perception and consciousness. In accordance with Ervin Laszlo's theories, I proposed a three-tiered model of human experience with the deep dimension at the base.[116] I was later surprised to discover that this model mirrors the tripartite soul concept of the shamanic worldview,[117] and also fits the concept of embodiment emerging in artificial intelligence theory and other cognitive sciences.

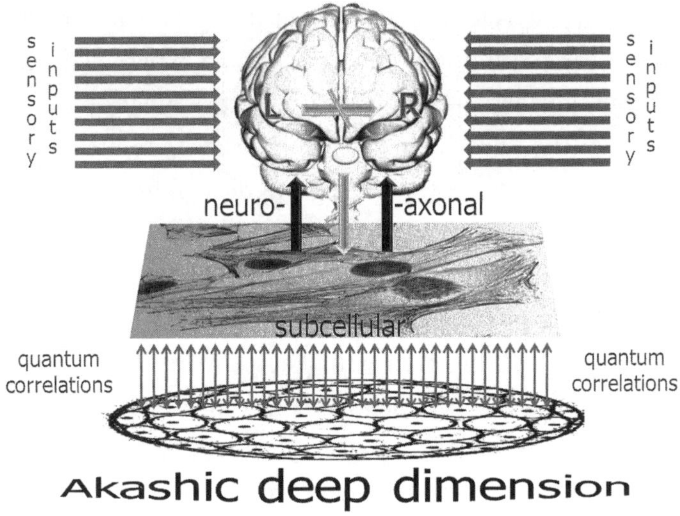

The Three-Tiered Networks of Human Perception and Consciousness

(copyright Ede Frecska, printed courtesy of the author)

The figure in this essay depicts two inputs for human knowledge and perception: (1) the sensory input linked to the spacetime domain and (2) quantum correlations linked to the domain beyond spacetime. Both inputs provide an inner representation of or an instant access to the environment: one through the brain, and the other through the body. Two networks, the neuroaxonal and the subcellular, process these representations: one in a symbolic and the other in a holographic form. Sensory signals provide the input for the ordinary states of consciousness.

The vast majority of cellular connections and even twenty percent of neuroaxonal communication occur through close connections, so-called gap junctions (electrical synapses between neurons). The cytoplasm of neighboring cells is directly connected by microchannels and a subcellular network of microtubular-microfilamental system passes through the junctions, linking every cell of the body.*

The neuroaxonal system of the brain is penetrated and informed by this immense microtubular-microfilamental matrix.

In the figure the crossed gray arrows between the left and right hemispheres, as well as between the neuroaxonal and subcellular networks, denote inhibitory effects (left-right hemisphere and up-down network dominances) in an ordinary state of consciousness. Quantum correlations (marked with uncrossed grey double arrows) are persistent and independent of the state of consciousness. Their function becomes manifest primarily during nonordinary states (e.g., during shamanic ecstasy and the trance state of mediums) when information enters from the subcellular matrix to the neuroaxonal system (shown by the black arrows). The nature of this transfer, an important coupling mechanism, is unclear; it may occur already at the synaptic membranes. The above duality in human information processing should not be confused with Julian Jaynes' "bicameral mind." Here we do not address the left-right hemispheric distribution of signal processing but the up-down differentiation of neural and subneural functions.

---

* The fine structure of the subcellular network may be responsible for the meridians, the channels of *chi* energy, and for the acupuncture points. The holographic feature of this subcellular network is reflected in the finding that the ear lobes, the feet, and the palms of the hand map the energy-information structure of the entire body.

The most important point of these interactions is that *the body is the interface between the brain and the beyond-spacetime Holofield.* This is also the lore of the headhunter Shuars and the Hawaiian Hunas: it is the "body soul'" component of the tripartite soul that conveys visions to the "mental soul." The former represents our bodily functions mediated by the subcellular matrix, while the latter is related to the brain. The deep dimension is the source of consciousness, and the brain is the receiver of this information. The body is the relay between the field and the brain.

An intriguing question is how the body functions as an interface when an out-of-body experience takes place simultaneously with a near-death experience. Perhaps after death the body still maintains its perceptive processes and after resuscitation the subject recollects his or her anomalous experiences—those that originate in the low-frequency domain of our coherence domain. Given that we are dealing with nonlocal processes, such information flows are possible. Bodily existence and consciousness are interwoven—an important point affirmed in this book. The subjective feeling of "I *am*" (the *sum* in Descartes' *cogito ergo sum*) is not part of the body's interface function: it is a nonlocal feature that is at the same time both "out there" and "in here."

The "free soul" (in Ralph Emerson's term, the "Oversoul"), that is, the immortal component of the tripartite soul cluster, is our imprint in the beyond-spacetime Holofield. According to the Hawaiian Kahuna tradition, the *'aumakua*, the Oversoul, is our personal creator: the primordial source of our self. It divides at birth, producing a seed that takes up residence in a new body. As the "divine source," it projects our immortal soul into the newborn. Similarly to other cosmogony myths, the Kahuna tradition emphasizes that our personal creator is the immortal part of our self. The personal Oversouls together create the spirit of humankind, the *ka po'e 'Aumakua*.[118]

This kind of traditional wisdom matches the new map of reality. Or, to be precise, the new map substantiates and clarifies the teachings of many branches of the wisdom traditions.

The New Map of Consciousness and the Neurosciences

Nitamo Federico Montecucco

In every part of the world we are witnessing today the birth of a global civilization with a global consciousness. Consciousness is the core of every living being and the key to human evolution. It is also the core of the paradigm emerging in field after field in science, culture, and spirituality. In this context, Ervin Laszlo presents in this book an important element, bringing together ancient spiritual wisdom and advanced scientific knowledge in a new paradigm in which consciousness is fundamental.

Two Paradigms

For centuries the old paradigm has divided consciousness from matter, the soul from the body, nation from nation, and science from religion, creating a world of divisions and wars without respect for the consciousness of human beings. Responsibility for the rise of ecological, economic, and social crises can be ascribed to the dominance of the old dichotomous paradigm. That paradigm is no longer tenable.

Today, we witness the constant and increasingly rapid development of a new way of thinking and living, a unitary paradigm capable of understanding the human being and all life in the integral way in which consciousness coexists with what we have called "matter" and forms a coherent whole. The emerging paradigm in science is part of a more ecological, humane, and sustainable trend in the world.

In this time of transition, we are observing an exponential evolution of research and understanding in the principal fields of science, such as physics, genetics, neuroscience and PNEI (psycho-neuro-endocrine-immunology). This supports the new paradigm and provides a unitary understanding of consciousness and its evolution from the level of quanta through proto-consciousness to developed human self-awareness.

The Old Paradigm and the Fragmented Neurophysiological Model

The dichotomous-fragmented model that forms the basis of the mainstream cultures is the philosophical and scientific expression of a human being without integrity—of an individual who experiences a deep inner division between body and soul, between heart and head, between male rational qualities and his female affective capacities, as well as between instincts and conscience. The dichotomous model results from a divided neurocognitive communication between areas of the brain, from a fragmented and dysfunctional interaction between the reptilian instinctive brain, the mammal emotional brain, and the human mental brain, and from a division between the brain from a fragmented and dysfunctional interaction between the reptilian instinctive brain, the mammal emotional brain, and the human mental brain, and from a division between the brain's rational and the intuitive hemispheres. Neuroscientist Paul Maclean called "schizophysiology" this divided state of consciousness. As we shall see, this neurophysiologically fragmented communication is detected, recorded, and quantified as low coherence in the electroencephalographic (EEG) waves emitted by the brain.

The New Paradigm: The DNA of a Global Civilization

Science's new paradigm offers a unitary conception of human being and existence. It is expressed by a person aware of his or her psychosomatic wholeness; a person living in a more natural and conscious way.

The research of the brain I conducted in the last two decades in Italy, as well as in some Himalayan monasteries, shows that in a state of depression, illness, or existential crisis, EEG waves show a low level of coherence, while in states of creativity, integrity, and mental and physical meditation the brain produces high EEG coherence: harmonic waves at a high level of synchronization. The figures below show the increasing rate of EEG coherence from the normal state *(left)* to the state of self-awareness *(right)*. The top two figures illustrate the increasing EEG coherence of the two hemispheres of a person's brain, and the bottom two figures show the increasing EEG coherence of the brains of twelve persons before meditation *(left)* and after meditation *(right)*.

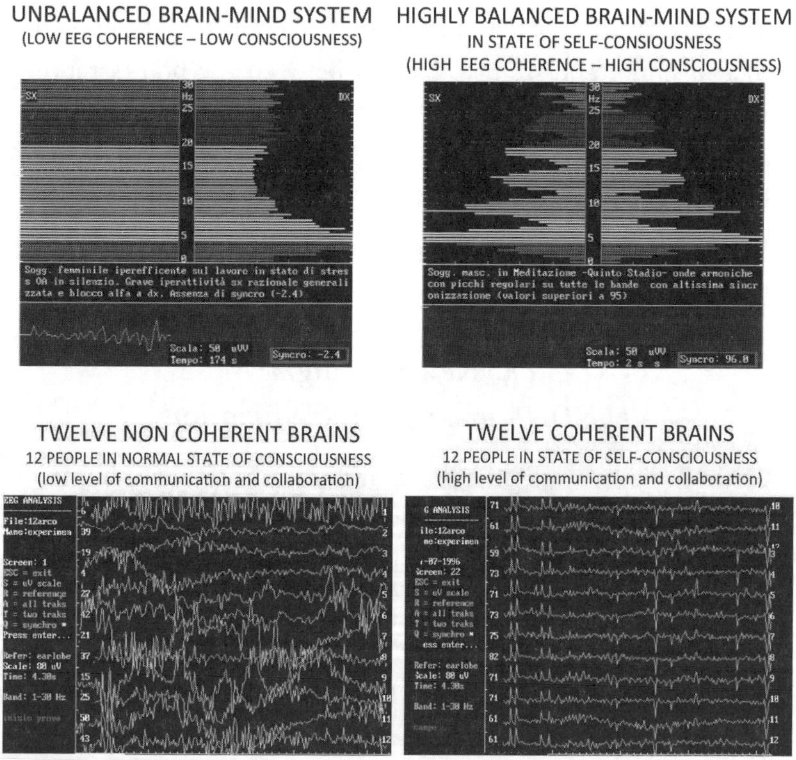
UNBALANCED BRAIN-MIND SYSTEM
(LOW EEG COHERENCE – LOW CONSCIOUSNESS)
HIGHLY BALANCED BRAIN-MIND SYSTEM
IN STATE OF SELF-CONSIOUSNESS
(HIGH EEG COHERENCE – HIGH CONSCIOUSNESS)
TWELVE NON COHERENT BRAINS
12 PEOPLE IN NORMAL STATE OF CONSCIOUSNESS
(low level of communication and collaboration)
TWELVE COHERENT BRAINS
12 PEOPLE IN STATE OF SELF-CONSCIOUSNESS
(high level of communication and collaboration)

© by Nitamo Federico Montecucco and provided courtesy of Dr. Montecucco

Alignment with the new paradigm's concept of reality comes about naturally in persons who live in harmony with nature's physical dimensions and are aware of being part of a delicate social balance and ecological equilibrium. The inner psychosomatic unity generate a different health and behavior and creates a unified way of perception of self and the world. This unified, harmonious, balanced, and nonviolent way to thinking and acting is the root of the Holos paradigm, and the unified vision of the human being and the planet. It represents the most important cultural revolution of our time. And it is only from this Holos paradigm that we can expect a radical transformation of our way of living and understanding the world.

The Dichotomous Paradigm and Evolution Driven by Chance

As Ervin Laszlo highlights in this book, the materialistic side of the old dichotomous paradigm is the mechanistic and reductionist neo-Darwinian interpretation that views evolution as a result of chance. The religious side of the old paradigm is the ideological and metaphysical interpretation keynoted by "creationism" and the affirmation of intelligent design. It considers a transcendental entity to be the sole creator of every "superior" form of biological life, refusing to recognize the relevant paleontological and scientific evidence. Both the materialistic and the metaphysical side of the old paradigm negate the fundamental role of consciousness in evolution.

The Neuro-Evolution of Consciousness

The fundamental understanding of all ancient and new holistic paradigms is that consciousness is pervading, informing, and organizing the whole of existence; it is the driver of the evolutionary process.

The new paradigm's first task is to enable a unitary understanding of the evolution of consciousness, from quantum physics to human self-awareness. Evolution is the most important phenomenon of life, because it is concerned not only with the already amazing processes of living beings, but also with their astonishing development toward higher levels of complexity, organization, perception, and understanding. The general laws of the evolutionary process allow us to understand how intelligence, compassion, and consciousness evolve in living organisms, and therefore the direction we can take to evolve individually and collectively toward a planetary consciousness: how we can shift from the fragmented and unsustainable eco-social condition of humanity to a more humane and sustainable planetary civilization.

The exponential development of research in neuroscience and psycho-neuro-endocrine-immunology (PNEI) conveys a new, comprehensive understanding of the unity of brain, mind, and consciousness. My own research focuses on brain-mind psychosomatic evolution—the "neuro-evolution of consciousness." Knowing the general laws of evolution conveys an understanding of the evolution of individual and collective self-awareness toward a planetary consciousness and a sustainable civilization.

Thus, it is fundamental to research and for the development of the unitary paradigm in regard to consciousness.

Consciousness Beyond Spacetime

Laszlo shows here that understanding the nature of both consciousness and a dimension beyond physical spacetime is an important and fascinating task. Modern science provides a basis for formulating hypotheses that can explain spiritual experience and provide a logical background to grasp the complex mechanisms that govern the elusive phenomena of consciousness.

When we "die," the psychosomatic unity of our body disorganizes and breaks apart: the atoms of the somatic biochemical body become separate elements, while consciousness (the "soul") becomes free of spacetime boundaries and experiences itself in a dimension of nonlocal information. Just as thermodynamics shows that there is a principle of conservation of energy and mass in nature, so there is a parallel principle of conservation of consciousness and information that is not subject to physical spacetime restrictions. In a Taolike universe, the spacetime Yang of the physical energy dimension and the nonlocal Yin of the dimension of consciousness and information are intrinsically interconnected and related. Quantum particles appear and disappear, shifting dimensions as we do when we are born and when we die. The physical dimension needs consciousness and information to organize and evolve, and the consciousness dimension needs the challenge and disorder (entropy) of physical reality to grow and realize itself.

Neuroscience Research on Consciousness of the Self and Nonlocal Interaction

Since 1991, I conducted a series of electroencephalograph (EEG) experiments to analyze the frequency spectrum of the brain through Fourier Transforms, and I also observed the coherence of EEG waves between the different parts of the brain.

The first discovery was that in a state of awareness and psychosomatic integrity, the brain spectrum consists of harmonic waves of increased coherence between the different areas of the brain, while in a state of disorientation and depression, the spectrum is disharmonious and EEG coherence is greatly decreased. In the following years, with the help of a computerized electroencephalograph, we began to study the interaction of the EEG waves of two people who are close to each other. We discovered that there is a "neuropsychic resonance" between the two brains, a synchronization we could record and quantify as EEG coherence.

In 1992 we began experimental research on the "Buddhafield," or a field of collective consciousness, and in 1994 we could demonstrate the existence of this field by measuring the collective EEG-wave coherence of twelve people in a state of meditation. This field could be explained as local electromagnetic interaction that decreases with the distance. But we also found a nonlocal aspect of this coherence. This became evident on May 20, 2007, when one million people were connected worldwide by the World Peace Prayer and Meditation Day hosted by Ervin Laszlo and the Club of Budapest, among others. We first carried out an experiment to evaluate the existence of a coherent collective consciousness field when two groups of subjects entered a state of meditation at a distance of about 200 km. The data confirmed the existence of a relatively low but statistically significant synchronization of the EEG waves of the two groups, with an average of 0.5 percent coherence peaking at 5 percent.

With these experiments we have shown that the collective consciousness of groups of people has a space-independent nonlocal component. We consider this a scientific evidence for the existence of a planetary consciousness. The mystery of understanding human consciousness remains, but now our consciousness can study itself in a more scientific way.

"That" reality and "this" reality are just one reality. The *Isa Upanishads* of India tell us,

That is the Whole, This is the Whole,
From Wholeness emerges Wholeness,
Wholeness return to Wholeness,
And Wholeness still remains.[119]

Two Experiences Beyond Space and Time

When I was fifteen, I was riding a motorcycle at night on a dark country road and a truck pushed me on to a rock at the side of the road. The bike turned over, I was thrown up in the air, and then crashed violently to the ground. A moment later I watched my inert body on the roadside from a height of about eight to ten meters. There was no pain; I felt very well. My perceptions had remained in my body while I was a free consciousness. Then I saw a car coming at high speed and knew that it would run over my body, as it was hardly visible on the dark road. I tried to return to my body, and woke up in that aching body. I rolled off the road and the car passed close by, but without hurting me. The experience was so clear that, despite its strangeness, I have no doubt that my consciousness is not only in the brain, but is somehow only connected with it.

On another occasion, in the winter of 1983, I was walking in the snow in Oregon when suddenly my breath, body, and mind stopped, and my consciousness expanded. It pulsated instantaneously as a bright light that embraced the whole valley. All things, the valley and the mountains, the houses and the people, became information and intelligent energy in a continuum of consciousness: an entanglement where everything was related to everything else. I felt like I do not exist—just being melted in an ocean of awareness. I was melted into that ocean and knew everything through spontaneous perception, beyond the normal dimensions of thoughts and words. Then I slowly returned to my body—but nothing was the same as before. Since then I have been engaged in research and experiment to understand the real nature of brain and consciousness.

CHAPTER 6

The New Map and the Nature of Existence

Existence Beyond the Body: The Tibetan View

TULKU THONDUP

IT IS HIGHLY INSPIRING TO READ these glimpses into the journey of consciousness beyond spacetime. It shows us that our experience after death is colored by our culture.

As this narrative suggests, and as Buddhism teaches, our identity is not our body or our career, but our mind—our consciousness. The body is merely a guesthouse. When we die, our mind leaves the body and takes rebirth in another life. In rare cases, if the person is a delog, they can cross the "boundary of no-return" and return to their former body.

According to Buddhism, all beings are reborn after death in some worldly realm—except if they become enlightened, transcending karma, cause and effect. Our future life depends totally on our current life's mental habits—on our karma. If we are drenched in negative thoughts and deeds, we will suffer in one of the hellish realms. If we are highly evolved, we could take rebirth in a pure land. None of this should be surprising, since our future existence is the reflection of our own mind.

I would like to add that there are many levels of pure lands in the Buddhist tradition. The highest levels of pure lands can be perceived only by fully enlightened ones, such as Buddhas. Other levels of pure lands, such as the one cited here, can be perceived by highly realized beings who do not have to be fully enlightened. In which level of pure land we take rebirth depends on our level of spiritual attainment.

If we wish to have a better rebirth, we need to improve the habits of our mind and the physical deeds inspired by our mind. Then and only then will the chains of our lives be ones that permit a happy existence.

Existence Beyond the Body: The Shamanic View

NA AAK

EVERY CULTURE HAS ITS OWN TECHNOLOGIES, disciplines, and practices to enter into the ethereal realm, such as meditation, sacred plants, extreme temperatures, fasting, prayer, sleep deprivation, contemplation, and others. What we call a nonordinary or altered state of consciousness is an experience beyond linear space and time, where the right brain functions expand and the person loses the limitations of the self-encapsulated ego. It is an experience in which I can identify myself as part of the environment that surrounds me, and my consciousness becomes amplified and open to the transpersonal realms, the realms beyond the individual. In these states I typically experience physical symptoms, perinatal and biographical memories with deep emotional charge, and a transpersonal expansion beyond space and time.

One of the most important steps in the evolution of our consciousness is to open up to experiences in these nonordinary or altered states. Indigenous communities created rituals and ceremonies to allow people to enter into an experience that takes them outside of the illusion of separation and into the realm of spirit, the realm of the Akasha. These practices have been misinterpreted as barbaric, primitive, and magical. They have been taken out of context and dismissed as empty. Yet the objective of these practices has been to overcome affliction, rise above ignorance, and merge beyond space and time while intuiting the sense of emptiness.

In indigenous societies these experiences come about in the ordinary states of our consciousness. The nonordinary is the experience of the physical/material aspect of life. The shaman or the medicine person can live permanently in the connected beyond-spacetime state. If I told a medicine person that my dead father has contacted me and walks around the house asking for my help, he would say that this is very good; talk to him and see what he wants. But if I told this to a doctor or an academic the most likely answer would be extreme concern for my mental health and a recommendation to seek psychiatric care.

The mystical experience is characterized by real yet extrasensory sensations, such as tasting color; seeing lights and shadows; experiencing rushes of coldness or heat in the body; hearing voices; talking to spirits; shifting shape with plants, animals, or deities; and seeing beyond time into the past and the future. These sensations are part of the ordinary state of consciousness for the mystic and shaman. Their lives are a continuous experience of the Akasha. If their mental state were to be analyzed in the context of mainstream medicine, the diagnosis might be paranoid schizoid disorder.

The mystic and shaman describe existence in the beyond-spacetime phase in terms of three basic forms or states: the astral, the causal, and the material. These are realms that correspond to attributes such as emotion, intellect, and materiality. Scriptures such as the *Upanishads* and other Vedic texts describe the forms that emerge in the various realms, but the most important realization is the existence of the fifth element: the ether. The ethereal realm, "the body of the universe," is that which allows things to be visible even when they are not solidified into gross existence.

The ethereal realm is the subtle body of the universe, the place where all things exist in potential. It is part of the beyond-spacetime hologram of the universe. It is not visible to the human eye but it is real; it is the origin of everything that is manifested in gross form. It has no separation in space and time. All things are together; all the information in the universe is here and now. In spacetime, things vibrate slowly enough to become perceptible, but beyond-spacetime they vibrate fast enough to be one. When we perceive this we enter the Akasha, the unbroken beyond-spacetime field of consciousness.

In the low-frequency realm separation is an illusion. We see, hear, touch, smell, and taste the world with our senses and analyze the data with our brain, but these are only the tools we use to experience the world. In the realm of gross existence, the consciousness of a human being is bound and restricted by its wrapping of bones, muscles, blood, and skin. The afflictions of this material body find a home in its attachments, aversions, and repulsions. Our eyes are blinded and we cannot see.

Beyond death we embark on a journey of detachment that helps us to recognize the true nature of the cosmos. The passage through the various bardos requires a trained teacher to guide consciousness through its many afflictions. When we embark on the journey beyond space and time our attachments become ropes that pull us away from pristine cognition into the drama and chaos of everyday experience. The journey beyond death is the most important event of the ongoing cycle of our existence. We spontaneously reconnect with the true nature of reality.

If things in space and time were left without arbitrary intervention, they would ultimately return to their origins. All of creation knows where home is, where to find congruence, peace, and liberation. This is why, despite misguided practices that numb the brain and consciousness, we conserve the instinct to return to the Akasha. A shaman or a mystic can provide support in this experience, yet most people wander around the world experiencing extrasensory sensations and feeling lost, having no clue what is happening to them. Spiritual emergence can be mistaken for a psychotic episode, and if it is treated as such, what could be a transformative initiation could become a destructive experience.

The journey beyond space and time can lead to the pristine cognition of the golden light that lies at its end. Can we behold that light? Can we love and accept unconditionally who and what we are? Or are we holding on to guilt and to shame? Guilt will become like lead for the ethereal body, locking us into an affliction we cannot overcome.

Religions have created rites of passage and told us that deities are waiting for us on the other side with lists of commandments and punishments. In indigenous cultures this is seen as a primitive idea. The passage is governed by a spirit that is actually the mirror of our deeds. For example, in the ancient Mayan tradition, the last space before total dissolution is the Etznab, a room of mirrors where we see a reflection of our own being. There is no "body" any longer; what was the unconscious is now the conscious.

This is the first phase of the journey of our discarnate consciousness, the phase where there are no hidden corners and all our merits and demerits are present to us. The final judgment comes from the state of our own consciousness: can we love and accept ourselves unconditionally? Or do we despise our self? This will decide the state into which we shall pass. Will it be reincarnation in a new body, or a trap created by the persistence of our incarnate afflictions?

When the material body has ceased to exist, the ethereal hologram of the individual remains in a transient state. In this state the ethereal self still suffers from attachments and ignorance, and its emotions and mental patterns determine the direction it will take. An evolved consciousness recognizes this transient state and prepares for the journey to reincarnation, or else into a higher, formless state of being.

At this stage, communication with the discarnate consciousness can be clear and effective. The individual still exists in the ethereal realm, its psyche persisting in a holographic form. If this consciousness does not manage to proceed to the following stages, it remains trapped in the in-between phase.

It is important to differentiate between the presence of a consciousness trapped in the in-between phase and evil entities or demons. The hologram of a person can wander around in familiar places and can become something like a guardian. It can take care of its loved ones until it is time for them to cross over. But consciousness can also remain in the in-between state, not knowing whether it is dead and where to go. When this happens, living people often have dreams and experiences in which the departed asks for help, and may even be insistent and demanding. In other cases the consciousness of the departed, having cultivated afflictions and attachments in life, finds it difficult to let go and it remains in a perturbed state, creating waves of affliction.

In traditional Egyptian culture the heart of the deceased is placed in a golden scale where Anubis, in the presence of Osiris, weighs the heart in relation to a *Maeig* (truth—a feather of a bird or of an ostrich). The heart riddled by guilt is as heavy as lead; only the heart that had cultivated truth is as light as a feather. It is our own afflictions and virtues that dictate how we experience death and continue our existence after death. The shaman or medicine person can only accompany the person's consciousness. His or her work has to be carried out while the person is alive.

The new millennium generations transform and perceive far beyond the physical dimension. Many children and young people live already in the world of the shaman and the medicine person: they have a natural connection to the domain beyond spacetime. This evolution is natural and must be cultivated if we hope to endure on this planet. The new man and woman have the consciousness and the capacities to drive the change needed in the world, to turn the tables on war and violence. As adults, we are either afraid of the change we see in our children, or we educate ourselves to be part of the evolution that unfolds in their consciousness.

A crucial step is to update the map we use to understand the human being. In ancient cultures there have been complex and sophisticated maps that, amazingly, turn out to match the current scientific understanding.

The map I find most congruent with reality is that of transpersonal psychology and quantum science combined with the cyclic structure of existence described in the Vedic scriptures. This map gives us a perspective on the human being that is independent of and distinct from the self-encapsulated ego of the modern world, and permits at the same time the realization that ultimately we are one with the Akasha. Embracing the perspective of the cyclic continuity of existence shifts our view of death and dying, transforming them into a glorious birth into the cosmos.

Existence Within and Beyond the Body: The Mystical View

JEAN HOUSTON

WHEN I WAS NINETEEN YEARS OLD I had a weekend hobby that few would consider intelligent. I jumped out of airplanes—with a parachute, of course. The training was simple and fast. We were taken to an old barn, where we learned to jump from its rafter into a pile of hay. Afterwards we were taught how to leap out from the plane into the sky, the countdown to pulling the rip cord, and some savvy advice on how not to break anything in our body upon landing. As an afterthought we were shown how to fold our parachute for the next jump. As jumps in those far off days were quite cheap—five dollars a jump—I took quite a few of them.

For a while, skydiving became a weekly event until one Saturday afternoon, I pulled my rip cord and nothing happened. I continued to tug away and still nothing happened. I must have folded my parachute wrong. I looked down at the ground, which was rising up to meet me forever, when, suddenly, my mind entered an amplitude of serenity and I found myself in life review. It seemed as if most of the events of my life from infancy to nineteen went by at their own time—not every little pork chop and chocolate bar, but the main events. The categories of time were strained by the tensions of eternity. Eternity had entered local time, and what was more, I seemed to be enveloped in a vast field of Consciousness that pervaded all and everything. I was a tiny dot in this Field, and yet, I was all and everything. It felt as if I had a vantage point from beyond spacetime wherein I could view the history of my life in spacetime. This glorious experience went on forever and then the parachute must have eventually opened for I found myself on the ground with a sore ankle. Needless to say, that was my last jump. (Or, perhaps, the chute never opened and you are reading this in Paradise.)

This experience helped to set me forth on a journey to explore the existence of Consciousness as the all-enveloping nature of reality. Of course, in the pursuit of such knowledge you come up against the rabid materialist agenda as exemplified by Francis Crick who essentially called us biological robots. In his book *The Astonishing Hypothesis* he informed us that "You, your joys and your sorrows, your memories and your ambitions, your sense of personal identity and free will, are in fact no more than the behavior of a vast assembly of nerve cells and their associated molecules."[120] In other words, he says we are robots. To me, his statement qualifies in the category *reductio ad absurdum*. Our being, our reality, our sense and sensibility is nothing but an assemblage of molecular components signifying nothing beyond the machinery that chances to manufacture Shakespeare, Mozart, Georgia O'Keefe, and Confucius. Delightful as this materialist fantasy is, I find greater truth in Ervin Laszlo's view that we are not biochemical machines destined to run down, but beings endowed with an infinite consciousness and a finite, but cyclically renewed body.

The theme of this remarkable book is that our consciousness continues beyond the death of the brain in the deep domain of the cosmos. This hypothesis is supported by exemplary reports of the continuity of conscious experience after the body dies. Ultimately, it comes down to the "deep domain of the cosmos" wherein Consciousness itself is the ground of all being, the source and sustenance of what we call "Reality."

Fractals and the Nature of Reality. One thing I know about reality is its fractal nature. Fractals are those patterns of repetition that are similar at all levels of magnification. You look at a huge coastline and see a certain wave pattern. But then look closely at the wave eddies in the sand and you see that they repeat fractally the coastline. They are not exactly the same, but they are certainly similar in process, if not exactly in form. Natural objects that are approximated by fractals to a degree include clouds, mountain ranges, lightning bolts, snowflakes, various vegetables (cauliflower and broccoli), and animal coloration patterns. Something under the microscope looks almost exactly like something that is 200 light years across the sky.

Looking at other patterns like trees, for instance, we see fractals of the brain and the circulatory system. Seashells are fractally related to the whorl pattern in flowers, to the ear, to the heart, to the DNA spiral, to the labyrinth, to our galaxy. And everything is patterned after the universe to which it is connected. The fractal dimensions in nature comprehend both outer and inner natures. Thus, the fractal repetitions of our lives with certain types of events repeating variations of themselves across time.

I am one who seeks to find a field of similarity and relevance between what may hitherto been seen as divided and distinguished worlds—art and science, theater and politics, reason and imagination, spirituality and economics, myth and history. And I can do this better when I see how one contains the fractals of the other. But now, with the understanding of the ways in which fractal resonance informs the whole, with increased observation of these patterns in both microcosmic and macrocosmic worlds as well as culture, we appreciate the ways in which ancient and indigenous people actually saw this and created symbolic structures that mediated and wove these together in mandalas, myths, and philosophies. "As above, so below. As within, so without."[121]

We have to consider that we are the stuff of photons and other subatomic matter, which compose the most basic properties of information. Our minds and the universe are mirrored realities. Just as matter and space evolved from a tiny dot to a universe of staggering proportions that seems to encompass body, soul, and mind, we too emerged from a pin-size dot of the fertilized egg into an immensely complex system that encompassed body, soul, and mind. Laws of form and emergence govern the genesis of ourselves and the universe: these include order and disorder, growth and entropy, determination and differentiation, and, above all, continuity. These laws are part of the matrix which we call Consciousness.

Understanding Consciousness is a journey that few have undertaken, perhaps most successfully in the spiritual journey of mystics in their pursuit of a larger reality. For what is mysticism but the art of union with Reality and a mystic, a person who aims at and believes in the attainment of such union. In its classical, spiritual form, it is a heroic journey, and valiant efforts are required to follow the path. Many of the spiritual teachers of the world have likened our lives to "a sleep and a forgetting." The mystic path, rather, is predicated on awakening, going off robot and abandoning lackluster passivity to engage co-creation with vigor, attention, focus, and radiance—characteristics, we might note, we can find in reports of near- and post-death experience. Thus, the mystical experience is perhaps the greatest accelerator of evolutionary enhancement. Through it, we tap into wider physical, mental, and emotional systems, thereby gaining entrance into the next stage of our unfolding, both individually and collectively. Once the province of the few, the mystic path may now be the requirement of the many—a unique developmental path for self and world.

In a lifetime of studying the art and science of human development, I have found no more powerful, practical, and evolutionary practice than what is known as the mystic path. When I have studied or talked with seekers who have had this experience, they have told me of a joy that passes understanding, an immense surge of creativity, an instant uprush of kindness and tolerance that makes them impassioned champions for the betterment of all: bridge builders, magnets for solutions, peacemakers, pathfinders. Best of all, other people feel enriched and nourished around them. Everyone they touch becomes more because they themselves are more. Perhaps we have needed the changes and accelerations of our time to put the flame under the crucible of becoming so that such inward alchemy could take place.

Mysticism seems to rise during times of intense change and stress. Add the sufficiency of current shadows and the breakdown of all certainties, and we have the ingredients for the current universal pursuit of spiritual realities. We live in a time in which more and more history is happening faster and faster than we can make sense of it. The habits of millennia seem to vanish in a few months and the convictions of centuries are crashing down like the Twin Towers of the World Trade Center in New York on September 11, 2001. And yet, the deconstruction of traditional ways of being may invite the underlying Spirit of which we are a part to break through. Similarly, the experience of dying is that of the most radical deconstruction followed, as we learn in this book and countless other accounts, by the most complete breakthrough into another order of being within the great Consciousness of the cosmos.

Many have written of the mystic path and tracked its myriad adventures and planes of development. I have found Evelyn Underhill, writing early in the twentieth century, to be one of the finest guides to the experience. In her great work *Mysticism*,[122] she presents the mystic path as a series of eight organic stages: awakening, purification, illumination, voices and visions, contemplation and introversion, ecstasy and rapture, the dark night of the soul, and union with the One Reality. In reflecting on these stages for this book, I've discovered that of the nature of each of these stages is remarkably similar to many of the descriptions reported of the after-life journey. These seems to be part of the hologram of fractally repeated experience that relate to both the experience of the mystic and many of the descriptions of the after-death experience. Indeed, the correlations both in description and in tone are remarkable. Here, for example, is a brief look at the stages of the mystical life both as they are found in classical mysticism as well as in reports of consciousness in the afterlife. Part of the description of stages of the mystical experience is adapted from my book, *Mystical Dogs*.[123]

In the first stage, "awakening," one wakes up, to put it quite simply. Suddenly, the world is filled with splendor and glory, and one understands that one is a citizen in a much larger universe. One is filled with the awareness that one is a part of an enormous Life, in which everything is connected to everything else and it is very, very good. This correlates with the many reports of the expanded awareness and happiness of the initial "awakening" of those who cross the threshold between death and the greater life.

The second stage of mystical development is called "purgation" or "purification." Here one rids oneself of those veils and obstruction of the ordinary unexamined life that keep one from the knowledge that one has gained from awakening. One is released from old ways of being and recovers one's higher innocence. In traditional mysticism it can take the form of a very intense pursuit of asceticism or rigorous work on oneself to rid the vestiges of negative behaviors. In the reports of afterlife experience, the fractal continues with some form of judgment, life review, and karmic work in which understanding, feelings, and emotions are purified and there is altogether greater clarity on the meaning and values of one's life and time.

The traditional third stage is called the path of "illumination:" one is illumined in the light. The light of bliss—often experienced as actual light—literally pervades everything. One sees beauty and meaning and pattern everywhere; yet, one remains who one is and is able to go about one's daily work.

The stage of illumination is also one that many artists, actors, writers, visionaries, scientists, and creative people are blessed to access from time to time. In the accounts of consciousness beyond spacetime, the experience of light as the all-pervading essence is a constant in the reports. "The light radiated from no one direction, it was a glowing, universal fact, bathing everything in its soft radiance so that the sharp shadows and dark edges which define objects on earth were missing. Each thing glowed or sparkled with its own light and was lighted as well by the circumambient splendor."[124]

The fourth stage is called "voices and visions." One sees, hears, senses—with more than five senses—an amplitude of reality, including things one has never seen before, such as beings of different dimensions, angels, archetypes, numinous borderline persons, or figures from other times and realms. It is a state of revealing and interacting with a much larger reality—including those spiritual allies that lie within us and the unfolding of the unseen gifts that we all contain. The afterlife experience is similar not only in one's encounter with family and friends who have also passed on, but with a panoply of higher beings, gods, higher planes of existence and other dwellers in the realms of spiritual existence.

The fifth stage is what Underhill and others call "introversion," which includes entering the silence in prayer and contemplation. It is a turning to the inner life, wherein one employs some of the vast resources of spiritual technology to journey inward to meet and receive Reality in its fullness. It results in daily life as a spiritual exercise, bringing the inner and the outer life together in a new way. In the correlate expression of life beyond death it takes the form of raising one's vibration to the frequency domain of the beyond-spacetime dimension.

The sixth stage is referred to as "ecstasy and rapture." Here the Divine Presence meets the prepared body, mind, emotions, and psyche of the mystic, which, cleared of the things that keep Reality at bay, now can ecstatically receive the One. It involves the art and science of happiness. There are similar reports in the experience of the afterlife of an expanse of feelings of joy, rapture, and exceeding happiness.

But, alas, after all this joy and rapture, the next stage, the seventh, is what is termed the "dark night of the soul," obeying the dictum that what goes up must come down. Suddenly the joy is gone, the Divine Lover is absent, God is hidden, and one is literally bereft of everything. Here one faces the remaining shadows of old forms and habits of the lesser self, preparing one to become more available to the final stage. Again, there appears to be a fractal of this in the higher frequencies before meeting with the One.

The eighth and last stage is called the "unitive life." At this stage one exists in the state of union with the One Reality all the time. One is both oneself and God. For those who enter this state, it seems as if nothing is impossible; indeed, everything becomes possible. They become world changers and world servers. They become powers for life, centers for energy, partners and guides for spiritual vitality in other human beings. They glow and set others glowing. They are force fields, and to be in their fields is to be set glowing. They are no longer human beings as we have known them. They are fields of being, for they have moved from Godseed to Godself. The experience in the world beyond spacetime appears to be remarkably the same, the entering into unity with Consciousness Itself, utter absorption into Spiritual union and grace.

In this book, we discover that these stages are not just for the mystic, but have their equivalence in the after-death experience. One appears to be the fractal resonance of the other. All of us have had experiences of to the beauty and wonder around us. And we have known the rigor of releasing old habits, and even the creativity and joy that come from new ways of being and thinking. We cannot avoid the depression and psychic flatland that accompany the dark night of the soul, and we may even have glimpsed or possibly experienced moments of transcendent union.

In studying the fractals of the mystic way of the journey beyond space and time, we find that love is the supreme quality that underlies the after-death experience. It is through the experience and practice of love that we travel both here and hereafter to the heart of the One, to Consciousness itself, lured by love to our infinite being wherever and however we exist.

Existence and the Intelligence of the Cosmos: Insights from a Psychedelic Communion

CHRISTOPHER M. BACHE

ERVIN LASZLO'S EXPOSITION OF the new map of reality evokes in me the same reaction I have had to all his books—a deep, instinctual, enthusiastic "Yes!" The scientific evidence he assembles for the new worldview makes my mind sing, but my Yes comes from a deeper place. It comes from the convergence of Laszlo's scientific vision with my personal experience. It comes from decades of exploring the farther bounds of consciousness using the psychedelic protocols developed by Stanislav Grof.

I believe that psychedelics represent a major turning point in philosophy, a true before-and-after advance. Their impact on Western thought has been delayed by the spasm of denial that branded them "hallucinogens" and locked them away as having "no currently accepted medical use and a high potential for abuse." But this reflex to criminalize psychedelics is exactly what we would expect when the stakes are this high, for these substances have the power to unravel and transform our culture's deepest convictions about what is real and true.

Laszlo's vision of the cosmos lifts science to a new horizon. He sees our universe floating in an invisible meta-universe of infinite potential, matter dancing in the quantum field, galaxies informed by a cosmic intelligence, a seamless wholeness that sustains and orders the diversity of life, every part driven by a relentless urge to grow and evolve, self-emergent creativity operating on timeline that staggers the imagination, our minds a fractal manifestation of the *logos*, the mind of All-That-Is.

The convergence of Laszlo's vision with insights arising from psychedelic research is deep and significant. The map of consciousness that Laszlo postulates can be experienced first-hand when psychedelics are used judiciously, systematically, and heroically. By methodically hyper-sensitizing our consciousness, by surrendering to the explosion of awareness that rises from within, by riding the cycles of death and rebirth that crush and liberate us, we enter into a deepening communion with existence. As the constrictive patterns of our private minds fall away, we awaken inside the mind of the universe itself.

It is difficult to overestimate the significance of this discovery coming at this precise moment in history. Just when Western culture had convinced itself that the entire universe is a machine, that it moves with a machine's precision and a machine's blindness, the capacity to experience the inner life of the universe is being given back to us. Because machines are not conscious, the appearance of consciousness in the universe has been interpreted as a cosmic accident, a remarkable stroke of good luck, nothing more. The entire human endeavor, with its vast range of sufferings and joys, has been emptied of existential significance because it has been judged to be merely a product of blind chance that disappears in a wisp of smoke when death finally snuffs our candle out.

When one gains access to the inner experience of the universe, however, one learns that far from being an accident, our conscious presence on this planet is the result of a supreme and heroic effort. Far from living our lives unnoticed in a distant corner of an insentient universe, we discover that we are everywhere surrounded by orders of intelligence beyond reckoning, that our consciousness does not end at death but continues in an ocean of time. In brief, we discover the universe that Laszlo describes so eloquently.

Waking to the Mind of the Cosmos

The most meaningful response I can offer to Laszlo's new map is to share a personal experience of the communion I speak of. I hesitate to do so, however, because it is dangerous to lift an experience out of its context, in this case the context of the larger visionary journey in which it was embedded. But there is space for only one example, so I offer this experience to illustrate the kind of contact with cosmic consciousness that psychedelics can facilitate. Nature exacts a price for such intimacies, but I will prune away the suffering that took place earlier in the session and skip over the many episodes of death-rebirth that prepared the ground in the preceding five years. Here we move directly to the fruition that took place in the second half of the session. This experience took place in the nineteenth of seventy-three high-dose LSD sessions I did between 1979 and 1999.

When I eventually moved beyond the field of collective suffering, I entered an exceptionally clear state that was vast and time-saturated. It felt both ancient and open-ended, a field of infinite possibilities. As I stabilized in this new environment, a circle opened around me and created a space that became an arena of dialogue between myself and a larger Consciousness. I discovered, much to my surprise, that the experiential field within the circle was responsive to my thoughts. When I first discovered this, I had the ecstatic sensation of confronting an enormous Intelligence that included and surrounded my own. "That's right," it communicated to me. "That's exactly what is happening." I began to ask It questions and It answered by orchestrating my experience in the circle. It was an extremely subtle process.

After some intervening experiences, I was brought to an encounter with a unified energy field underlying all physical existence. I confronted an enormous field of blindingly bright, incredibly intense energy. Experiencing it was extremely demanding and carried with it a sense of ultimate encounter. This energy was the single energy that comprised all existence. All things that existed were but varied aspects of its comprehensive existence.

The experience then changed into a powerful and moving experience of the Cosmic Tree. The energy became a massive tree of radiant energy suspended in space. Larger than the largest galaxy, it was comprised entirely of light. The core of the tree was lost to the brilliant display but limbs and leaves were visible around its edges. I experienced myself as one of its leaves. The lives of my family and close friends were leaves clustered near me on a small branch. All of our distinguishing characteristics, what made us the individuals we were, appeared from this perspective to be quite minor, almost arbitrary variations of this fundamental energy.

I was taken around the tree and shown how easy it was to move from one person's experience to another, and indeed it was ridiculously easy. Different lives around the globe were simply different experiences the tree was having. Choice governed all experience. Different beings who were all part of Being Itself had simply chosen these manifold experiences.

At this point I was the tree. Not that I was having the full range of its experience, but I knew myself to be this single, encompassing consciousness. I knew that Its identity was my true identity. I was actually experiencing the seamless flow of consciousness into crystallizations of embodiment. I was experiencing how consciousness manifests itself in separate forms while remaining unified. I knew then that there was fundamentally only One Consciousness in the universe. From this perspective my individual identity and everyone else's appeared temporary and almost trivial. To experience my true identity filled me with a profound sense of numinous encounter. "So this is what I am." The freedom was sheer bliss.

For the next several hours, this Consciousness took me on an extraordinary tour of the universe. It was as though It wanted to show me Its work. It appeared to be the creator and generative intelligence of our physical universe.

It would "take me somewhere" or open me to some experience and I would come to understand some aspect of the working of the universe. Over and over again I was overwhelmed at the magnitude, the subtlety, and the intelligence of what I was witnessing. "That's incredible." "I'm beginning to understand." The beauty of the design was such that I was repeatedly left breathless by what I was seeing. Sometimes I was so staggered that I would stop and It had to come back for me. "Keep up. Keep up," It said, taking delight in my awe. Sometimes I was not sure what I was seeing and It would do something and everything would suddenly become larger and I would understand. Then It would take me on to something else.

These experiences were the most ecstatic, most cognitively marvelous, most existentially satisfying experiences of my life. My elevation into the field I was now in had the subjective quality of remembering, as did all my experiences on the tour. I was reawakening to levels of reality that I had previously known but forgotten. I was lifted into one "higher" and "larger" experiential field after another. With each transition I entered a deeper level of quiet and bliss-filled peace. It was as though an amnesia lasting billions of years was being lifted from me, layer by layer. The more I remembered, the larger I became. Wave after wave of awakening was pushing back the edges of my being. To remember more was to become more.

Finally I was lifted into a particularly spacious and peaceful dimension. As I remembered this dimension I was overcome by an overwhelming sense of homecoming and felt fully the tragedy of having forgotten this dimension for so long. I cannot describe how poignant this was. Being fully restored to this dimension would be worth any cost. I asked what had happened and It explained that we had left time. Then It said, "We never intended so many to get caught in time." It felt like time was simply one of the many creative experiments of the multidimensional universe I was being shown.

Though these experiences were extraordinary in their own right, the most poignant aspect of today's session was not the discovered dimensions of the universe themselves but what my seeing and understanding them meant to the Consciousness I was with. It seemed to be pleased to have someone to view Its work. I felt that It had been waiting for billions of years for embodied consciousness to evolve to the point where we could at long last begin to see, to understand and appreciate what had been accomplished. I felt the loneliness of this Intelligence, having created such a masterpiece and having no one to appreciate Its work, and I wept. I wept for Its isolation and in awe of the profound love that had accepted this isolation as part of a larger plan. Behind creation lies a love of extraordinary proportions, and all of existence is an expression of this love. The intelligence of the universe's design is matched by the depth of love that inspired it.

CHAPTER 7

Wider Horizons

The Tao, Consciousness, and Existence

Dr. and Master Zhi-Gang Sha

I am honored to contribute my thoughts to this book. From my perspective as a Tao servant and teacher, I appreciate the new map of reality presented by Ervin Laszlo as well as the insights provided by Deepak Chopra, Stanislav Grof, Gary Zukav, Jean Houston, and the other contributors to this path-breaking book.

The great Tao sage Lao Tse explained that the Tao is the source of all life and all creation. Many thinkers understand the concept of the Tao as the source that creates *yin* and *yang* as two, and the ability of two to create three and from three to create all things. This is the process of Tao creation. What fewer scientists have studied is what Tao scholars call "the blurred condition" as the reality indicated by Laszlo's concept of the low-frequency band of our coherence domain. It is from this deep dimension that all things arise in the universe, and into which all things return. We can comprehend the cycle of existence as all things arising from and then moving back to the Tao. The reverse of creation is the return of all things to Tao, their source. This is a major insight that Laszlo's theory shares with the Tao.

Laszlo speaks of the cosmos as the wider reality that is more inclusive than the universe. The universe contains all the things we had called matter. The cosmos contains not only these things but also consciousness. The cosmos is boundless.

In my teaching I emphasize that each human being can access this consciousness which is not just created from the Tao but—at the same time—is the Tao itself. When we access this deeper reality, the Tao-field, miracle healings can occur.

My personal mission is to teach others not only how to access this deeper reality, to heal themselves and others, but eventually to return to the Tao as more evolved beings. This return can include entering the state of Tao awareness or Cosmic Consciousness even while still in human form. In my tradition it is reported that those who achieve the state of Tao are able to transcend the limits of space and time. All things are unified in the Cosmic Consciousness, in the ground-state *logos* of the cosmos.

It is impossible to talk about the Tao. The Tao is larger than the largest and smaller than the smallest. The Tao has no beginning nor end and is infinite in every direction. All comes from the Tao and all will return to the Tao. The journey of the individual soul is to incarnate as a human being and through unconditional service to the life force and other souls to return to the Tao. In being of service to other souls, purification takes place, and with perfect purification a human being can reach immortality.

This is not an easy or quick path. Millions of lifetimes of service will be required and even then a single misstep of pride or wrong action could cause a soul to fall in vibration and require further purification.

Ervin Laszlo has identified many scientific principles that corroborate my teaching. Not just human beings but every rock, tree, and element on earth and throughout the universe has a soul, a consciousness. Every DNA, RNA, cell, and quantum has a consciousness. Modern science does not have the ability to measure these consciousnesses, but I believe that the principle of a deeper dimension of reality will be, and it already is, understood by science. It is important that we progress to this level of understanding because it will alter human behavior in positive and significant ways. If we knew that every element in our world has a consciousness we would be more careful how we treat each other as well as Mother Earth and its creatures, plants, air, water, and all elements.

Laszlo writes that there is a directionality in the world, a trend that expresses a deeper meaning and purpose in our existence. I could not agree more. For me, that trend is to follow the Tao. Those who follow the Tao principles flourish, and those who go against them must learn their lessons. I advise my students to purify, purify, purify and practice, practice, practice the chants and actions that will assist the journey of their consciousness. Every word, every action, every thought in every moment impacts on that journey. The paradox of individual existence is that our individual consciousness and our spacetime-bound bodies are ultimately part of a universal consciousness, a pure field which I call Tao and Laszlo calls the ground state of the cosmos. This deep reality beyond spacetime is without beginning and end and it encompasses all that we are, all that we think, and all that we feel in a unitary presence that transcends space and time.

Laszlo developed the theory of the low-frequency Akashic domain to explain the fundamental reality of the cosmos. That domain is the Tao. Align yourself with the Tao and you may reach not just an understanding of immortality but immortality itself. This may seem impossible to traditional scientists focused exclusively on measurable phenomena. But allow your consciousness to evolve and you may experience the deep reality, the condition in which you are both part of the domain of space and time, and of the domain beyond spacetime—the domain that is limitless, boundless, and eternal.

The New Map of Reality: Who Are You Really?

JOHN R. AUDETTE

THERE IS A FAMOUS QUOTE attributed to Mark Twain, known for the many astute observations he kindly and brilliantly bestowed upon his fellow humans: *It's not what you don't know that will get you into trouble. It's what you think you know for sure that just ain't so.*

This has indisputable relevance to life's ultimate questions . . . the really big ones that we wrestle with for most of our conscious existence. They are the lingering, nagging questions that roll around in our heads and nip at our heels incessantly in search of satisfying answers. This book addresses the most important among them. It outlines a new paradigm—a new map of reality. In light of this map we get fresh, although basically timeless, answers to the big questions. *Who am I? Why am I here? What is life's true meaning and purpose? What happens to me and my loved ones when the time comes for us to die?*

As this book shows, oftentimes actual truth, that is to say uncompromised objective truth, is not what we think it is. It can be very different from that which we perceive or believe to be true. This certainly applies to what we think of ourselves and the world around us, as well as to reality as whole. What we think and perceive to be true, even though real to us in its impact and consequences, can be markedly different than what is actually true in the context of objective reality.

Laszlo's new map of reality tell us that this is the case when it comes to our thinking about the nature of reality, about consciousness and its disposition after bodily death, as well as to life's meaning and purpose. When it comes to sorting out these weighty issues, in the everyday context all of us are truly looking through a glass darkly. At best, we fumble around attempting to make educated guesses, using the tools of classical science to make discoveries that can be validated by replication under the intense scrutiny of peer review. Still, our knowledge is lacking, incomplete and imperfect.

My Life's Experience and Quest

I am not a scientist. I make no claim to be one. But I embrace science. I share the rigor and discipline of scientists in questing for truth. I have no interest in falsehoods, illusions, half-truths or dogmas. I hold no opinions or beliefs except those which I believe are defensible and fully supported by credible evidence. When I come to regard something as true, it is not necessarily because I want it to be true or need it to be true, but rather because I have determined it to be true through observation and research.

I learned long ago through trial and error that chasing butterflies in the field while walking along the primrose path wearing rose-colored glasses is a complete waste of one's time and energy. Truly, it serves no purpose to indulge in fiction or fantasy. So I do my best as a matter of discipline to seek out only truth and represent only truth, objectively speaking. Therefore, I go to great lengths to make sure my expressed positions are fully consistent with the best evidence and data available on any given subject.

In search of objective truth, I have been a diligent student of spiritually transformative experiences (STEs) and non-local consciousness experiences (NLCEs) since 1974. I began this work as an agnostic, having been raised in the Catholic faith, which I abandoned at age 18 when I was first able to live apart from the impositions of my well-meaning parents. Once independent, my life's path blessed me with two distinct advantages over most people in my quest for truth.

First, my life's path brought me into hospice work where I received the privilege of learning a great deal from dying patients. Second, it also brought me the opportunity to meet and interview hundreds of people over the years who had STEs and/or NLCEs of one kind or another, as well as the scientists who study them. This work also bestowed upon me the honor of meeting and working with some of the various leaders in the human potential/spiritual awakening movement who have written many of the leading books on these subjects.

These two distinct advantages empowered me with an uncommon vantage point. I was indeed privileged to form direct relationships with dozens of dying patients as they made their transition, and also with hundreds of people who reported NDEs and/or other kinds of STEs and/or NLCEs. These marvelous people, imbued with very special insights and wisdom from their astronaut-like journeys to the great beyond, were and are my greatest mentors.

I truly believe that if my fellow human beings could be gifted with the same opportunities I had to be in relationship with dying patients and those who report STEs and/or NLCEs, most would arrive at the same grounded conclusions I did.

What I learned from them in forty-two years of incessant study, and what I assert they can teach us all, is summarized in the following fifteen insights:

1. Consciousness is not dependent on the brain, nor is it a product or by-product of it.

2. Consciousness survives death. It is timeless and eternal. It is not bound by space, time, or form. It is neither matter nor energy. It is both individuated and immortal and indestructible.

3. There is no eternal salvation or eternal damnation or judgment by a superior being. Rather, there is only eternal existence and the ongoing evolution of souls into Christ or cosmic consciousness, which is best defined as the universal imperative to love all things unconditionally, including oneself.

4. The meaning and purpose of all existence is to evolve into a pure expression or manifestation of unconditional love for all things. Unconditional love is the abiding ultimate organizing principle of the universe/metaverse.

5. We all come from and return to the same Source or Creator, best described as total perfect unconditional love, absolute truth, and total knowledge.

6. All living things are one, all aspects of an interconnected whole, all vital elements in the matrix of creation. There is no real or true dichotomy

between animate and inanimate objects. All matter and energy, regardless of its manifest form in physical reality, participates equally in the web of creation through the unseen processes of quantum cohesion, coherence, and entanglement. Therefore, everything is "alive" at some level of being and with some basic level of awareness, if only by virtue of participation in the quantum processes that are incorporated within and among all matter.

7. What we sow we reap. What we do to others we do to ourselves, in full measure. This includes what we do to animals, trees, the oceans, the rivers, the earth, its atmosphere, and to outer space, for all of creation is an interconnected and interdependent matrix.

8. After death, there will be a comprehensive life review in the presence of Source/Creator and All That Is, to include every feeling, thought, word, and action, as well as the total impact we have had on the whole of creation. All is revealed. Nothing is concealed.

9. In this life review, we judge ourselves in the presence of pure unconditional love, total knowledge, and absolute truth. There is no external judgment,

just we who judge ourselves before indescribable love, beauty, and perfection.

10. In our life review, we feel the joy and love we brought one hundred times over, whereas we feel the pain and suffering we caused one hundred thousand times over.

11. Wherever and whenever we brought pain and suffering, we eagerly commit ourselves to a process of full atonement (and then some) to compensate or atone for the hurt we caused to those we hurt. This atonement occurs over the course of future lifetimes in various forms, times, and places.

12. Throughout eternity, we manifest in various forms and in various places as needed to atone to those we hurt and to learn to love all things unconditionally, ourselves included, until we master it perfectly and consistently.

13. When we master the consistent practice of unconditional love, as Jesus Christ did in physical form on the cross when He said, "Forgive them Father for they know not what they do," we reunite as One with Source again, from whence we came, because we match or equal the vibration of Source. This is the sublime blissful state commonly known as "Heaven." There is no higher

form of being. This is total perfection, love, and bliss. Rebirth into form ends except for voluntary incarnations to serve the greater good.

14. We can be only as strong as our weakest link. The good of the one and the good of the many are symbiotic. Both flourish in our natural ideal state of perfect unity, harmony, peace, and love.

15. All collective suffering is collectively self-inflicted, born of illusions and misperceptions, caused by a failure to see ourselves and the larger reality as they truly are in the bigger picture and the grander design. Source/Creator is not responsible for the ills or suffering we bring upon ourselves and our planet of our own choosing and free will.

These insights, also flowing from the new map of reality presented in this book, are not new discoveries or revelations. Rather, they are a distillation of timeless wisdom from ancient mystics, sages, and saints coupled with the cornerstone traditional teachings of the world's major religions and combined with research findings from the cutting edge of contemporary science.

Therefore, I assert that these insights reflect the best comprehension of reality and timeless universal truth formulated by human beings over millennia of reflection, contemplation, mystical experience, scholarly effort, and formal research. Perceptual, attitudinal, and behavioral alignment with these insights by most of humankind could result in the collective co-creation of an optimal, sustainable future for Earth and all its inhabitants.

Over the past four decades, I have made every effort to carefully consider every single alternative explanation within the materialist model of reality in an effort to explain STEs and NLCEs within this framework. In my opinion, no one explanation or grouping of explanations, other than the survival hypothesis, can adequately account for the full range of phenomena reported by persons who undergo extensive significant transformative experiences and nonlocal consciousness experiences.

Therefore, without ever having an STE myself, I evolved spiritually from being a detached agnostic in early 1974 to one who fully embraces these insights to be valid and true today. This insight grabbed hold of me in 1974 and has transfixed me ever since, enabling me to rethink, re-evaluate and redefine myself and my worldview to be fully consistent with the new map of cosmos and consciousness outlined in this book.

The Meaning and Importance of the Emerging Insights

Living in accordance with these insights, and rethinking ourselves in light of them, could dramatically change human nature and behavior, as well as the overall complexion of life on earth. Through a global process of reinforcing their validity with credible scientific research and promoting their popular acceptance through educational campaigns and personal growth programs, the spiritual evolution of humanity and the advancement of human civilization could be enhanced for the greater good of all.

To be sure, many individuals will avoid life's deeper questions until the proverbial hand grenade is in the trench. Only when the death of a close loved one occurs or a personal terminal illness strikes will they begin a deeper thought process in an effort to discover what more there may be to reality and to themselves apart from the body and the things of this world.

Yet, from common experience, we know that tomorrow is promised to no one. Most assuredly, it is not. Tomorrow never knows if it will find any one of us still here living on planet Earth in physical form to enjoy the company of our loved ones and the things we treasure in this existence.

As Buddha once said long ago, "Things appear only to disappear." And, to quote a popular cliché that conveys the same insight, "We're here one minute and gone the next." And, to quote another: "Now you see me. Now you don't."

Inarguably, the death of our physical form can come at any time. For some, with warning or advance notice, and for others with none. Death stalks us moment to moment, hovering over us like the proverbial sword of Damocles, lying in wait for the time when time runs out on our physical existence. Whether we live here for a short while or a long while, our lifetime in physical form on planet Earth still races by, passing from start to finish like the blinking of an eyelid.

Every single one of us suffers from a terminal condition called physical existence. Life as we know it in the body we occupy will surely end, predictably and invariably, as all matter does when the time comes for ultimate fate to strike. This holds true for all physical creation, even for our planet, our sun, our solar system, our galaxy, and the entire universe. Behold the sand mandala.

One day, all things in this universe must pass and transcend manifest form. But it is this finiteness that gives meaning and purpose to physical existence, not as the end all and be all, but as what is truly tantamount to being a proving ground for our continuous consciousness. Death challenges us to make our lives meaningful, and in that sense, all of physical life should be a continuous preparation for death.

This qualifies death to be the great common denominator . . . the great equalizer, for it affects us all equally and renders us all equal when we pass on, reducing our once vibrant physical form to an unremarkable lifeless corpse. The sooner we acknowledge this fact to ourselves, the sooner we can begin the very important inner work of discovering our larger spiritual identity beyond the body—beyond the physical container that temporarily houses our infinite consciousness.

Of course, we can delude ourselves into thinking otherwise, and many of us do, by denying the prospect of our own death. We can and do fool ourselves into thinking, “To thee and to thee and to thee but never to me.” Eventually, however, death will find each one of us, like it or not, with a rude command to "shuffle off our mortal coil." When that time comes, it will teach us in visceral terms the meaning of the poet John Donne's famous observation, "And therefore never send to know for whom the bell tolls; It tolls for thee."

There is a Native-American Indian expression that was commonly used among some tribes to convey their philosophy of life and death. *Today is a good day to die,* some would say or think at the start of each new day. This saying was a recognition that any given day could be their last on Earth in the body. It was a daily effort some of them made to acknowledge their association with or belonging to "the Great Spirit." It was reflective of their understanding that their earthly existence was temporal and transient. To say it another way, "life is but a dream."

Even though death is always lurking and looming, many of us in Western culture do not think about it. We busy ourselves with mundane earthly pursuits, dramas, and distractions that keep us quite preoccupied, all the while pretending we will live forever in this body and in this world. But such an attitude keeps us from confronting our own mortality and from asking ourselves the deeper questions about the true meaning and purpose of our existence. We can play this game of pretend only for so long. In a sudden flash, like all games, it must come to an end.

Without question, many of us lead relatively superficial lives transfixed by pursuit of the things of this world: material possessions, sports, romance, sex, wealth, fame, power, personal beauty, anti-aging strategies, popular entertainment, drugs, alcohol, and the like. In the end, none of these things hold any meaning for us whatsoever. In the end, we see all these things for the imposters and dead ends that they truly are.

If this describes your current reality and style of life, then know that you too are playing an imprudent game of make-believe. Kudos for reading this book to benefit from its wisdom. Kudos for taking the first step out of the box. To quote scripture, "For how does it profit a man to gain the world but lose his soul?"

The late Dr. Elisabeth Kubler-Ross would often remark in her lectures and interviews that "Dying patients are the greatest teachers in the world if we would only put aside our own fear of death long enough to listen to them and learn from them." Elisabeth was a long-time friend and pivotal mentor dating back to our first meeting in 1975.

A Swiss-born psychiatrist, Elisabeth founded the hospice movement in the United States and elsewhere. She is singularly credited with revolutionizing care for terminally ill patients and shattering the persistent cultural taboo concerning open discussion of end of life issues. In her classic work from 1969, *On Death & Dying*, she conceived the well-known five psycho-emotional stages of grief that most dying patients experience when they face death: "Anger, Denial, Depression, Bargaining, and Acceptance."

Elisabeth would frequently comment that many of us in Western culture have "a very erroneous view of death." She would often observe that "If we truly understood death and what it means to die, we would lose our fear of it. We would live our lives very differently, and treat one another very differently." She could not have been more right then, or more right now, or a thousand years from now.

When people who lack spiritual depth or conviction come to grips with their own impending death, they realize they can no longer define themselves in familiar customary terms. Their long held ego-identity begins to quickly disintegrate under the weight of so many long-harbored false illusions and assumptions concerning physical existence. They realize that it is no longer possible or viable to define themselves as the sum total of their physical body, or net worth, or material possessions, or accomplishments in life, or academic degrees, or the social roles they played in this lifetime, (husband, wife, sister, brother, father, mother, etc.).

These realizations spark an identity crisis of the first order, and give rise to a series of gut-wrenching questions. People ask themselves, if I am no longer any of these things, then who am I? What am I? What will become of me?

One day all of us will face these same issues. The sooner we face them, the better, ideally long before the onset of one's end of life drama. When that time comes for you, if you're still thinking you are your body or your social identity, this same towering identity crisis may take hold within your psyche. It can be a most challenging struggle indeed, mentally, in addition to the angst you may face over the pending demise of your physical form.

There is no better time than right now to become acquainted with one's inner eternal essence, one's soul, which in the end is all that survives the ordeal of physical death. So, if you are still of the opinion that your body is the sum total of who you are, then please examine the evidence closely as I have done and consider reevaluating your position. In fact, having now read these thoughts and observations, and this book from start to finish, please consider making Laszlo's New Paradigm of Reality your New Reality.

The first step is to begin to see yourself as more than your body, because you are. Your body dies, but you do not. Clearly, there is much more to reality than what meets your five senses. Clearly, there is more to you than your physical body. This is the truth that will set you free.

The next step is to use this as an opportunity to rethink, re-evaluate and redefine yourself. This could be an important wake-up call for you. Can't you hear the tolling of the bell? It tolls for you and me and for every one of us.

Albert Einstein, possibly the world's brightest scientist ever, is reputed to have said: *There are only two ways to live your life. One is as though nothing is a miracle. The other is as though everything is a miracle.*

It seems to me that the latter point of view is the most accurate way of thinking and perceiving reality. How can life and all creation be anything other than an amazing miracle? Consider how an acorn grows into an oak tree, or how simple stardust gathers together to form complex galaxies and other life forms. Consider how you and I became the people we have become from mere zygotes, from the simple union of sperm and egg. Consider that you are alive and breathing and thinking complex thought forms right now while a zillion other complex processes are simultaneously happening in your amazing body. If one cannot see all these things and so much more as astonishing awesome miracles, then one is not looking closely enough at the truly intricate nature of all things.

When one fully opens one's eyes and heart to truly comprehend the unfathomable complexion of nature and the breathtaking wonder of creation, a magnificent interconnected and interdependent matrix emerges from the depths of our observation that simply cannot be explained away by random chance.

As Albert Einstein and Max Planck and other great classical physicists concluded late in their remarkable scientific careers, the universe and all life within is much too precise and elegant to be the result of pure accident or coincidence. This is why in the latter years of their historic work, they and other great scientific thinkers began talking more like spiritual mystics than materialist scientists, precisely because they drilled down to the depths, as far as they could, to discover a universe that was much more an intentional brilliant construction than mere accidental happenstance.

Another well-known statement Einstein made in a private letter he wrote in February 1950 to Mr. Robert Marcus of New York City is further food for thought. In this correspondence, he said:

> *A human being is part of the whole world, called by us 'Universe,' a part limited in time and space. He experiences himself, his thoughts and feelings as something separated from the rest—a kind of optical delusion of his consciousness. The striving to free oneself from the delusion is the one issue of true religion. Not to nourish the delusion but to try to overcome it is the way to reach the attainable measure of peace of mind.*[125]

To free ourselves from this delusion that Einstein refers to in order to see ourselves as we really are in relation to the whole of creation, a new way of thinking is needed. This is not one based on faith, dogma, conjecture, or fantasy, but rather one that is deeply rooted in what Einstein called "true religion" based on facts, evidence, and knowledge derived from credible science.

What is that new manner of thinking? Could it be Laszlo's New Map of Reality? Could it be the insights expressed by Einstein, which are fully consistent with Laszlo's map? Could it be Buddha's call for us all to get "right in our thinking?" Could it be the teaching of Jesus Christ for us to discover and accept the "truth that will set you free?" Yes, indeed, but this is a conclusion you must reach for yourself—just as Einstein and Planck did, along with many other bright scientific minds like them, whose disciplined inquiry into the nature of creation brought them, analytically, to the inescapable intellectual conclusion that materialism is a flawed and archaic interpretation of reality. Godspeed on your journey to this same destination, which is where all roads of serious open-minded inquiry ultimately lead.*

Conscious Agency for Planetary Wholeness

Kingsley L. Dennis

As Ervin Laszlo so eloquently and clearly shows in this book, the cosmos is a self-organizing and self-actualizing whole. Holotropic evolutionary trends underlie all manifestation of its unfolding reality. Evolution in the known physical universe—in its laws and processes—as well as in and among living organisms, it appears, tends toward more sensitive and stable coherence, as well as toward conscious interconnectivity. On this planet the ultimate physical manifestation of coherence may very well be social order at a planetary scale—a planetary civilization. Could this be the arena where immanent universal order meets a transcendent emergent consciousness?

* The Laszlo Institute of New Paradigm Research and Eternea, together with the Club of Budapest and other like-minded organizations, join forces in a collaborative effort to provide humanity with a sound empirical basis to accept the validity of the above insights. We believe this could bring about profound change in human nature and the nature of social, educational, medical, political, and economic systems, as well as religion. We are advancing a holistic blueprint to aid the evolution of human consciousness and human civilization by changing individual perceptions of reality, as well as the basic understanding of life's meaning and purpose. We invite you to join us in this most urgent of all pursuits.

Social Coherence on a Planetary Scale

A grand sweep of history shows the rise and fall of countless civilizations, empires, and cultural impulses. From another viewpoint it also shows a marked shift in the perceptive traits of human consciousness. How we *see* the world, and our place in it, has influenced how we participate in the world around us. Until very recently, the consensus has been to view the world as exterior to us—separate and fragmented. Empires sought to conquer and control; and to create, as far as was possible, their idea of a unipolar world. Yet no empire ever truly succeeded in this endeavor. Previous city-states, societies, civilizations, and empires have represented the emergence of groupings ("systems") seeking greater stability and outreach—in a word, coherence. This fundamental need for coherence and stability that came with complex groupings was often critically centered on resources. The overshoot of a society/social system in the face of dwindling resources often resulted in sudden collapse. As in the physical, chemical, and biological examples mentioned in this book, the dominant attractor is coherence. The drive toward achieving greater levels of coherence—especially amongst increasingly complex systems—appears to be a universal trend, or vector. According to this hypothesis, by applying the coherent attractor to social systems then the ultimate scale-up on this planet would be a planetary civilization. Are we currently on the cusp of a developmental impulse toward a planetary civilization? Is this the purpose/drive behind the coherent order underlying existence in our spacetime?

We have entered a period where a unipolar world is no longer possible—the age of empires is at an end. Our present multipolar world reflects a level of deep interconnectivity between the dominant, and also not-so-dominant, nations, states, and regional blocks. Paradoxically, however, this early stage of global interconnectivity and interdependence is creating conflict amongst the major players—the very opposite of what we would expect to see in a drive toward coherence. So, where is the underlying coherence behind this display of social disruption?

In recent years we have witnessed the rise of an empathic consciousness among the diverse peoples of the world. A major catalyst behind this emergence has been our global technologies of communication. As Laszlo notes, a developing degree of "perception" (or "prehension") of the interconnection between parts of a whole serves as both an expression of coherence as well as a driver toward further coherence. The Internet—which is expected to have a sixty-six percent global reach by 2020—represents an exterior form of this underlying need for manifesting interconnectivity. Earlier commentary on the rise of global interconnectivity discussed this in terms of a "Global Brain." We know from recent neuroscience that the mind operates throughout the human body, and is largely centered in the human heart. The concept of the human brain and its functioning is increasingly referred to as an extended mind. Our technologies of connection and communication serve as the tangible expression of our species extended mind, and as such function as channels for our conscious communication.

The postindustrial world is establishing a global environment where unprecedented information flows, through distributed (and wireless) networks, are allowing for new levels of connection, collaboration, consciousness, and compassion.

We have become increasingly conscious of our inherent interconnectivity upon a social/physical level, as well as upon a digital and nonlocal one. Moreover, as the older borders and boundaries (both real and invented) separating us on this planet further dissolve, we find that there is greater unity within our diversity than we realized—and our social fears dissolve too. And how we *see* the world also influences how we interpret our *received* consciousness. It is likely that the current drive toward social coherence on planet Earth will first emerge through the individual consciousnesses of us, the people. From the Internet to smartphones, from social media and video sharing, from blogging to vlogging—we are connected, passionate (and compassionate), and striving to collaborate like never before in our history as a species. And much of this shift is taking place *under* the radar of the mainstream systems. The fundamental universal drive toward greater coherence may very well be manifesting through a marked shift in human consciousness that is now increasingly being played out on a global field.

The Emergence of Planetary Consciousness

The philosopher Karl Jaspers referred to the period from 800–200 BC as the Axial Age. It was a time that, according to Jaspers, new yet similar ways of thinking appeared in Persia,

India, China, and the Western world. He indicated also that the Axial Age represented an in-between period, where old certainties had lost their validity and new ones were yet to emerge. The new religions that arose in this time—Hinduism, Buddhism, Confucianism, Taoism, and monotheism—influenced new thinking in terms of individuality, identity, and the human condition. These new emerging religions helped to catalyze new forms of thinking and expressions of human consciousness. And yet, over time, we have seen how they were not wholly successful in developing coherence in a social context. Author and educator Duane Elgin has recently referred to our present time as the Second Axial Age, in that religions of separation are being replaced by a new spirit of communion. The world is moving into a spiritual communion and empathic connection with a living universe. A major feature of this emerging empathic consciousness is that it actively seeks conscious participation. Furthermore, it exhibits a direct-intuitive perception, rather than a linear-rational one. The more individual consciousnesses that connect across the planet, the greater will be the perception ("prehension") of this interconnectivity, which in turn catalyzes the innate fundamental drive toward seeking further coherence. This realization of our communion *in* consciousness further initiates the *receiving* of a consciousness seeking to manifest coherence as a universal natural order.

The purpose of sentient human life on this planet may well be the drive toward manifesting a coherent planetary consciousness. In other words, toward "bringing in" the consciousness field (outside spacetime) into greater manifestation in spacetime—in our case, here upon the earth. There is a correlation here with Aurobindo's concept of the Supermind, in that a form of higher consciousness can be made immanent upon the material plane. This would require the preparation of the human biological system in order to transceive (transmit and receive) and thus actualize this—a form of *transcendence* in consciousness. That is, raising localized aspects of consciousness (individual perceptions and awareness) in order to increase the coherence of consciousness amongst the whole. And this can be made tangible by local conscious actors—each one of us—becoming aware and participating through our everyday acts of right thinking, right behavior, and right being.

We are no longer either isolated individuals or an inarticulate mass—we are localized consciousness acting through aware individuals who seek to consciously connect, collaborate, and care about the future. Each one of us—as localized consciousness—is a reflection of nonlocal consciousness; and in this way we are also a reflection of each other. This analogy was beautifully expressed in the concept of Indra's Net where each jewel in the net reflects all the other jewels—it is a simple metaphor for the interconnectedness of our reality.

This energetic reality, validated by the new sciences outlined by Laszlo in this book, is now increasingly manifesting in our localized spacetime environment. We now have the means to interconnect nonlocally—through our technologies—as well as through our physical networks (made easier through increased social mobility). These are the signs of an emerging planetary civilization that respects diversity as well as unitary coherence. And as we connect and share our consciousness—our thoughts, ideas, visions, etc.—we will be helping to strengthen the signal—the *reception* or *prehension*—of consciousness and thus the *bringing in* of a coherent cosmic consciousness. A planetary consciousness on Earth, expressed through a sentient, individualized humanity, may not only be a real possibility but the expression of the fundamental cosmic purpose.

Human Consciousness and Purpose in the Cosmos

Laszlo suggests that a cosmic matrix beyond spacetime codes the spacetime universe, which then behaves in a way consistent with what we know as a holographic projection. The universe is *in-formed* by the deep consciousness beyond. It acts as a nonlocal consciousness field, of which sentient life is the localized manifestation.

It has been inferred through various religious and sacred texts and traditions that the universe (material reality) came into being as a way for its Source to know itself—"*I was a hidden treasure and wanted to be known.*" This is reminiscent of *Know Thyself*, the famous maxim from the Delphi oracle. Self-consciousness is ascribed to those creatures at the peak, or greater actualization, of consciousness. Self-reflection is one of the prized attributes of self-consciousness—yet how can the whole reflect upon itself? Self-realization is something we credit to each attained individual consciousness. As speculation, I wonder what self-realization upon a greater scale would be like. Self-realization as a planetary consciousness? As a galactic consciousness? And finally as a cosmic consciousness fully realized and self-conscious through all of its localized manifestations? Astounding initiation.

Human consciousness is a part of the greater whole. As sentient beings we receive part of the consciousness that pervades spacetime, and thus we are affected by it—*animated by it*—as well as feeding back into the whole. Our individual expressions of consciousness in spacetime reflect back into the greater nonlocal consciousness field, the ground-state *logos* of the cosmos. The greater our individual perceptions and conscious realization, the greater the total reflection of the cosmic consciousness in its entirety—just like the further polishing of any jewel in Indra's Net enhances the overall radiance of the whole net. The cosmic matrix of consciousness is in-formed through emerging conscious awareness of its parts. As each one of us wakes up, the cosmic net shines that little bit brighter. If enough localized consciousnesses awake upon this planet we may catalyze a localized planetary field into conscious awareness—a planetary net that is sufficiently prepared (polished) to "bring in" the greater consciousness that is pervasive in the cosmos: the immanence of the Supermind, to use Aurobindo's terminology. Then we are each a conscious agent of cosmic realization and immanence.

We each have an obligation in our existence on this planet to raise our individual, localized expressions of consciousness. In doing so, we both infect and inspire others in our lives to raise theirs, as well as reflecting back our conscious contribution into the source *THAT IS*. The hidden treasure that is at the very core of our existence wishes to be known—for *us* to be known—by our individual journeys of self-realization, and to "bring it all back home," (to paraphrase Bob Dylan).

After individual self-consciousness comes collective and planetary consciousness. The emerging technologies and social movements on this planet may well be part of this process, in-forming an extended mind and empathic embrace across the face of the earth. And one day we may witness a grand awakening, unprecedented on this planet—and this may very well underlie the meaning of sentient life, as conscious agents of evolutionary unfolding.

Laszlo's Map of Reality and the New Human Consciousness

Gary Zukav

Ervin Laszlo's map of reality offers a substantially new scientific concept to replace the most commonly held beliefs about the world. It is a revolution in the science that followed the discoveries of Isaac Newton. It is a powerfully open paradigm with wonderfully spacious ways of approaching the nature of the cosmos and our role in It.

A paradigm is a way of looking at the world and experiences. For example, a paradigm that the universe is inert (read: dead) and phenomena within it are inexorably controlled by rigid regularities (read: constants) within an overall context of chance (read: we don't know how the whole thing started or why) is a closed paradigm. Paradigms that the universe is mechanistic (read: a big machine) and/or that our experiences are predetermined (read: free will is an illusion) are also closed paradigms. Their assumptions prevent exploration of alternatives from inside and outside the paradigm just as the fortified walls of medieval cities kept inhabitants in and marauders out.

A paradigm that the universe is alive, wise, and compassionate, on the other hand, is an open paradigm. So too are paradigms that the world is meaningful even if we cannot always detect, deduce, or conclude the meaning, and many other paradigms that are not defended by indestructible dogmas—including dogmas once considered heretical (think Copernican astronomy). They open adherents to possibilities of meaningful explanations that are "nonsense" (literally) in the closed courtyards of rational inquiry. These paradigms are academic anathemas to verifiable veracity.

So powerful and pervasive is the ability of a paradigm to shape our experiences that they appear to be *products* of our experiences. The more our experiences conform to a paradigm, the more indisputable it becomes. Empirical science, by definition, assumes that only experiences of the five senses can validate the maximum economy and elegance of a theory that is at once consistent within itself and also consistent with experience. This assumption was the strength of science and adherence to it lifted human understanding above superstition.

Now we have come to an entirely new circumstance in human history. An expanded perception is emerging in hundreds of millions of individuals that is not confined to the limitations of the five senses! Were it not rapidly becoming a shared perception, individual examples of it would continue to be dismissed as hallucination or fantasy—near-death experiences, experiences of beauty, wonder, and awe; premonitions of events that have not yet occurred; communication with deceased loved ones; grounded sense of self as immortal; experiences of one's life as meaningful; intuitions of gifts within us—gifts that we were born to give—and the thirst to discover and give them. None of these are new in the human experience. What is new is the *species-wide* appearance of them in a startlingly brief period of time. Never before has the consciousness of a species as complex as our own transformed so dramatically and thoroughly, much less so quickly.

What are we to make of this—apart from denying its existence? When a question is asked that cannot be answered with conventional understanding, the way of the seeker—the true scientist—has always been to expand into a larger context. When the question was asked, for example, if forms of life exist that are smaller than we can see, the microscope was invented. Now questions that we have asked since our origin are being asked with new relevancy: do domains of the universe exist beyond the confines of the five senses? As humankind expands into its larger awareness, answers are arriving through direct experience. But how can science account for this?

This brings me back to Ervin Laszlo's wonderfully open integral paradigm. It bridges the domain of space and time (the physical world) and the domain beyond spacetime (the transcendent nonphysical reality). It provides a model that invites discourse and intellectual inquiry into the most fecund, profound, and relevant questions now before us while honoring the rigorous requirements of scientific certitude. The certitude it seeks is not the surety of knowing how the universe works, but of exploring a model that opens us to understanding our new experiences from the context in which we find ourselves—a five-sensory world. It does not deny or condemn the expanded, multisensory experiences of millions. On the contrary: it begins with them and seeks a cogent explanation that can help us explore them more deeply, that opens portals of awe and leaves them open. It begins the discussion that could transform the five-sensory (empirical) discipline of science into the multisensory investigation of new multisensory experiences that are coming to the foreground of human awareness.

Ervin Laszlo's unitary paradigm does not attempt to define Divinity. A set cannot be defined in the terms of one of its subsets. Five-sensory perception is a subset of a larger set, and that larger set is the nonphysical domain from which we come and to which we will return. This larger domain has no place, and no possibility of being recognized, in the self-defined discipline of a five-sensory science that is limited in its ability to address the most vital issues before us. Laszlo's map of reality accommodates and defines this domain. It opens the door through which yet unappreciated ways to welcome wisdom and compassion may pass. A new species of multisensory humans is now encountering domains of experience that invoke full, deep, and reverent appreciation of the universe. Only a paradigm such as Laszlo describes can support this irreversible encounter.

A Significant Coincidence

The Dancing Wu Li Masters: An Overview of the New Physics, a book about quantum mechanics, particle physics, relativity, and quantum logic that I wrote in 1979 won the American Book Award for Science. *The Seat of the Soul*, a book I wrote a decade later about evolution, the soul, karma, and authentic power remained on the list for thirty-one weeks as *The New York Times*' Number 1 bestseller. I refer to them because they show, in my opinion, that science which invites exploration of human consciousness (for example, some interpretations of the quantum formalism) and our new and expanded human perception are both moving swiftly into mainstream awareness. This is the context in which Ervin Laszlo's new map of reality appears.

Below Ervin Laszlo has put his fundamental terms, "high-frequency band physical phenomena" and "low-frequency band transcendent phenomena" (or "high-frequency band" and "low-frequency band" for short) in brackets beside some of the fundamental terms I used in *The Seat of the Soul*, such as "domain of the five senses," "Earth school," and "nonphysical reality." This cross-referencing does not seem to present any obstacles to understanding. It indicates (in my opinion) a significant compatibility of Laszlo's map of cosmos and consciousness and my observations of the transformation that is occurring in human consciousness. (Page numbers in parentheses are from *The Seat of the Soul*, twenty-fifth Anniversary Edition).[126]

> *(30)* This is the framework of our evolutionary process: the continual incarnation and reincarnation of the energy of the soul into physical reality [high-frequency band] for the purposes of healing and balancing its energy in accordance with the law of karma. Within this framework we evolve, as individuals and as a species, through the cycle of being unempowered to becoming empowered.
>
> *(145)* When you return home [low-frequency band], when you leave your personality and body behind, you will leave behind your inadequacies, your fears and angers and jealousies. They do not, and cannot, exist within the realm of spirit [low-frequency band]. They are the experiences of time and matter [high-frequency band]. You will once again enter the fullness of who you are [low-frequency band]. You will perceive with

loving eyes and compassionate understanding the experiences of your life, including those that seemed so much to control you [high-frequency band]. You will see what purposes they served. You will survey what has been learned, and you will bring these things into your next incarnation [high-frequency band] if you choose one.

(85) Your soul knows its guides and Teachers. It drew upon their wisdom and compassion in charting the incarnation that became you [high-frequency band], and that part of your soul that is you will be gathered into their waiting arms when the incarnation that is you comes to an end—when you go home [low-frequency band "reach the cosmic *logos* at the lowest-frequency band of vibration"].

(225) When a soul incarnates [high-frequency band], its memory of the agreement that it has made with the Universe becomes soft. It becomes dormant, awaiting the experiences that will activate it [high-frequency band]. These experiences are not necessarily experiences that the personality would choose. They are nonetheless necessary to the activation of the awareness of the power and the mission of the soul within the consciousness of the personality [high-frequency band] and to its preparation for that task.

(167) When we speak of souls entering the physical arena [high-frequency band] to heal, to balance their energy, to pay their karmic debts, we are speaking of the evolution of Life as we know it upon our Earth [high-frequency band]. We are not speaking of other galaxies, or of Life on other levels [low-frequency band] that are not physical as we know them [high-frequency band]. The experience of physicalness [high-frequency band] is not always necessary to certain advances. If it is, it is encouraged.

(167) There comes a point when the physicalness experience [high-frequency band] no longer serves the soul's awareness, and, therefore, the soul chooses to learn in the nonphysical realm [low-frequency band]. It may choose to learn, for example, through the task of becoming a nonphysical guide.

(167) Our nonphysical Teachers are from these levels of Light [low-frequency band]. Therefore, it is not appropriate to consider them from the dynamic of the personal [high-frequency band]. Rather, it is more appropriate to think of them as impersonal consciousnesses, which is that which they are, from realms that cannot be understood in human terms [low-frequency band].

(167–168) Duality only exists in certain levels [high-frequency band], and not in others [low-

> frequency band]. Duality is a dynamic of learning. It is its own rhythm and tension and does not exist beyond another level of learning and development. You are existing in duality [high-frequency band] and your nonphysical Teachers [low-frequency band] are not.
>
> *(168)* We are destined to evolve beyond the nature of duality [high-frequency band]. Duality is that which is understood in time and space [high frequency band]. As you evolve beyond that, and also when you leave your physical body and journey home to your nonphysical plane of reality [low-frequency band], you will not exist in dualism [high-frequency band], and that sense of the wrathful, or sorrowful, or fearful self that you think of as present to you now will evaporate. It has no power in the realm beyond duality [low-frequency band] where there exists the perfection of all that is. When you leave your physical form [high-frequency band], you will join the nonphysical level of reality [low-frequency band] that is appropriate to your vibrational frequency at the time that you leave your incarnation.

The ability to cross-reference Laszlo's fundamental terms in his new map of reality and mine in *The Seat of the Soul* points, in my opinion, toward an emerging science that is not anchored in the limitations of the five senses and that accounts for a range of multisensory experiences that are becoming the substance of human consciousness. If so, Ervin Laszlo's wonderfully open unitary scientific paradigm could be the acorn that grows into a great future tree.

Seeking Syntony with the Intelligence of the Cosmos

ALEXANDER LASZLO

THE MEANING OF EXISTENCE, according to the conclusions reached on the basis of the new map of reality, is to participate in and enable the evolution of consciousness. Participating in and enabling the evolution of consciousness lends meaning to existence in the world. It lends meaning to our own existence. The question to ask is how we can live in accordance with that meaning.

Ignorance can be compared to a dark room in which you sleep.
No matter how long the room has been dark, an hour or a million years,
the moment the lamp of awareness is lit the entire room becomes luminous. . . .
You are that luminosity. You are that clear light.

—TENZIN WANGYAL RINPOCHE
The Tibetan Yogas of Dream and Sleep

Let us recall the understanding offered by the new map. We are here/now/finite, and we are eternal/ever-changing/infinite. The paradoxical nature of the new understanding is due to the fact that the map charts territories beyond those portrayed by the five senses. We live in a domain described by the map as nonlocal and entangled, with the clear implication that whatever we think and do is reflected in the rest of reality, just as the rest of reality is reflected in us. We are not individual and separate; we are interconnected and whole.

Experiments in macro-cellular biology confirm this insight. If we place two living heart cells next to each other—not touching, but a short distance apart—they soon begin to beat in unison. They start contracting, pulsing at their own rhythm, and soon they are doing it at the same time, even though they are not touching.

Here we witness the intelligence of the cosmos at work. This intelligence is omnipresent and ever-present, it surrounds and flows through everything. And everything flows through it, too—not just metaphorically, but quite literally. This means that things—stars, atoms, you and me—continually flow into existence through the in-forming action of the intelligence that creates and guides all things in the universe.

> *There is a soul force in the Universe, which if*
> *we permit it,*
> *will flow through us and produce miraculous results.*
>
> —Mahatma Gandhi

Biophysicist Mae Wan Ho tells us that the living organism is like an immense superorchestra. The orchestra's instruments span a spectrum of size ranging from a piccolo of 10^{-9} meter to a bassoon or bass viol of one meter or more and they jointly span a range of seventy-two octaves. The orchestra never ceases to play and its members never cease to maintain a recurring rhythm and beat with ever changing variation. They change the key, the tempo and the tune, with every player enjoying maximum freedom in improvising while remaining in beat and in tune with the others.[127]

The various sections of the orchestra (classically divided into strings, woodwinds, brass, and percussion—though in the superorchestra of the living organism there are many more sections, each of their own sort) perform with local coherence among themselves as well as in overall coherence with all the other sections. The resulting embedded and dynamically connected harmonies express each player and the entire orchestra as one. This is very much the sort of play and interplay commissioned by the intelligence of the cosmos.

Group behavior in animals often demonstrates levels of coherence like this. A school of herring, a murmuration of starlings, a herd of zebra—all act as one, with such coordination that the whole group seems to be one organism. For humans to achieve such choreographed behavior they have to train for years as artists and athletes.

Nevertheless, it is possible to tune in and flow with grace and ease without having to train for the synchronized swimming event at the Olympics. In fact, events and performances that require such high levels of synchronization tend to break down when the team is asked to engage in free-form synchronization or respond to unforeseen changes. But it is possible to master the dynamics of coherence. It is a matter of making ourselves available to the "in-formation" reaching us from the deep dimension of the cosmos.

Practices of Attunement: Ways of Tuning into the Deep Dimension

How do we make ourselves available to the in-formation that reaches us from the cosmos? There are many ways of doing so, and they all involve some form of "tuning in." Doing so is the simplest and most natural thing in the world, but at the same time it requires focus, attention, and above all, practice. One does not have to become a yogi to master this—after all, herring and starlings and zebras know how. Indeed, worrying about how to do it just complicates matters and makes things worse, cluttering consciousness with a constant stream of commentary about what is going on, moment by moment. As soon as we reflect on what is going on, or think about it in any way, we are no longer in the connected flow, no longer in tune, and no longer living in the moment. We end up thinking about what just happened, distilling it into words and freezing the moment so as to reflect on it an instant after it happens.

But we can turn off what psychologists call "the monkey mind"—that part of our consciousness that keeps up the constant chatter, commenting on everything. Quieting the monkey-mind, releasing into the moment and allowing our perceptions to flow with whatever arises in our field of awareness accords with the teachings of "mindfulness." This is a practical path that essentially involves three simple steps, and the more we practice them, the more we can tune into the in-formation reaching us from the deep dimension.

If you decide to tune in, here is how you can go about it.

The first step is to quiet the chatter in your mind; the second step is to release into the moment—without the need to "do anything," just being fully present—and the third step is to allow your perceptions to flow with whatever arises in your awareness. This will produce greater coherence with yourself, and with all things around you. These are the steps that have been practiced in all forms of yogic meditation for millennia and which more recently have formed the core of Otto Scharmer's celebrated Theory U and his practice of "presencing."[128]

Imagine that you are a heart cell, beating out the rhythm of your life. You are aware of all the other cells around you, beating out their rhythms, too. And you sense that you are part of a great being that is always becoming, a pattern that flows and informs, infusing everything with coherent life. What if you knew that something as fantastic and amazing as a heart were possible—something that could pump massive amounts of blood and animate an entire body—if only you and the cells around you were to beat as one? This type of integral coherence is possible for us as a species—not only possible, but vitally necessary if we are to shift out of our all-too-prevalent disconnected and destructive modes of strident individualism. The challenge is to read the new map of reality and incorporate its insights in a practice through which we enact each moment as an integral expression of the holographically in-formed universe.

David Price writes about engaging in a "daologue" with Earth.[129] He asks, "how might we listen and act differently given this perception of the conversation of the Earth, this enveloping planetary layer, this connecting and collecting intelligence, this sum of all dialogues: this Daologue?" The dimensionality of Daologue evokes exploration of and engagement with the way in which conversation, play, dance, and all aspects of life connect us to ourselves, to each other, to the more-than-human world, and across time and space to past and future generations.

There are four spheres through which you can tune your consciousness to the intelligence intrinsic to the cosmos. When you engage across all four spheres to consciously connect and curate the emergence of the bigger story of your individual and collective being, you participate in the authoring of a World Narrative—the story of the universe becoming itself; continually actualizing to "higher" (or actually deeper) levels of coherence. The quality and character of this story depends on the way in which we each author our life in and across four spheres of attunement.

1. In the first sphere, the practice involves centering, quieting the monkey mind, listening with every cell of your being. This practice cultivates intu-

ition, empathy, compassion, insight that matches outsight, and a willingness to explore and follow your deepest calling.

2. In the second sphere, the practice involves deep dialogue and collaboration. Coming together to learn with and from each other and to engage in coordinated action with considerateness, openness, and joy to enable the emergence of collective wisdom.

3. In the third sphere, the practice involves communing: listening to the messages of all beings (whether they be waterfalls, animals, mountains or galaxies) and acknowledging our interdependence and ultimate unity with them.

4. In the fourth sphere, the practice calls for learning to read the patterns of change of which we are a part; learning to hear the rhythms of life and becoming familiar with the improvisational jam session that nature has been playing since time immemorial. This practice cultivates your ability to play your own piece; to sing and dance your own path in harmony with the nature of existence in the universe.

The purpose of these exercises is to aid you in developing rhythms and rituals in your daily life that enable you to further the evolution of your consciousness by creating consonant coherence simultaneously at the intra-personal, inter-personal, trans-species, and trans-generational levels.

The Quest for Syntony

As you practice attuning yourself to the deep dimension of the cosmos, it will be increasingly important to continue exploring ways of fitting your individual melody with those of others within the broader symphony of life on Earth. This is not just a metaphor: it is the essence of "syntony."[130]

In its most basic expression, syntony is evolutionary consonance. By seeking to engage with life through syntony, you enhance your participation in the evolution of consciousness both in yourself and in the universe. The path of syntony involves aligning conscious intention with evolutionary purpose and thereby fostering and co-creating consonant pathways of development in partnership with the logos that in-forms the universe.

Kingsley Dennis wrote about the post-Millennials in his book *Phoenix Generation: A New Era of Connection, Compassion, and Consciousness.*[131] This era is only just dawning, but intimations of hope, pragmatism, and spiritual awakening can be sensed in the way in which young people choose to express their lives. As cybercowboy novelist and technology futurist William Gibson noted, "the future is already here—it's just not evenly distributed."[132] Knowing where to look for it, how to recognize it, what to do with it, and how to cultivate it are part of the mind set, the skill set and the heart set of the Phoenix Generation, the new generation of syntony seekers.

This act of listening into what Stuart Kauffman calls "the adjacent possible"—of curating that which appears as though it were almost seeking to emerge—is the act of intuiting, imagining, and co-creating a narrative of holotropic thrivability.[133] It is what is deliciously captured by Arundhati Roy's evocative assertion: "Another world is not only possible, she is on her way. On a quiet day, I can hear her breathing."[134] Cultivating this sense-ability—and the corresponding response-ability that it calls for—is part of the new set of competencies needed for a thrivable human presence on Earth; an expression of integral coherence and resonance that flows from accessing the "in-formation" of the deep dimension of the cosmos. Living into the adjacent possible involves both knowing how to read the new map of reality and furthering the evolution of consciousness that is its essence.

Charles Eisenstein asks, "Why is it assumed without much debate that no one can have direct access to the subjective experience of another person (or nonperson)?[135] This is obvious only if we conceive and experience ourselves as fundamentally separate from each other. There are other stories of self, however. We could see ourselves, as many spiritual traditions do, not as separate beings but as "interbeings," not just interdependent but interexistent." The emergence of narratives of systemic sustainability, of evolutionary syntony, of "glocal" thrivability (that is, of patterns of being and becoming that express both local and global thrivability) draw upon this wellspring of understanding. As Wendy Wheeler suggests, there are collective ways to be more than we can be by ourselves alone; ways that express a larger sense of being and a greater sense of self.[136] With the new map of reality it is possible to understand and "sense into" patterns that are coherent and consistent with the interconnected narrative of cosmic emergence.[137]

When we approach the issue of evolutionary coherence from the standpoint (or rather, the flowpoint) of the quest for syntony, the aim is not to find "the best way" or "the right way," or even "the most convenient and gratifying way," but rather the ways (for there are many) that increase our consonant alignment with the evolutionary trend toward ever greater coherence as an integral expression of consciousness. It is important to develop what can be thought of as the competency of integral-coherence—the state of self-actualization of individuals and of groups marked by the mastery of the knowledge, the abilities, the attitudes, and the values required for co-evolutionary actions, and thereby for the pursuit of thrivable modes of being and becoming. By connecting, listening, paying attention, integrating, intuiting what is emerging, and giving full expression to your sense of syntony, you can re-member the intimate connections by which you and your community — and every frog, tree, stone and star in the cosmos—are in-formed by the wisdom of the deep dimension of the cosmos.

> Everywhere transience is plunging into the depths of
> Being. . . .
> It is our task to imprint this temporary, perishable
> earth into ourselves so deeply,
> so painfully and passionately, that its essence can rise
> again, "invisibly," inside us.
> We are the bees of the invisible. We wildly collect the
> honey of the visible, to store
> it in the great golden hive of the invisible.
>
> —RAINER MARIA RILKE
> From a letter to his Polish translator, Witold Hulewicz,
> November 23, 1925

One tale of the emerging consciousness is related in the story of a conversation with a bee-keeper. In this story, an old bee-keeper said that he knew he would be a keeper of bees when he was three years old. With loving pride, he told me that all the species of plants and animals know what role the bees play in their ecosystems, and that they depend on the bees to fulfill their role. This observation raises the question of what role the animals and plants know that humans play in their ecosystems and whether or not they depend upon us to play that role.

When this question was posed to my daughter Kahlia Paola Laszlo, who was thirteen at the time, she replied that she thought that perhaps the role humans play is to be the connectors: connecting life with life, connecting what is with what might be. This answer seems to affirm the spirit of Janine Benyus's observation that life creates conditions conducive to life.[138]

It is a far cry from the species-centrism and zoophobia that characterizes much of what Darwinism became at the hands of Herbert Spencer and others over the last hundred years. At the time of the popularization of Darwinian evolutionary theory, T.H. Huxley noted that the life-affirming values that underlie the sort of notions expressed by Benyus actually affirm life in a markedly different way: "The practice of that which is ethically best—what we call goodness or virtue—involves a course of conduct which, in all respects, is opposed to that which leads to success in the cosmic struggle for existence. In place of ruthless self-assertion it demands self-restraint; in place of thrusting aside, or treading down, all competitors, it requires that the individual shall not merely respect, but shall help his fellows; its influence is directed, not so much to the survival of the fittest, as to the fitting of as many as possible to survive. It repudiates the gladiatorial theory of existence."[139]

"Re-membering" your community—not as a human being with myopic self-centered interests, but as a human becoming consciously participating in and enabling the evolution of consciousness—is fast becoming an evolutionary imperative. As the new map of reality makes clear, the writing is already on the wall, we just seem to have trouble reading it. The movement that underlies the broader process of cosmic evolution requires that each of us rebalance all four spheres of attunement together. When we do so we re-member our integral process of becoming by making the new map come alive in our very being, and in doing so we enact conscious coherence in our day-to-day life.

The collective consciousness of our species is gaining new and surprising capacities. In his contribution to this book, Kingsley Dennis notes that the generations of humans now coming onto the scene are equipped with more highly developed sense-abilities (what I would call a more refined syntony sense), allowing them to listen into and curate holotropic emergence more easily and more naturally. What Kingsley refers to as "the rise of an empathic consciousness" is a hallmark of these generations, and it is well worth looking for signs of its expression.

Attunement to the evolution of consciousness offers practical benefits. When you achieve a higher level of attunement, you are filled with—

1. *Passion:* vibrant, intense, and compelling enthusiasm
2. *Integrity:* dignity or elevation of character; worthiness, honor and respect
3. *Grace:* simple elegance, considerateness and a composed way of being
4. *Control:* personal mastery in (not of) the situations in which you find yourself
5. *Flow:* tuning your actions and attitudes to harmonize with your surroundings.

These are the "five movements of syntony."[140] They constitute the ground upon which the sense-abilities of syntony can be cultivated and the response-abilities of the syntony seeker can be brought into coherent expression. Working with them takes dedication and practice, even if learning to develop your sense of syntony with the universe is more like learning to love than like following an instruction manual.

> The day will come when, after harnessing the ether, the winds,
> The tides, gravitation, we shall harness for God the energies of love.
> And, on that day, for the second time in the history of the world, man will have discovered fire.
>
> —Pierre Teilhard de Chardin
> "The Evolution of Chastity" (February 1934),
> as translated by Rene Hague in *Toward the Future* (1975)

To participate in and enable the evolution of consciousness in you and around you, you need to practice with purpose and vision. Then you can make syntony. And as with love, making it happen should not be confused with forcing it to happen. One is a creative, constructive, life-affirming act. The other is a restrictive, imposing, life-constraining act. True love is something we can make, but never force. The same holds true for peace and for harmony—and for participating in and enabling the evolution of consciousness in the world.

Do you wish to be a part of the numinous dance of evolution—a conscious part? When you dance (or rather, when you allow yourself to be danced), your every step creates ripples that interact with and in-form not only your own time and place, but the time and place of everyone on the floor. The way you dance affects the quality of the flow—and the extent to which it sustains you and the other processes and patterns that co-arise with you. The syntony of this dance expresses the integral coherence of in-formation in the cosmos.

Having the new map of reality is the first thing. Next thing is to know how to read it. And the ultimate thing is to bring it alive in all we do/are, feel/think/express, relate to, and connect with. It is syntony, it is holotropy, it is love, and in its essence, it is life in its fullest and most meaningful expression.

PART THREE

Meaning

CHAPTER 8

In Search of Meaning

As expert as they are at collecting and analyzing data, most modern scientists tend to shy away from the question, "What does it all mean?" To them, the question seems so vague as to be, well, meaningless. But it was not always so. The boundaries separating science from other ways of understanding reality—mysticism, theology, and philosophy—used to be more fluid. In ancient Greece Pythagoras was both a rigorous mathematician and a charismatic shaman. Sir Isaac Newton was both a hard-nosed empirical physicist and an obsessive Christian theologian. Albert Einstein and Niels Bohr elucidated physics and at the same time wrestled with issues concerning the basic nature and meaning of reality. . . . At a deep level, largely unanalyzed and rarely acknowledged, the quest for meaning is what drives frontier physics and cosmology today.

—Nobel physics laureate FRANK A. WILCZEK and DEEPAK CHOPRA in *The San Francisco Chronicle*, July 13, 2015

From time immemorial, thinking people have raised questions of meaning. Philosophers have asked, *why is there something in the world, rather than nothing?* Reality is a collection of "things," why and how did they come about?

To this day, philosophers as well as philosophically minded scientists ask, *how is it, that what there is in the world, is intelligible?* The world could also be a random collection of unrelated things, without further rhyme or reason. These are questions of meaning, and they are meaningful questions.

In this concluding chapter we raise the issue of meaning and ask, *Is there a reason for the existence of the things that furnish the world? And is there a reason for their intelligibility?*

These questions have been asked for millennia, and the answers given to them have varied. Skeptics as well as hard-nosed "realists" have dismissed the questions as having no answer—at least none that could be reasonably put forward. Religious and spiritual leaders said that there is an answer: the reason for the existence, and for the at least partial intelligibility of things is the will of the Divine intelligence that created them. Scientists and secular thinkers mainly said no. There is no reason for the existence of things because only things created on purpose have a reason for their existence—that reason being the purpose for which they have been created

In the new map of reality we find an answer that recalls the old spiritual answer but joins it with the answer we can now give through science. As Max Planck, Albert Einstein, Wolfgang Pauli, Carl Gustav Jung, and scores of scientists believed and did not fail to assert, there is an intelligence intrinsic to the universe. That intelligence, acting through the laws of nature, is responsible for shaping the nature of things in the world. It ensures that the world is not merely a random heap of unrelated things, but an ensemble of coherently interrelated events and processes.

This is a perfectly logical and reasonable hypothesis, yet mainstream scientists are reluctant to embrace it. They prefer to maintain that the processes that bring things into existence are basically random. Because if they are, we need not inquire into the reason for their existence. Things come about in the welter of actions and interactions in nature without any particular reason and intention.

Physicist Nassim Haramein noted,

> [T]he fundamental axioms and basic assumptions at the root of physical theories . . . presume that evolutionary systems emerge from random interactions initiated by a single "miraculous" event providing all of the appropriate conditions to produce our current observable universe, and our state of existence in it. This event, typically described as a "Big Bang," astonishingly is thought to have produced all of the forces and constants of physical law and eventually biological interactions under random functions.[141]

Even Thomas Kuhn, the father of the concept of paradigms in science, has been hesitant to allow that there would be a purpose underlying the existence of things. He wrote,

> The developmental process has been an evolution from primitive beginnings—a process whose successive stages are characterized by an increasingly

> detailed and refined understanding of nature. But nothing makes it a process of evolution toward anything. . . . The entire process may have occurred as we now suppose biological evolution did without benefit of a set goal, a permanent fixed scientific truth of which each stage in the development of scientific knowledge is [an improved] exemplar."[142]

Although Kuhn recognized that each new paradigm is an "improved exemplar" in the history of science, and that it brings increasingly detailed and refined understanding of nature, this understanding, he said, does not disclose anything like a goal or purpose in nature—evolution in nature, according to Kuhn, is not evolution toward anything. This, however, may not be the best assessment of the facts. Let us take a fresh look.

Purpose in Nature

In our day considerable evidence has surfaced that things and events in the universe are not random but coherent. (Here coherence means that the elements that make up a thing or system are precisely coordinated, so that every element responds to every other.) Coherence in nature is the outcome of evolutionary processes that are themselves coherent.

The Argument from Coherence: (1) The Coherence of the Physics of the Universe

How coherent and complex systems would have evolved in nature has long puzzled mystics, prophets, scientists, and inquiring people in all walks of life. Hermetic, vedic, and daoist thinkers and the leaders of the great religions ascribed the emergence of systems to a supernatural agency. A Divine Being or intelligence created the systems, or at least the conditions and the impetus for them. Scientists searched for natural causes. Henri Bergson, for example, postulated an *elan vital* that would counter the trend toward the degradation of energy in living systems, and biologist Hans Driesch perceived a counter-entropic drive in the universe he termed *entelechy*. Some scientists spoke of *syntropy* as the force that would underlie the evolution of coherent systems, and others, such as Teilhard de Chardin and Erich Jantsch, invoked *syntony*.

The evolution of coherent systems does call for an explanation: chance, even if involving a large number of systems over historical time scales, fails to account for the facts. The search space of possible combinations of the elements that make up complex systems is so vast that random trial-and-error would have greatly exceeded the available time frames. There were over thirteen billion years available for the evolution of the combinations of the basic elements that make up the known universe, and four billion years for the combination of the macromolecules and cells that make up living systems on this planet. These time frames are enormous, yet they are insufficient to explain the coherence we observe in nature.

The probability that even the simplest and most fundamental biological systems would have come about through a random shuffling of their elements is practically nil. The DNA-mRNA-tRNA-rRNA transcription and translation system, basic to living systems, is so complex and precise that it is astronomically improbable that it would have been assembled by chance. It is likewise improbable that complex systems could evolve by a chance modification of their genetic pool. Mathematical physicist Fred Hoyle said that the probability that new species would emerge through a chance mutation of the gene pool is comparable to the probability that a hurricane blowing through a scrapyard would assemble a working airplane. If attempted randomly, even unscrambling the six faces of a Rubik's Cube at the rate of one move per second would take longer than the age of the universe.

Already the basic parameters of the universe exhibit staggering coherence. Cosmologist Menas Kafatos demonstrated that many of the ratios among the fundamental parameters can be interpreted on the one hand in terms of the relationship between the masses of elementary particles and the total number of nucleons, and on the other in reference to the relationship between the gravitational constant, the charge of the electron, Planck's constant, and the speed of light. The mass of elementary particles, the number of the particles, and the forces between them display harmonic ratios. Sir Arthur Eddington and Paul Dirac noted that the ratio of the electric force to the gravitational force is approximately 10^{40}, and the ratio of the size of the universe to the size of elementary particles is likewise around 10^{40}. This is surprising, since the ratio of the electric force to the gravitational force should be unchanging (these forces are constant), whereas the ratio of the size of the universe to the size of elementary particles should be changing (given that the universe is expanding). In his "large number hypothesis," Dirac speculated that the agreement between these ratios, one variable the other not, is more than random coincidence. But if so, either the universe is not expanding, or the force of gravitation varies proportionately to its expansion.

The cosmic microwave background radiation—the remnant of the energies of the Big Bang—is likewise astonishingly coherent, it is dominated by a large peak followed by smaller harmonic peaks. The series of peaks ends at the longest wavelength Lee Smolins termed R. When R is divided by the speed of light we get the length of time independent estimates tell us is the age of the universe. When we divide in turn the speed of light by R, we get a frequency that equates to one cycle over the age of the universe. And when R is squared and divided by the speed of light (c^2/R) we get the measure of the acceleration of the expansion of the galaxies. These and related "coincidences" suggest that all the parameters of the universe are finely tuned to all the other parameters, and together are coherent with the universe's overall dimensions.[143]

The Argument from Coherence: (2) The Evolution of Coherent Systems

There is a coherent basis in the universe for the evolution of coherent systems, but this does not in itself explain the actual evolution of such systems. The fact is that living systems are astonishingly coherent. The human body, for example, consists of anywhere from 37.2 trillion to 100 trillion cells, and each cell produces 10,000 bio-electrochemical reactions every second. Every twenty-four hours 10^{12} cells die and are replaced.

The coordination of this vast number of cells and of their electromagnetic and chemical signaling cannot be ensured by classical physical and chemical interactions alone. The conduction of signals through the nervous system cannot proceed faster than about twenty meters per second, and cannot carry a large number of diverse signals at the same time. Yet molecules, cells and cellular assemblies resonate at the same or compatible frequencies throughout the body, whether they are proximal or distant. They interact at various speeds, ranging from the slow (among hormones and peripheral nerve fibers), to the very high (along the Ranvier rings of myelin-shielded nerves). The interactions are precisely correlated, involving quantum-type "entanglements" in addition to classical physical-biological interactions.

Complex systems emerged in the universe in the course of the evolution of the universe itself. In 1927 Georges Lemaitre, a Belgian priest turned scientist put forward the hypothesis that the universe, rather than being infinite and unchanging, is expanding. This was confirmed by astronomer Edwin Hubble two years later. When the Friedman equations that decode the structure of the universe turned out to be unstable, cosmologists accepted the idea that the universe changes over time. At the beginning of the evolutionary process the parameters that lead to the evolution of complex systems must have been already given. They were extraordinarily finely tuned: variations of the order of one-billionth of the value of some universal constants (such as the mass of elementary particles, the speed of light, the rate of expansion of galaxies, and two dozen others) would not have produced stable atoms and stable interaction among the atoms. Even a minute variation of some of the constants would have precluded the evolution of multiatomic, molecular, and then biological systems.

Complex systems began to evolve in the universe. Planck-scale ripples appeared in the primordial Minkowski vacuum: quanta such as leptons (electrons, muons, tau particles, neutrinos), mesons (pions) as well as hadrons (baryons including protons and neutrons). In the course of time they clustered into atoms, and these clustered into molecules and molecular assemblies. On the astronomical scale stars and stellar systems, galaxies and galactic clusters came into existence.[144]

On some planets, and even in some regions of interstellar space, organic molecules emerged. On suitable planetary surfaces they cohered into cellular and multicellular systems. On Earth the initial forms of life emerged more than four billion years ago and evolved intermittently but unceasingly into more and more complex organic and multi-organic systems.

This evolution could not have been the product of mere chance. Yet, until the beginning of this century most scientists believed that life is the result of a series of fortunate coincidences. It was known that the evolution of life is physically improbable: physical processes tend to run down to states of higher entropy, and not up to complex structures that conserve and process energy. In the absence of an *elan vital* or other life force, the evolution of life on Earth must be a case of stupendous serendipity.

Serendipity is clearly suggested by the position of our planet in this galaxy. Earth is a planet is in the "Goldilocks Zone," neither too far nor too close to its sun, a main-sequence G2 dwarf star.[145] It has the right atmosphere and the right amount of water for producing and sustaining life. It has the right mass and it occupies a nearly circular orbit. It has an oxygen/nitrogen rich atmosphere, and a moderate rate of rotation. There is liquid water on its surface, and a correct ratio between water and land-mass. Its surface temperature fluctuates within the narrow range required for life. It is also at the right distance from the center of the galaxy, and is protected from asteroids by giant gas planets. In this position the sun's heliosphere protects its surface from cosmic rays and pressures lethal for biological systems, and its own magnetosphere protects it from dangerously high energies emanating from the sun's heliosphere.

However, the hypothesis of serendipity is moderated by the finding that our planet is not unique in the universe; it is not even extraordinarily rare. Some 2,000 "exoplanets" have been identified, planets orbiting stars other than the sun. Scientists working with the Kepler space telescope detected several thousand candidate planets. On the average, each star in the Milky Way galaxy has at least one planet, and one in five sunlike stars have an Earth-size planet in the Goldilocks zone. With 200 billion stars in our galaxy, there are 11 billion Goldilocks-zone Earth-size planets in this galaxy alone—and there may be 10^{22}

to 10^{24} galaxies in the universe. It is more than likely that life, even intelligent life, is present in many places in the universe.

Moreover it turned out that the evolution of life is not merely a statistically permissible fortunate development, but a basic evolutionary process. The first strand of evidence in this regard was the discovery that organic molecules occur under a wide range of conditions. In 2011 a team of astrophysicists headed by Sun Kwok and Yong Zhang at the University of Hong Kong found 130 such macromolecules in the vicinity of active stars.[146] They include glycine, an amino acid, and ethylene glycol, the compound associated with the formation of the sugar molecules necessary for life. They are present around hot and active stars and are ejected into space in the course of the thermal and chemical evolution of the stars. Organic molecules were discovered in interstellar clouds as well. The incidence of the most complex of these molecules, isopropyl cyanide, has been reported in 2014 by a team of researchers headed by Arnaud Belloche at the Max Planck Institute for Radio Astronomy. Its branching carbon structure is similar to that of the amino acids that form the basis of proteins.

Second, there is evidence that under certain conditions primordial DNA, the basis of all complex forms of life, self-creates spontaneously. Research by Tommaso P. Fraccia, Gregory P. Smith, Giuliano Zanchetta, et al, reported in the journal *Nature Communications* indicates that "homology recognition" between sequences of several hundred nucleotides occurs quasi "telepathically," without physical contact among the nucleotides, and without the presence of proteins. The spontaneous self-assembly of DNA fragments a few nanometers in length into liquid crystals drives the formation of chemical bonds and creates chains of DNA. The self-organizing properties of DNA-like molecular fragments over billions of years may have produced the first DNA-like molecular chains also on Earth.[147]

Third, we now know that on this planet life evolves wherever it possibly can, even under highly unfavorable thermal and chemical conditions. So-called extremophiles survive in active volcanoes and deep within the seas, demonstrating an astonishing capacity to withstand a vast range of temperatures and pressures. Under low-energy and biochemically and climatically unfavorable conditions extremophiles are necessarily simple organisms, but more advanced forms of life tend to evolve wherever conditions are more benign.

Searching Deeper

Evolution is nonlinear but incessant, and consistently coherence-oriented. The presence of coherent systems on this planet, and very likely elsewhere in the universe, cannot be the outcome of random processes. There must be a factor that orients the developmental process. Max Planck said that there is an intelligence that brings the nucleons and electrons of atoms into coordinated vibration. The same intelligence constitutes clusters and superclusters of in-formed vibrations: physical, biological, and ecological systems. This is a coherent and consistent evolutionary process, and it should be possible to discover its *logos*, the purpose behind it.

We can discover the *logos* of a nonrandom process by considering the direction in which it unfolds. What kind of conditions would obtain when the process has run its course—when no further development could take place because everything that could possibly develop had already done so? This would be the Omega Point in the evolution of coherent systems in the universe, and we can ask what kind of conditions would reign at that point.

We would expect that at the Omega Point all systems in the universe would be fully coherent. But this is not the case. Coherent systems cannot exist indefinitely in space and time. At the Omega Point there will not be coherent systems in the universe: there will not be systems of any kind. This astounding prediction is not based on assuming some cosmic catastrophe, but on the extrapolation of the evolutionary processes already under way.

Physical cosmology tells us that the build-up of systems in space and time is not infinitely extendable. Conditions under which complex and coherent systems can exist come to an end. There are various scenarios describing how these conditions come to an end, but they all agree that they do.

Extrapolations based on the relation between the expansive force liberated by the Big Bang and the contracting force of gravitation show that, unless the universe remains balanced at the razor's edge between expansion and contraction, it either expands infinitely (the open universe scenario), or it contracts in finite time to quantum dimensions (the closed universe scenario). Whether it collapses to quantum dimensions, or disperses in cosmic space, the universe becomes incapable of supporting systems above the energy level of the vacuum, its ground state.

If we live in an open universe, the second law of thermodynamics predicts that in its continuous expansion all systems will run down to maximum entropy. According to this "Big Freeze scenario," after a time no irreversible reactions will take place; not even a candle will burn. Spacetime will be a lukewarm domain of distributed heat, locked into inactivity. By contrast, the "Big Crunch scenario" of a closed universe maintains that the force of gravitation overtakes the force of expansion, and the last remnants of black holes, stripped nuclei of hydrogen, are super-compacted. The entire "matter-content" of the universe returns to quantum dimensions—compressed into a space smaller than the head of a pin.

It may also be that due to the action of dark energy, distances in the universe will become infinite before either the Big Freeze or the Big Crunch scenario would play out. According to this "Big Rip scenario," there will be a time when no finite system could exist in space and time.

Even the optimally stable scenario of equilibrium between expansion and contraction does not ensure the existence of complex systems. An international team of astronomers at the University of Leiden in Holland investigated the quantities of hydrogen nuclei—so-called alpha particles—currently present in the universe.[148] (These substances are necessary for the formation of stars.) They found that the amount of hydrogen nuclei present in the galaxies is only sufficient to form another five percent of the already formed stars. Fifty percent of the existing stars formed about 9 billion years ago, and they are ninety-five percent of the stars that can possibly form.

Stars have a finite lifespan: they either undergo supernova explosions, or become absorbed in black holes. The time until all stars vanish in the universe is thought to be of the order of tens of billions of years. Thus the time horizon of the equilibrium scenario, the same as that of the Big Bang, Big Freeze, and Big Rip scenarios, is finite. When the processes described in these scenarios have run their course, no system of any kind will persist in the universe.

The fate of coherent systems remains unchanged even if our universe is not the only universe in the cosmos. Some cosmological scenarios envisage multiple universes, existing simultaneously. Periodically universe-creating events—"Bangs"—occur, and they give birth to new universes. The universes each follow their own evolutionary trajectory, at the end of which coherent systems can no longer be sustained in their spacetime. Whether there is one universe in the cosmos or many, coherent systems cannot exist infinitely in the world.

If the evolution of complex systems were the purpose of existence, whether in our unique universe or in multiple universes, the purpose of existence would be doomed to be unachieved. But what would then be the purpose of existence in the cosmos?

CHAPTER 9

The Vision of Ultimate Meaning

COSMIC PURPOSE AND THE EVOLUTION OF CONSCIOUSNESS

The evolution of coherent systems is not likely to be the purpose of existence in the cosmos. But could it be that the evolution of consciousness is that paramount purpose? Consciousness, we have said, is a basic phenomenon in the universe. Object-like as well as mind-like Gestalts are manifestations of evolving clusters, superclusters and hyperclusters of vibrating waves.

The consciousness—the mind-like Gestalt—associated with a particle, an atom, or a molecule is embryonic compared with the consciousness associated with a living organism, and the consciousness associated with a simple organism is primitive compared with the consciousness of an evolved organism. An evolved organism is a highly coherent system, and such a system can carry a highly evolved consciousness.

The evolution of higher species of organisms may be the necessary condition for the evolution of higher forms of consciousness. In that event the evolution of higher organisms, while not the intrinsic purpose of existence, is the instrumental purpose of existence: the condition necessary for the evolution of consciousness.*

The Visionary Scenarios

The hypothesis that the purpose of existence is the evolution of consciousness is *ipso facto* cogent because, unlike the clusters that constitute coherent object-like systems, the clusters that manifest consciousness are not doomed to vanish. These low-frequency long-wave clusters could persist when conditions in the universe approximate the cosmological scenarios known as the Big Freeze, Big Crunch, and Big Rip, and even when no further stars and can form and those that did form reached the end of their life-cycle. In these ultimate cosmic epochs the high-frequency, high-amplitude, and relatively short-length waves that create object-like clusters flatten. But the mind-like Gestalts created by low-frequency, low-amplitude and long wavelength clusters could persist. At the end of time, there could be mind and consciousness in the universe, and "no-thing" else.

We can envisage the following single-universe consciousness-evolution scenario:

---

* That consciousness evolves conjointly with the evolution of organisms has been affirmed by Frederic Myers in a message "from beyond." He described the evolution of consciousness ("essence" or "soul") in the following terms:

> The essences or souls of plants, after dying, gather together in their myriads and in time form one whole. These . . . go up one step in the ladder, and are one when they enter the body of insects. Myriads of insect lives again make one being which, in due course, enters the body or a bird. And so the process continues.

> *A stage is reached in the evolution of systems in the universe in which clusters of high-frequency waves ("bodies") can no longer exist in space and time. The high-frequency clusters vanish, but the low-frequency clusters persist. These clusters are now discarnate consciousnesses journeying on the transcendent Planes of existence. They evolve, and ascend from one Plane to the next. They enter deeper and deeper domains of vibration, reaching higher and higher etheric Planes. Ultimately they reach the highest Plane where their descending rate of vibration approaches that of the ground state of the cosmos. In that condition the evolved consciousnesses resonate with the intelligence inherent in the ground state of the cosmos. They reach the condition the Eastern wisdom teachings call Nirvana and the Western teachings regard as the gates of heaven. They enter communion with the Cosmic Mind, the intrinsic intelligence of the cosmos and persist, perhaps infinitely, beyond space and time.*

We can also envisage a more embracing and ultimately also more meaningful multiuniverse consciousness–evolution scenario.

> *The cosmic ground state, although eternal and immutable, is excitable. It is periodically excited by injections of energies; events signalling the birth of new universes. Each injection creates a universe*

in which clusters, superclusters and hyperclusters of vibration—particles and systems of particles—emerge and evolve. Each cluster is in-formed by the vibration of the consciousness intrinsic to the cosmic ground-state from which it has emerged. The clusters in each universe evolve independently, but are in-formed by the same ground-state intelligence.

At the apex of their evolution, the consciousnesses evolving in association with the clusters in each universe enter enter into communion with the ground-state intelligence of the cosmos. They articulate and potentiate that cosmic intelligence. As a result in each successive universe the intelligence of the cosmic ground-state in-forms the consciousnesses that appear in that universe and in all universes more articulately and potently. The communion of the highly evolved consciousnesses with the ground-state intelligence of the cosmos creates a trans-universal learning cycle that produces more and more evolved organisms carrying more and more evolved forms of consciousness.

The self-evolution of the consciousness intrinsic to the cosmos through the evolution of the consciousness carried by clusters of vibration in this and in other universes may be the ultimate purpose of existence. Then the purpose of our existence is to enable and foster the evolution of the consciousness intrinsic to the cosmos through the evolution of our own consciousness.

This insight lends meaning to our existence. We are here to evolve the consciousness of the cosmos by evolving our consciousness. We can pursue this task throughout the cycle of our existence. During the incarnate phases, when our consciousness appears to reside in our body, we can evolve our consciousness by fostering its capacity to enter in the deep domains where nonlocal intuitions and experiences of oneness and unconditional love appear. Doing so provides optimum conditions for embarking on the after-death transcendent journey of our consciousness. Experiencing the etheric Planes and ascending to higher Planes continues our evolution in the discarnate phase of our existence.

When the discarnate phase ends, our evolved conciousness encounters optimum conditions for reincarnation to earthly existence. In the new incarnate phase further opportunities are given for experiencing and for learning, and for evolving to ever-higher forms of consciousness.

The cycle repeats. The evolved consciousness ascends to higher and higher Planes of existence, vibrating more and more deeply, resonating in syntony with the intelligence of the ground state of the cosmos. At the apex of this evolution the manifest universe vanishes, and the evolved consciousness becomes one with the intelligence that is the ultimate, and then the sole, reality of the cosmos.

Afterword

Meaning and Purpose in the New Map of Reality and in the Wisdom Traditions

Shamik Desai

In his brilliant exposition of the new map of reality, Ervin Laszlo validates in light of contemporary scientific research ancient truths espoused by the mystical branches of the world's principal wisdom teachings: Hinduism, Buddhism, Taoism, Kabbalah, Christian mysticism, Sufism. He has accomplished the spectacular feat of harmonizing and validating these truths through the empirical realm—in the language of quantum physics. He has elevated physics to the level of metaphysics and placed consciousness in its rightful place: anywhere and everywhere.

All the great wisdom traditions agree that every "thing" is a manifestation of a larger Oneness. They hint regarding the meaning of existence: the One Source yearns deeply to know and love Itself. Hence, it has manifested in a material form (at a higher band of vibration, in Laszlo's language) with the intention of realizing Itself through a process of respiritualization. This process unfolds as each sentient being in the universe "opens the spiritual eye" and perceives the universe through the lens of Oneness, and then turns its superperceptions into reality through loving, mindful engagement.

The Semitic traditions—Judaism, Christianity, Islam—tell us that our highest duty lies in growing our souls by hallowing the world and bringing heaven upon earth by the end of time. The religious project in Semitic faiths is for man to make heaven and earth one by sacralizing the world (through acts of righteousness, love, *jihad*), transforming it into a vast undivided sacred space, a shoreless unbroken ocean of "brotherly love"—a Philadelphia, a Zion, a Promised Land: what physicists would call the spacetime domain of elevated vibrations. The essence of the divine project as understood in the Abrahamic faiths (and particularly by their mystical representatives) is to not rest until the One Truth becomes fully embodied. The unidirectional linearity of time as understood by the Semitic peoples adds to the urgency of this mission.

In the Eastern traditions—Hinduism, Buddhism, Taoism—life's primary task is to align oneself with *dharma*—the moral order of the universe—and, in times of societal imbalance, to restore *dharma* by re-aligning with others as well as with oneself. Alternatively, they tell us that the task is to wake up and help others to wake up, or in the Mahayana branch of Buddhism, to seek *nirvana* (ego-extinguishing) for all. Or again—by each of us assuming that state of unselfconscious playfulness—*wu-wei*—which allows us to draw maximum *ch'i* from the cosmos—to manifest the Tao, making it a living presence in the world. Collectively, we are urged to peel back the layers of *maya* and reveal the core of consciousness behind the veil of appearances, elevating that which is Immanent to the level of the Transcendent until *advaita*, or nonduality, is laid bare. This objective is achieved when we all do what we ought to do—i.e., dispatch our highest duties with detached equanimity, act purely with uncalculating intentionality, walk the path and the way, tap into the Source, achieving spontaneous creative resonance with ourselves and the world by entering into the flow of love and life.

The meaning and purpose of existence is to align and harmonize our relations with the unseen order, the Ultimate Reality, as individuals—and those among us with an evolved consciousness are to seek such alignment also at the societal and planetary levels. The Hindu and generally Eastern obsession with moral order and restoring *dharma* is analogous to the Judaic-Semitic preoccupation with world-hallowing.

It might be argued that there is a subtle difference in emphasis and tone between the Semitic faiths and the Eastern systems—that the Semitic traditions are more life-affirming and world-embracing ("God saw all that he had created, and beheld that it was very good", Genesis 1:31), and that the Eastern traditions are more world-denying (recall Buddha's many reflections on the repulsiveness of the human body). The Semitic systems imply that the missionary work of elevating the consciousness of one's external surroundings—the hallowing of the world—will lead to the elevation of one's own consciousness by default. And in the somewhat more inward-facing Eastern traditions it is implied that the elevation of one's own consciousness will elevate the consciousness of the whole universe (i.e., shall restore *dharma*), likewise by default. But these are variations of nuance only. For internal and external coherence are mutually reinforcing and cannot be decoupled, even if internal coherence is given a higher valuation. The end result is the same: every instance of mindful engagement by any sentient being advances the vector of evolution, increasing the creative intelligence of the cosmos and the sum total of consciousness in the world.

Ervin Laszlo's understanding of the ultimate meaning and purpose embedded in the universe is strikingly similar to that of the wisdom traditions. The particular symbolic and linguistic manifestations vary across spiritual traditions, but the underlying premise and storyline remain the same. So, too, with Laszlo's new paradigm map of reality does a familiar metaphysical narrative come to light.

In Laszlo's interpretation, evolution leads to higher and higher levels of coherence and to increasing alignment in our thoughts and actions with the intelligence that underlies and orients evolution. As we scale the ladder of consciousness and express our oneness with people and nature through loving engagement—we might equally say, as we practice "at-one-ment"—increasingly complex and coherent systems emerge and spread over widening spheres.

In Laszlo's view, by the end of time consciousness ascends (or, in terms of wave frequency, descends) to the level of the immutable intelligence of the ground state of the cosmos in an almost mystical merging. The immutable intelligence of the cosmos is in religious terms the Godhead itself (Yahweh, Lord God, Allah, Brahman, the Void, the Tao). "God"—the Infinite—is both the beginning and end-goal of history, the primal cause and effect: "I am the Alpha and the Omega" (Revelation 22:13). Arguably, this is the same story—the mystical and mythic story—retold in this book for modern ears in the language of science.

In fact, Laszlo goes a step further, conjecturing that the evolution of consciousness may continue beyond the end of time itself, taking place not only through the cycles of incarnation within each universe, but also through the cycle of *successive universes.* After the universe retracts into nothingness (via any of the current cosmological scenarios), it could be aroused again by an injection of energies and another universe could be born. This vision is not unfamiliar to many of the wisdom traditions. Eastern traditions have always maintained a cyclical, oscillating view of cosmic time. In the Hindu picture of time flow, spatiotemporal reality continually re-hatches from a cosmic egg every cosmic day (defined as a *kalpa* of 8.64 billion years). For a half-day, *Brahma* (the creative, manifested aspect of the Brahman) grows and evolves, after which he sleeps for another half-day (during which the material world collapses and dissolves into nothingness and potentiality), only to awake and repeat the cycle. In Buddhism (which conceives of time as a wheel, or *Kalachakra*) and Taoism (which envisages space-time revolving around its spiritual center—the Tao—in endless cycles of transformation; indeed, the very symbol of Taoism—the *yin-yang* symbol—evokes a sense of eternal cycling), similar beliefs are held.

Laszlo gives this notion of cyclicality an uplifting and somewhat Western spin—as he infuses the Eastern conception of time with a sort of Semitic optimism and progressive buoyancy. Having now realized (we might equally say known, loved, beheld) itself through one lifecycle of the Universe, It—the eternal, transcendent Brahman—is enriched after the journey of its self-discovery, and infuses the succeeding iteration with its enhanced potency. Hence, each cycle of the universe is more coherent, more evolved, than the one that precedes it in an ever-escalating arc. Laszlo 'improves' upon the Eastern view, so to speak, by leaving open the possibility for the Brahman/Godhead to improve upon Itself. Indeed, we may feel closer to the divine if we pause to consider that, just as we become more fully ourselves with each of our lifetimes, so too does the intelligence of the cosmos.

There cannot be a fundamental contradiction between religion and science. The empirical data supplied by science—the partial truths revealed by the five senses—when interpreted through a lens of sufficient width and depth and invested with enlightened intuition point to the same truth that humanity's collective unconscious already knows and feels. It confirms what the greatest seers have been telling us for thousands of years.

It follows from Laszlo's analysis of the meaning of evolution in the universe—and the prophets of the wisdom traditions would agree—that *our* purpose is to help the universe fulfill *its* purpose. As our impulse to self-realize is woven into the fabric of Nature, our collective self-realization is Ultimate Reality realizing itself. By participating in the teleological evolution of Nature, we co-create the Divine.

We should rejoice that the latest discoveries in quantum physics affirm the ancient truths. Let us hope that Socrates was right when he said that "to know the good is to do it." Because we find ourselves today at a critical crossroads—at a unique moment in the history of consciousness, which we must not fail to turn to advantage. We are faced with a stark choice: the Path of Creativity or the Path of Consumption and Destruction. The ultimate choice will flow from our level of consciousness. The prevailing orientation to reality—consumptive, short-term, numbers-maximizing—occupies only an adolescent level of consciousness. It has led to dangerous, unsustainable imbalances at the individual, societal, and planetary levels—and hence must be urgently, collectively, reconsidered and revised.

Today, few places on this planet remain where an ethics of pure intention can be practiced. We typically find ourselves coerced into reverse-engineering our actions and instrumentalizing people and nature to achieve narrow bottom-line outcomes—enslaved by what I call (in my own forthcoming dystopian novel) the "Tyrant of Numbers."[149] But utilitarians tend to choke on their own base ends—because utility, when aimed at directly, is always missed. Consciousness precedes and informs material outcomes. Creativity arises from acts of love and ensues on its own. This is the ultimate irony—that only a respiritualized world can flourish materially, can beget real and sustainable wealth and save us from civilizational collapse. Real flourishing can only occur in sacred, conscious spaces. Hence, in one sense, we still live in economically, socially, ecologically imbalanced and even bankrupt times.

But, simultaneously and paradoxically, there is tremendous cause for hope. Perhaps as a counterbalancing response to the crises of our time, there are clear signs of a collective evolution in consciousness. We are starting to see across various fields of human endeavor vivid examples testifying to the rise of a new civilizational paradigm. The emerging paradigm affirms ancient truths and is beginning to increase creativity, harmony and justice in and across all social systems. It is now shaping global trends and infecting institutions. With new social modes of being (global, open, organically unfolding movements; socio-spiritual, purpose-driven enterprises on the market landscape; and technological innovations of distributed and democratic architecture), the emerging conditions are biased in favor of connection, collaboration, compassion—in one word, *coherence*.

Unlike the counterculture movements of the 1960s and 1970s, the new integral paradigm is already integrating itself into mainstream institutions and processes. For the first time in recent history, there is a globally permeating acknowledgement that consciousness lies at the base of all things—and that our ultimate duty lies in uncovering and expanding this consciousness to the best of our ability. A planetary consciousness is unfolding as we elevate ourselves above the timeworn currencies of blood and money and begin to trade in that ultimate currency which emanates from our true selves: the currency of consciousness. This singular currency is augmented rather than depleted with use.

Our age is ripe for an awakening based on an ancient truth: All is One. If indeed All is One, then selfless, loving action is rational—aligned with the ultimate nature of reality. The Hebrew Bible's Ten Commandments and the ethical framework they imply of a just social order as well as the Genesis account of man's essence being equivalent to the image of God; Christ's exhortations to cultivate humility, veracity and charity and to obey the Golden Rule; the very meaning of the word *Islam*—"the peace of surrendering to the Ultimate"; the indispensable Hindu axiom, "*atman* (individual soul) is *Brahman* (Universal Soul)"—which becomes realized by a *rishi* when he achieves *moksha*, or liberation from spacetime; Buddha's identification of the "three fires" of "greed, hatred and delusion" as the cause of *dukkha*, or human suffering (extinguished through generosity, compassion and ego-emptiness); and the Taoist mode/posture of non-active action—of making oneself quietly receptive to the universal flow of life, to the tide of *elan vital* which animates all Reality: all of these mandates and mantras point to the notion of supreme integration and unity, to the fact that we are all stitched into the fabric of a larger whole. Laszlo's map of reality corresponds to and confirms this premise.

The implications are staggering and a reason for jubilation. The vector of evolution has not veered off course; in fact, it is bang on target and gaining steam.

Acknowledgments

It gives me pleasure to express my heartfelt thanks to many of my wise friends and colleagues who have contributed to this book. They include Deepak Chopra, Gary Zukav, Stanislav Grof, Nassim Haramein, Jude Currivan, Stephan A. Schwartz, Allan Combs, Stanley Krippner, Ede Frecska, Nitamo Federico Montecucco, Na Aak (Paola Ambrosi), Tulku Thondup, Jean Houston, Christopher Bache, Shamik Desai, Master Zhi-Gang Sha, Kingsley L. Dennis, and John R. Audette. My long-term collaborator Maria Sagi provided constant information and vital inspiration as my theories and ideas evolved from the inception of this summation to their current shape. I have had the benefit of expert advice from Giuseppe Vitiello of the University of Salerno and had illuminating conversations and correspondence with Sylvie Ouellet, Anne Deligne, David Rousseau, Katya Walter, as well as my long-term agent and friend William Gladstone. A special thanks to the dedicated team of SelectBooks headed by Kenzi Sugihara, the publisher, with Nancy Sugihara as managing editor, Kenichi Sugihara in charge of publicity and marketing, and Yoji Yagamuchi as editor. Their care and expertise and patient commitment was a vital support for me as we worked our way through the multiple drafts of this book.

The discussions I had with my elder son, Christopher, a leading exponent of the new discipline of ethical and responsible business management and a true new-paradigm business leader himself, and the moral and emotional support of Carita, my constant companion and better half for more than a half-century, have been essential. And I am truly grateful for the constant love and care of my younger son, Alexander, a true "cultural creative" if there ever was one, for accompanying me throughout the adventure of drafting this study.

Notes

Foreword

i. Erwin Schrödinger, *My View of the World* (London: Cambridge UP, 1964), 30.

ii. Erwin Schrödinger, *Mind and Matter* (London: Cambridge UP, 1967), 135.

iii. Erwin Schrödinger, *What is Life? The Physical Aspect of a Living Cell* (London: Cambridge UP, 1967), 129.

iv. J.W.N. Sullivan, "Interviews with the Great Scientists VI: Max Planck," *The Observer*, Jan. 25, 1931, 17.

Introduction

v. Thomas Kuhn, *The Structure of Scientific Revolutions* (Chicago, IL: University of Chicago Press, 1962).

vi. David Bohm, *Wholeness and the Implicate Order* (London: Routledge & Kegan Paul, 1980); Karl Pribram, *Languages of the Brain* (Englewood Cliffs, NJ: Prentice Hall, 1971); Rupert Sheldrake, *A New Science of Life: The Hypothesis of Formative Causation* (Los Angeles, CA: J. P. Tarcher, 1981); Ilya Prigogine, *From Being to Becoming: Time and Complexity in the Physical Sciences* (San Francisco, CA: W. H. Freeman, 1980).

vii. Ervin Laszlo, *Science and the Akashic Field: An Integral Theory of Everything* (Rochester, VT: Inner Traditions, 2007).

viii. Stanislaw Grof, *Beyond the Brain: Birth, Death, and Transcendence in Psychotherapy.* (Albany, New York: State University of New York Press, 1985); Stanisloff Grof, *Psychology of the Future* (Albany, New York: State University of New York Press, 2000).

ix. Stanislaw Grof, *When the Impossible Happens: Adventures in Non-Ordinary Realities* (Louisville, Colorado: Sounds True, 2006).

x. Ibid.

xi. Aldous Huxley. *Perennial Philosophy* (New York and London: Harper and Brothers,1945).

xii. Stanislaw Grof, *Beyond the Brain: Birth, Death, and Transcendence in Psychotherapy* (Albany, New York: State University of New York Press, 1985); Grof, *Psychology of the Future.*

xiii. Grof, *Beyond the Brain*; Grof, *Psychology of the Future.*

xiv. C. G. Jung, *Symbols of Transformation.* Collected Works, vol. 5, Bollingen Series XX (Princeton, N.J.: Princeton University Press, 1956); C. G. Jung, *The Archetypes and the Collective Unconscious,* Collected Works, vol. 9,1, Bollingen Series XX (Princeton, N.J.: Princeton University Press, 1959).

xv. Grof, *When the Impossible Happens.*

xvi. Ibid.

xvii. C. G. Jung, *Synchronicity: An Acausal Connecting Principle.* Collected Works, vol. 8, Bollingen Series XX (Princeton: Princeton University Press, 1960).

xviii. Alfred Korzybski, "A Non-Aristotelian System and Its Necessity for Rigor in Mathematics and Physics," A paper presented before the American Mathematical Society at the meeting of the American Association for the Advancement of Science (New Orleans, Louisiana, December 28, 1931); Gregory Bateson, *Steps to An Ecology of Mind* (San Francisco: Chandler Publications, 1972).

xix. Ervin Laszlo, *The Creative Cosmos: A Unified Science of Matter, Life and Mind* (Edinburgh: Floris Books, 1993); Ervin Laszlo, *The Interconnected Universe: Conceptual Foundations of Transdisciplinary Unified Theory* (Singapore: World Scientific Publishing, 1999); Ervin Laszlo, *The Connectivity Hypothesis: Foundations of an Integral Science of Quantum, Cosmos, Life, and Consciousness* (Albany, NY: State University of New York Press, 2003).

xx. Grof, *When the Impossible Happens.*

xxi. Bohm, *Wholeness and the Implicate Order*; Pribram, *Languages of the Brain*; Sheldrake, *A New Science of Life*; Alfred North Whitehead, *Process and Reality* (New York: Macmillan,1929); Bateson, *Steps to an Ecology of Mind.*

xxii. Leibniz G. W. *The Principles of Philosophy Known As Monadology.* Cambridge: Cambridge University Press, 2010.

xxiii. Whitehead, *Process and Reality.*

Chapter 1: Cosmos

1. Alain Aspect, Jean Dalibard, Gerard Roger, "Experimental Test of Bell's Inequalities Using Time-Varying Analyzers," *Physical Review Letters* 49 (1982).
2. A. Einstein, B. Podolsky, N. Rosen, "Can Quantum-Mechanical Description of Physical Reality be Considered Complete?" *Physical Review* 47 (1935): 777–80.
3. B. Hensen, H. Bernien, A. Dreau, et al., "Loophole-Free Bell Inequality Violation Using Electron Spins Separated by 1.3 Kilometers," *Nature* 256 (2015).
4. Abraham Pais, *The Genius of Science* (Oxford: Oxford University Press, 2000).
5. The American Indian M. Scott Momaday described the vision of reality of the Plains Indians of the northern Americas as follows.

> If I can try to find an analogy, it's rather like looking through the viewfinder of a camera, the viewfinder which is based upon the principle of the split image. And it is a matter of trying to align the two planes of that particular view. This can be used as an example of how we look at the world around us. We see it with the physical eye. We see it as it appears to us, in one dimension of reality. But we also see it with the eye of the mind. It seems to me that the Indian has achieved a particularly effective alignment of those two planes of vision. He perceives the landscape in both ways.

N. Scott Momaday, "Native American Attitudes to the Environment," in Capps, Walter Holden (ed.), *Seeing With A Native Eye: Essays on Native American Religion.* (New York: Harper & Row, 1976): 81.

6. Swami Vivekananda, *Raja Yoga*. Advaita Ashrama, Calcutta, 1982 (eighteenth impression).

7. David Bohm, *Wholeness and the Implicate Order* (London: Routledge & Kegan Paul, 1980).

8. Karl Pribram, *Languages of the Brain,* (Brandon House, 1971); *Brain and Perception: Holonomy and Figural Processing,* (Laurence Erlbaum, 1991).

Chapter 2: Consciousness

9. Jean Jacques Charbonier, *Seven Reasons to Believe in the Afterlife* (Inner Traditions, Rochester, VT, 2015), originally published in French as *Les 7 bonnes raisons de croire à l'au-delà* (Paris: Guy Tredaniel Editeur, 2012). See also Stephan A. Schwartz, this volume.

10. Cited by Charbonier, *Seven Reasons.*

11. Charbonier, *Seven Reasons.*

12. Kenneth Ring and Sharon Cooper, Near-Death and Out-of-Body Experiences in the Blind: A Study of Apparent Eyeless Vision. *Journal of Near-Death Studies* 16:2 (Winter 1997), 101–147.

13. Kenneth Ring and Sharon Cooper, *MindSight: Near-Death and Out-of-Body Experiences in the Blind* (Bloomington, IN: iUniverse, 2008).

14. Stephan A. Schwartz with R.J. De Mattei, . "The Mobius Psi-Q Test: Preliminary Findings" in *Research in Parapsychology 1982*, eds. William G. Roll, et al. (Metuchen, N.J. & London: Scarecrow, 1983), 103–105.

15. Stephan A. Schwartz, *Opening to the Infinite* (Budha, TX: Nemoseen, 2007).

16. Stephan A. Schwartz, "Numinosity, Entropy, Intention, and Remote Viewing: Three Variables Subject to Manipulation," *Proceedings of Neuroscience and Consciousness conference.* Seattle, March 17–19, 1983.

17. Ervin Laszlo with Anthony Peake, *The Immortal Mind* (Rochester, VT: Inner Traditions, 2014).

18. The decades-long research of Annabella Cardoso, an ambassador of her native Portugal, is particularly noteworthy in this regard. See the periodical edited by Cardoso, *ITC Journal*, <cuadermostci@itcjournal.org> and the references to her work in Laszlo, *The Immortal Mind.*

19. William James, *Ingersoll Lecture on Immortality* (Boston: Houghton Mifflin, 1899).

20. David Darling, "Supposing Something Different: Reconciling Science and the Afterlife," *OMNI* 17:9 (1995), 4.

21. Eben Alexander, *Proof of Heaven: A Neurosurgeon's Journey into the Afterlife* (New York: Simon & Schuster, 2012); Eternea, The Convergence of Science & Spirituality for Personal & Global transformation, www.eternea.org/Postulates.aspx.

22. Stephan A. Schwartz, "Six Protocols, Neuroscience, and Near-Death: An Emerging Paradigm Incorporating Nonlocal Consciousness." *Explore* 11:4 (2015): 252–260. A slightly different version can also be found in *The Mysteries of Consciousness*. ed. by Ingrid Fredriksson. (Jefferson, NC: McFarland, 2015), 5–20.

23. Open Sciences Campaign, http://opensciences.org/about/manifesto-for-a-post-materialist-science.

Chapter 3: Existence

24. Rosemary Brown, *Immortals by My Side* (London: Bachman & Turner, 1974).

25. Jane Sherwood, *The Country Beyond* (Saffron Walden: C.W. Daniel Ltd., 1969), 64–65.

26. Tulku Thondup, *Peaceful Death, Joyful Rebirth* (Boston: Shambala, 2005), 189–190.

27. Anthony Borgia, *Life in the World Unseen* (London: Psychic Press, 1974).

28. W.Y. Evans-Wentz, *The Tibetan Book of the Dead* (Oxford: Oxford University Press, 1960).

29. Neville Randall, *Life After Death* (London: Robert Hale, 1975).

30. Paramhansa Yogananda, *Autobiography of a Yogi* (London: Rider, 1969).

31. Sylvie Ouellet, series of personal communications, Spring 2015.

32. Geraldine Cummins, *Beyond Human Personality* (London: Psychic Press, 1935). The passages that follow are also from this book.

33. Frederic Myers, *Human Personality and Its Survival of Bodily Death* (London: Longmans, Green, 1907).

34. Geraldine Cummins, *Beyond Human Personality* (Guildford, England: White Crow, 1935).

35. Jane Sherwood, *The Country Beyond*, Chapter 15.

36. Poonam Sharma and Jim B. Tucker, "Cases of the Reincarnation Type with Memories from the Intermission Between Lives," *Journal of Near Death Studies* 23:2 (2004).

37. Interview of James Tucker by Miriam Gablier, January 2014.

38. Masayuki Ohkado, *Children with Life-Between-Life Memories* (Aichi, Japan: Chubu U, and Charlottesville: U of Virginia, 2013).

39. Rosemary Brown, *Immortals By My Side,* Chapter 11.

40. Jane Sherwood, *The Country Beyond*, 54.

41. Ervin Laszlo, *Quantum Shift in the Clobal Brain* (Rochester: Inner Traditions, 2006), 153–156.

42. Sir James G. Frazer, *The Golden Bough*, vol. 8 (London: MacMillan, 1937).

43. Cecil Day Lewis, *The Aeneid: Translated from the Latin* (Oxford: Oxford University Press, 1986).

44. Dzogchen Ponlop, *Mind Beyond Death* (Ithaca, NY and New York: Snow Lion Publications, 2006).

Chapter 4: The New Map in Physics

Nassim Haramein, The Physics of Oneness

45. Fred Hoyle, *The Intelligent Universe* (London: Michael Joseph, 1983).

46. John Archibald Wheeler with Kenneth Ford, *Geons, Black Holes, and Quantum Foam: A Life in Physics* (New York: W.W. Norton, 1998), 146.

47. To better understand the scales involved, here is an analogy. There are approximately 100 trillion cells in the average human body and each typical cell consists of approximately 100 trillion atoms. If you were to take one of those minute atoms and make it the size of the dome at the

Vatican (138 feet or 42 meters) the proton in the middle nuclei would be approximately the size of the tiny head of a pin. Now, if we were to put a Planck unit on the end of your finger and then grow it to the average size of a grain of sand then the minuscule proton would all of a sudden have a diameter equal to the distance from here to the nearest star, Alpha Centauri or approximately 25.5 trillion miles or 40 trillion kilometers in diameter.

48. The analogy is best visualized as a rubber duck in a bathtub. Imagine a bathtub full of water with a drain on one end. Pulling the plug on the drain will produce a gradient, generating a spinning dynamic in that region where all molecules of water are co-moving in a highly coherent manner. If a rubber duck is placed far from that region, it appears to be very little affected by the event on the other side of the tub. But if the rubber duck is placed close to that region of co-moving particles, it appears to start orbiting and be attracted to the drain (the black hole). One could describe this event as the attraction being equivalent to the amount of curvature of the surface of the water towards the drain, the more curvature the more the rubber duck appears to be attracted. This is analogous to Einstein's field equations, which utilize complex metric tensor space to describe the surface of spacetime curving to produce gravity. On the other hand, a proper analysis of what is occurring will reveal that it is in fact the spin dynamics of the co-moving water particles that are producing the effects appearing as curvature and thus producing the apparent gravitational force.

49. Indeed, the surface-to-volume Planck ratio for the proton, when multiplied by the Planck mass to get the mass-energy (just like the cosmological solution I had found for black holes), generates a mass for the proton (1.603498×10^{-24} grams) that is within 0.069×10^{-24} g of the experimentally measured value ($1.672621777 \times 10^{-24}$ grams).

50. Aldo Antognini, François Nez, Karsten Schuhmann, et al., "Proton Structure from the Measurement of 2S-2P Transition Frequencies of Muonic Hydrogen," *Science* 17 (2013): 417–420.

51. Nassim Haramein, William Brown, Amira Val Baker, "The Unified Spacememory Network: From Cosmogenesis to Consciousness," *The Journal of Conscientiology* 1 (2015).

52. Albert Einstein, "Relativity and the Problem of Space,"Notes to the Fifteenth Edition.

53. Mari Jibu, Scott Hagan, Stuart R. Hameroff, et al., "Quantum Optical Coherence in Cytoskeletal Microtubules: Implications for Brain Function," *Biosystems* 32:3 (1994).

54. Rupert Sheldrake, *The Sense of Being Stared At: And Other Unexplained Powers of Human Minds* (Oark Street Press, 2013).

55. Miroslav Hill, "Adaptive State of Mammalian Cells and Its Nonseparability Suggestive of a Quantum System," *Scripta Medica* 73:4 (2000): 211-222.

56. I would like to acknowledge the critical contribution of molecular biologist William Brown for his contribution to the cross-fertilization from physics to biology and for the ongoing discussions and support of astrophysicist Dr. Amira Val Baker.

Jude Currivan, The In-formed Cosmos

57. Antoine Bérut, Artak Arakelyan, Artyom Petrosyan, et al., "Experimental Verification of Landauer's Principle Linking Information and Thermodynamics," *Nature 483 (2012): 187–189.*

Allan Combs and Stanley Krippner, On Consciousness

58. H. Nomura and T. Okoshi, "Storage Density Limitation of a Volume-Type Hologram Memory: Theory," *Applied Optics* 15 (1976): 550–555.

59. Jean Clottes and David Lewis-Williams, *The Shamans of Prehistory: Trance and Magic in the Painted Caves*, S. Hawkes, trans. (New York: Harry N. Abrams, 1998).

60. Mircea Eliade, *Shamanism: Archaic Techniques of Ecstasy*, Willard R. Trask, trans. (Princeton: Princeton UP, 1951). See also Michael Harner, *The Way of the Shaman* (New York: Harper & Row, 1980).

61. Benny Shanon, "Ideas and Reflections Associated with Ayahuasca Visions," *MAPS Bulletin* 8 (1998): 18.

62. Stanislav Grof and Christina Grof, *Beyond Death: The Gates of Consciousness* (London: Thames & Hudson, 1980). See also Stanislav Grof and Joan Halifax, *The Human Encounter with Death* (New York: Dutton, 1977); and D. J. Trisker, *Spirits Alive: Confrontations with the Spirits of Brazil* (New York: Vantage, 1996).

63. Joan Halifax, *Shaman: The Wounded Healer* (Spring Valley, NY: Crossroad, 1982). See also Stacy B. Schaefer and Peter T. Furst, *People of the Peyote: Huichol Indian History, Religion and Survival* (Albuquerque: University of New Mexico, 1996).

64. Stanley Krippner, "Mythological Aspects of Death and Dying," in *Perspectives on Death and Dying*, Arthur Berger, Paul Badham, Austin Kutscher, et al., eds. (Philadelphia: Charles Press, 1989): 3–13.

65. Raymond A. Moody, Jr., *Life after Life* (New York: Bantam, 1975). See also Raymond A. Moody, Jr. with Paul Perry, *The Light Beyond* (New York: Bantam, 1988); Kenneth Ring, Life at Death (New York: Coward, McCann and Geoghegan, 1980); Carol Zeleski, *Otherworld Journeys: Accounts of Near-Death Experiences in Medieval and Modern Times* (New York: Oxford University Press, 1987).

66. Pim van Lommel, Ruud van Wees, Vincent Meyers, Ingrid Elfferich, "Near-Death Experience in Survivors of Cardiac Arrest: A Prospective Study In The Netherlands," *Lancet* 358 (2001): 2039–2045. doi: http://dx.doi.org/10.1016/S0140-6736(01)07100-8.

67. A. Heim, "Remarks on Fatal Falls," *Swiss Alpine Club Yearbook* 27 (1892): 327–337.

68. Stanley Krippner, ed., "Tribal Shamans and Their Travels into Dreamtime" in *Dreamtime and Dreamwork: Decoding the Language of the Night* (Los Angeles: Tarcher/Perigee, 1990): 185–193.

69. Henry Corbin, *The Man of Light in Iranian Sufism* (Boston: Shambhala, 1978), 400.

70. Raymond Frank Piper and Lila K. Piper, *Cosmic Art* (New York: Hawthorne, 1975).

71. John Leslie, *Universes* (London: Routledge, 1989).

Chapter 5: The New Map in the Study of Consciousness

Stephan A. Schwartz, A New Map of Reality Based on Consciousness

72. "How Many Stars are There in the Universe?" European Space Agency. http://www.esa.int/Our Activities/Space Science/Herschel/. Accessed September 27, 2015.

73 Larry Dossey, *Recovering the Soul* (New York: Bantam, 1989): 1–11.

74. Mike Parker Pearson, *The Archeology of Death and Burial* (College Station, TX: Texas A&M, 1999).

75. Julien Riel Salvatore and Geoffrey A. Clark, "Grave markers, Middle and Early Upper Paleolithic burials," *Current Anthropology* 42/4 (2001): 481–90.

76. Plato, *The Republic*, Book VI. https://www.gutenberg.org/files/1497/1497-h/1497-h.htm. Accessed November 12, 2015.

77. George Sidney Brett, *A History of Psychology, Vol. 1. Ancient and Patristic* (London: George Allen & Co., 1912) 302. https://babel.hathitrust.org/cgi/pt. Accessed: 2 June 2016.

78. "Interview with Max Planck," *The Observer*, January 25, 1931.

79. Max Planck, 'Das Wesen der Materie' [The Essence of Matter], Florence, Italy (1944). *Archiv zur Geschichte der Max-Planck-Gesellschaft*, Abt. Va, Rep. 11 Planck, Nr. 1797.

80. Albert Einstein quoted in Harold Eves, *Mathematical Circles Adieu* (Boston: Prindle, Weber and Schmidt, 1977).

81. Erwin Schrödinger, *My View of the World* (Cambridge: Cambridge UP, 1960): 62.

82. Abraham Pais, *The Genius of Science* (Oxford: Oxford University Press, 2000).

83. O. Costa de Beauregard, "The paranormal is not excluded from physics," *J Sci Exploration* 12 (1998): 315–320.

84. William James, Lecture XX, "Conclusions & Postscript," *The Varieties of Religious Experience* (Public Domain). E-book location: 7162.

85. Gitt Panitchayangkoona, Dugan Hayesa, Kelly A. Fransted, et al., "Long-Lived Quantum Coherence In Photosynthetic Complexes At Physiological Temperature," *Proceedings of the Nationall Academy of Sciences USA* 107:29 (2010):12766–70. doi: 10.1073/pnas.1005484107. Epub 2010 Jul 6. PMID: 20615985.

86. Andrew B. Newberg, *Principles of Neurotheology* (Burlington, VT: Ashgate, 2010).

87. "Making Music Together Connects Brains," *Science Daily* November 29, 2012. http://www.sciencedaily.com/releases/2012/11/121129093417.htm. Accessed November 29, 2012.

88. Edward M. Bowden, Mark Jung-Beeman, "Aha! Insight Experience Correlates with Solution Activation in the Right Hemisphere," *Psychonomic Bulletin &Review* 10:3 (2003): 730–737. PMID: 14620371.

89. Mark Jung-Beeman, Edward M. Bowden, Jason Haberman, et al., "Neural activity when people solve verbal problems with insight," *PLoS Biology* 2:4 (2004): E97. PMID: 15094802.

90. Jeanne Achterberg, Karin Cooke, Todd Richards, et al., "Evidence For Correlations Between Distant Intentionality And Brain Function In Recipients: A Functional Magnetic Resonance Imaging Analysis," *Journal of Alternative and Complementary Medicine* 11:6 (2005): 965–71. PMID: 16398587.

91. Stephan Schwartz, "Six Protocols, Neuroscience, and Near Death: An Emerging Paradigm Incorporating Nonlocal Consciousness," in *Mysteries of Consciousness*, Ingrid Fredriksson, editor (Jefferson, NC: McFarland, 2015).

92. Stephan Schwartz, "Through Time and Space: The Evidence for Remote Viewing," *The Evidence for Psi*, Damien Broderick and Ben Groetzel, eds. (Jefferson, NC: McFarland, 2015).

93. Pim van Lommel, *Consciousness Beyond Life* (New York: HarperOne, 2007): 62.

94. van Lommel, et al., "Near-Death Experience in Survivors of Cardiac Arrest."

95. Bruce Greyson, Janice Miner Holden, Pim van Lommel "There Is Nothing Paranormal About Near-Death Experiences"revisited: comment on Mobbs and Watt," *Trends in Cognitive Science* 16:9 (2012):445; author reply 446. doi: 10.1016/j.tics.2012.07.002.

96. Julie Beischel, *Modern Mental Mediums* (Tucson, AZ: Windbridge Institute, 2015).

97. Ian Stevenson, *Reincarnation and Biology* vols. I-II (Westport, Conn: Praeger, 1997).

98. Carl Sagan, *The Dragons of Eden* (New York: Random House, 1977), 7.
99. Carl Sagan, *The Demon Haunted World* (New York: Random House, 1996), 302.
100. Stephan Schwartz, *Opening to the Infinite* (Budha, TX: Nemoseen, 2007), 33–34.
101. Schwartz, *Opening to the Infinite,* 33–34.
102. Ibid., 33-34.
103. Ibid., 33–34.
104. Ibid., 33-34.
105. Jacques Hadamard, Subconscient intuition, et logique dans la rechere scientifique. *Les Conférences du Palais de la Découverte* le 8 Decembre 1945, (Alencon n.d.): 7–8.
106. Stephan Schwartz, "Nonlocality and Exceptional Experiences: A Study of Genius, Religious Epiphany, and the Psychic," *Explore* 6:4 (2010): 227–236.
107. John Mihalasky, "ESP: Can It Play a Role in Idea-Generation?" *Mechanical Engineering* (Dec. 1972).
108. Kuhn.
109. "Minority Rules: Scientists Find the Tipping Point." *Discovery,* August 4, 2011. http://news.discovery.com/human/opinion-minority-rules-110804.htm. Accessed March 1, 2015.
110. G.S. Stent, "Prematurity and Uniqueness in Scientific Discovery," *Scientific American* 227:6 (Dec. 1972): 84–93. doi: 10.1038/scientificamerican1272-84.
111. Stephan Schwartz, *The Secret Vaults of Time* (New York: Grosset & Dunlap, 1978).
112. Schwartz, *Secret Vaults of Time.*
113. Dossey, 1–11.
114. Coleman Barks, translator, *Rumi: The Book of Love: Poems of Ecstasy and Longing.* (New York: Harper-Collins, 2003).
115. Stephan Schwartz, *The 8 Laws of Change* (Rochester: Park Street, 2015): 118–119.

Ede Frecska, The Deep Roots of Consciousness

116. Ede Frecska, "Nonlocality and Intuition as the Second Foundation of Knowledge," *Neuroquantology* 10:3 (2012), 537–546. doi:10.14704/nq.2012.10.3.599.

117. Ede Frecska, Levente Móró and Hank Wesselman, "The Soul Cluster: Reconsideration of a Millennia Old Concept," *World Futures: The Journal of New Paradigm Research* 67:2(2011): 132–153. doi:10.1080/02604027.2010.532464.

118. Hank Wesselman, Henry Barnard Wesselman, Jill Kuykendall, *Spirit Medicine: Healing in the Sacred Realms* (Carlsbad: Hay House, 2004).

Nitamo Federico Montecucco, The New Map of Consciousness and the Neurosciences

119. Osha, *I am That: Talks on the Isa Upanishad,* (Mumbai: Jaico Publishing House, 2008).

Chapter 6: The New Map and the Nature of Existence

Jean Houston, Existence Within and Beyond the Body: The Mystical View

120. Francis Crick, *Astonishing Hypothesis: The Scientific Search for the Soul* (New York: Touchstone, 1995), 3.

121. "Hermes Trismegistus quotes," Goodreads. Accessed November 22, 2015. https://www.goodreads.com/author/quotes/272885.Hermes_Trismegistus.

122. Evelyn Underhill, *Mysticism: A Study in the Nature and Development of Spiritual Consciousness* (New York: Dutton, 1930).

123. Jean Houston, *Mystical Dogs: Animals As Guides to Our Inner Life* (Novato, California: New World Library, 2004).

124. Jane Sherwood, *The Country Beyond: The Doctrine of Re-birth* (London: C.W. Daniel, 2004), 65.

Chapter 7: Wider Horizons

John R. Audette, The New Map of Reality: Who Are You Really?

125. Alice Calaprice, *Albert Einstein's Letters to and from Children* (New York: Prometheus Books, 2002), 184.

Gary Zukav, Laszlo's Map of Reality and the New Human Consciousness

126. Gary Zukav, *The Seat of the Soul: 25th Anniversary Edition* (New York: Simon & Schuster, 2014).

Alexander Laszlo, Seeking Syntony with the Intelligence of the Cosmos

127. Mae Wan Ho, *The Rainbow and the Worm: The Physics of Organisms* (Singapore: World Scientific, 1998).

128. Otto Scharmer, *Theory U: Leading from the Future as it Emerges* (San Francisco: Berrett-Koehler, 2009).

129. David Price, "Daologue" in Open to Persuasion ... Open reasoning in a complex world. http://opentopersuasion.com/2014/05/22/daologue/. Accessed May 29, 2015.

130. Alexander Laszlo and Kathia Castro Laszlo, "Syntony and Flow: The Artscience of Evolutionary Aesthetics" in *The View: Mind over Matter, Heart over Mind: From Conan Doyle to Conversations with God*, David Patrick, ed. (London: Polair, 2009).

131. Kingsley L. Dennis, *The Phoenix Generation: A New Era of Connection, Compassion, and Consciousness* (London: Watkins, 2014).

132. William Gibson, "The Science in Science Fiction," NPR *Talk of the Nation, November 30, 1999, discover.npr.org/features/feature.jhtml?wfId=1067220. Accessed May 7, 2012.*

133. Stuart Kauffman, "The Adjacent Possible: A Talk with Stuart A. Kauffman," November 9 2003. Edge Foundation. http://edge.com. Accessed May 28, 2015.

134. Arundhati Roy, *War Talk* (London: South End Press, 2003).

135. Charles Eisenstein, "Qualitative Dimensions of Collective Intelligence: Subjectivity, Consciousness, and Soul," *Spanda Journal* 2 (2014).

136. Wendy Wheeler, *The Whole Creature: Complexity, Biosemiotics and the Evolution of Culture* (London: Lawrence and Wishart Ltd, 2006).

137. An excellent game through which to practice these skills of awareness and increase our availability to the information flow of the deep dimension is called Psyche—the Game of Decisions. As a synchronistic game for the transformation of conscious energy, it was conceived to serve as a universal guide for human affairs in the form of a game combining the wisdom of highly developed ancient civilizations with the discoveries of modern psychology (as described in the foreword to the Psyche game manual). The game, developed by Mexican psychologist Armando Perez, is a contemporary synthesis of ancient systems of self-discovery from Mexico, China, Greece, India, and Persia drawing upon the archetypal ludic patterns at the heart of such learning systems as the I Ching, Leela, Asha, Patoli, and Magic Squares. The classical version is played as a board game but more recently it has been transformed into an interactive downloadable App called "Decisions by Psyche." It is a wonderful tool for self-reflection and for the intentional exploration and transformation of your conscious energy.

    Another good practice has been developed by Jungian scholar and Martial Artist Richard Squeri. His work lies more in the somatic and kinesthetic engagement with flow: with tuning and alignment of self in dynamic relation to the in-formation flows through which we emerge. Squeri has developed a body of practice known as Flowing Dragon Swords (FDS) which, to use his words, "is a language of the soul. It provides a direct route to what my heart wants to reveal to me. . . . Practicing this dance over time teaches us to tune in to the body, mind, and Spirit while we remain engaged with another human being. . . . As I put away my sword and ease into the rest of my day, I find that this remarkable game transforms all my encounters in a positive way." (Squeri, 2015). Squeri goes on to explain that FDS is "part martial art, part psychological self-exploration and spiritual practice. It is based primarily in nonverbal methods of communication and the gradual acquisition of a new awareness of the self. The spontaneous co-creation of movement in the game provides part of this important new dialog, though all that is necessary is the ability to simply hold a wooden sword." (Ibid.) Simplicity, attention, care and a willingness to learn and be in-formed are at the heart of this practice of flow, alignment, tuning and grace. It is an excellent practice for anyone interested in heightening their cosmic in-formational availability. (See Richard Squeri, "The Power of The Game" in *Flow Dragon Swords: A Practice of Life and Learning. https://flowingdragons.wordpress.com/the-power-of-the-game.) Accessed December 9, 2015.*

138. Janine Benyus, "Innovations Inspired by Nature" in *Doors of Perception 7: Flow* (Conference in Amsterdam: 14,15, 16 November 2002). http://flow.doorsofperception.com/content/benyus_trans.html. Accessed May 28, 2015.

139. Thomas H. Huxley, "The Struggle for Existence in Human Society" in *Evolution and Ethics and Other Essays* (New York & London: Appleton, 1925), 81–82.

140. Alexander Laszlo, "Living Systems, Seeing Systems, Being Systems: Learning to Be the Systems We Wish to See in the World" in *Spanda Journal* 6:1 (2015).

Chapter 8: In Search of Meaning

141. Nassim Haramein, The Resonance Project, see article in this volume.

142. Thomas Kuhn, *The Structure of Scientific Revolutions (Chicago: University of Chicago Press, 1962).*

143. Robert Nadeau and Menas Kafatos, *The Non-Local Universe: the New Physics and Matters of the Mind* (Oxford: Oxford UP, 2001).

144. The buildup of complex systems is due to the action of the so-called Pauli Exclusion Principle. This principle specifies that no two electrons orbiting the nucleus of an atom can occupy the same quantum state at the same time. Thus, as electrons enter the atom's energy shells, they are shifted to different orbital pathways. In consequence atoms acquire internal structure. In the course of time they fill the Periodic Table of the Elements from hydrogen to uranium and beyond. Without the action of the exclusion principle only the inner energy shells would surround the atomic nucleus, and heavier atoms, hadrons and the molecules built of them, would not exist in the universe.

145. "Goldilocks zone" refers to the fairytale of Goldilocks and the three bears. Goldilocks found the house of the three bears and in their absence tried the porridge and the beds and discovered that some are too hot or too big, and others too small and too cold. Finally she found those that are just right—like our planet did in the galaxy.

146. Sun Kwok and Yong Zhang, "Astronomers Discover Complex Organic Matter Exists throughout the Universe," *Science Daily* (October 26, 2011).

147. Tommaso P. Fraccia, Gregory P. Smith, Giuliano Zanchetta, et al., "Abiotic Ligation of DNA Oligomers Templated by Their Liquid Crystal Ordering," i*Nature Communications* 6 (2015): 6424. doi:10.1038/ncomms 742.

148. D. Sobral, A. M. Swinbank, J. P. Stott, "The Dynamics of z=0.8 Ha-selected Star-forming Galaxies from KMOS/CF-HiZELS," *The Astrophysical Journal*, 779:139 (2013): 428, 1128.

Afterword

Shamik Desai, Meaning and Purpose In the New Map of Reality and In the Wisdom Traditions

149. Shamik Desai, *2020: The World Through Troogol Glass* (unpublished manuscript).

Bibliography

Aldo Antognini, François Nez, Karsten Schuhmann, et al. "Proton Structure from the Measurement of 2S-2P Transition Frequencies of Muonic Hydrogen." *Science* 17 (2013): 417–420.

Gregory Bateson. *Steps to an Ecology of Mind*. San Francisco: Chandler, 1972.

David Bohm. *Wholeness and the Implicate Order*. London: Routledge & Kegan Paul, 1980.

Jurgen Brosius, Thomas Dull, and Harry Noller. "Complete nucleotide sequence of a 23S ribosomal RNA gene from Escherichia coli." *PNAS* 77:1 (1980): 201–204.

Jurgen Brosius, Margaret Palmer, Poindexter Kennedy, and Harry Noller. "Complete nucleotide sequence of a 16S ribosomal RNA gene from Escherichia coli." *PNAS* 75:11 (1978): 4801–4805.

William Cantara, Pamela Crain, Jef Rozenski, James McCloskey, Kimberly Harris, Xiaonong Zhang, Franck Vendeix, Daniele Fabris, and Paul Agris. "The RNA modification database, RNAMDB: 2011 update." *Nucleic Acids Research* 39:1 (2011): D195–D201.

Jean Clottes and David Lewis-Williams. *The Shamans of Prehistory: Trance and Magic in the Painted Caves*. Translated by Sophie Hawkes. New York: Harry N. Abrams, 1998.

Henry Corbin. *The Man of Light in Iranian Sufism*. Boston: Shambhala, 1978.

Emilio Del Giudice, Antonella De Ninno, Martin Fleischmann, et al. "Coherent Quantum Electrodynamics in Living Matter." *Electromagnetic Biology and Medicine* 24:3 (2005): 199–210.

Mircea Eliade. *Shamanism: Archaic Techniques of Ecstasy*. Translated by Willard R. Trask. Princeton: Princeton UP, 1951.

Ede Frecska. "Nonlocality and Intuition as the Second Foundation of Knowledge." *Neuroquantology* 10:3 (2012): 537–546. doi: 10.14704/nq.2012.10.3.599.

Ede Frecska, Levente Móró and Hank Wesselman. "The Soul Cluster: Reconsideration of a Millennia Old Concept." *World Futures: The Journal of New Paradigm Research* 67:2 (2011): 132–153. doi:10.1080/02604027.2010.532464.

Stanislav Grof. *Beyond the Brain: Birth, Death, and Transcendence in Psychotherapy*. Albany, NY: SUNY Press, 1985.

———. *The Cosmic Game: Explorations of the Frontiers of Human Consciousness*. Albany, NY: SUNY Press, 1998.

———. *Psychology of the Future*. Albany, NY: SUNY Press, 2000.

———. *Realms of the Human Unconscious: Observations from LSD Research*. New York: Viking Press, 1975. Republished as *LSD: Doorway to the Numinous*. Rochester, VT: Inner Traditions, 2009.

———. *When the Impossible Happens: Adventures in Non-Ordinary Realities*. Louisville, CO: Sounds True, 2006.

Stanislav Grof and Christina Grof. *Beyond Death: The Gates of Consciousness*. London: Thames & Hudson, 1980.

Stanislav Grof and Joan Halifax. *The Human Encounter with Death*. New York: Dutton, 1978.

Herb Gruning. *God and the New Metaphysics*. Nevada City, CA: Blue Dolphin, 2005.

Joan Halifax. *Shaman: The Wounded Healer*. New York: Crossroad, 1982.

Nassim Haramein. "Quantum Gravity and the Holographic Mass." *Physical Review and Research International* (2013): 270–292.

Nassim Haramein, William Brown, and Amira Val Baker. "The Unified Spacememory Network: From Cosmogenesis to Consciousness." *The Journal of Conscientiology* 1:1 (2015). Accessed December 6, 2015. Retrieved from http://icc.iacworld.org/portfolio/nassim-haramein-william-brown-and-amira-val-baker/.

Michael Harner. *The Way of the Shaman*. New York: Harper & Row, 1980.

A. Heim, "Remarks on Fatal Falls," *Swiss Alpine Club Yearbook* 27 (1892): 327–337.

Miroslov Hill. "Adaptive State of Mammalian Cells and It's Nonseparability Suggestive of a Quantum System." *Scripta Medica* 73:4 (2000): 211–222.

Jean Houston. *Mystical Dogs: Animals As Guides to Our Inner Life*. Novato, California: New World Library, 2004.

Fred Hoyle. *The Intelligent Universe*. London: Michael Joseph, 1983.

Aldous Huxley. *Perennial Philosophy*. New York: Harper and Brothers, 1945.

Mari Jibu, Scott Hagan, Stuart Hameroff, Karl Pribram, and Kunio Yasue. 1994. "Quantum optical coherence in cytoskeletal microtubules: implications for brain function." *Biosystems* 32 (1994): 195–209.

Carl G. Jung, *Symbols of Transformation. Collected Works,* volume 5. Bollingen Series 20, Princeton: Princeton UP, 1956.

———. *The Archetypes and the Collective Unconscious. Collected Works,* volume 9. Bollingen Series 20, Princeton: Princeton UP, 1959.

———. *Synchronicity: An Acausal Connecting Principle. Collected Works,* volume 8, Bollingen Series 20. Princeton: Princeton UP, 1960.

John H. Kennell and Marshall H. Klaus. "Parental Bonding: Recent Observations that Alter Perinatal Care." *Pediatrics in Review* 19:1 (1998): 4–12. doi: 10.1542/pir.19-1-4.

Marshall H. Klaus, John H. Kennell, and Phyllis H. Klaus. *Bonding: Building the Foundations of Secure Attachment and Independence.* New York: Perseus, 1995.

Alfred Korzybski. "A Non-Aristotelian System and Its Necessity for Rigor in Mathematics and Physics." Paper presented before the American Mathematical Society at the meeting of the American Association for the Advancement of Science, New Orleans, Louisiana, December 28, 1931.

Stanley Krippner, "Mythological Aspects of Death and Dying." *Perspectives on Death and Dying.* Edited by Arthur Berger, Paul Badham, Austin Kutscher, et al. Philadelphia: Charles Press, 1989, pp. 3–13.

———, editor. "Tribal Shamans and Their Travels into Dreamtime." *Dreamtime and Dreamwork: Decoding the Language of the Night.* Los Angeles: Jeremy P. Tarcher/Perigee, 1990, 185–193.

Thomas S. Kuhn. *The Structure of Scientific Revolutions.* Chicago: U of Chicago, 1962.

Ervin Laszlo. *The Connectivity Hypothesis: Foundations of an Integral Science of Quantum, Cosmos, Life, and Consciousness.* Albany, NY: SUNY Press, 2003.

———. *The Creative Cosmos: A Unified Science of Matter, Life and Mind.* Edinburgh: Floris, 1993.

———. *The Immortal Mind: Science and the Continuity of Consciousness Beyond the Brain.* New York: Simon and Schuster, 2014.

———. *The Interconnected Universe. Conceptual Foundations of Transdisciplinary Unified Theory.* Singapore: World Scientific Publishing, 1999.

———. *Science and the Akashic Field: An Integral Theory of Everything.* Rochester, VT: Inner Traditions International, 2004.

———. *The Self-Actualizing Cosmos.* Rochester, VT: Inner Traditions, 2014.

———. *The Systems View of the World: A Holistic Vision for Our Time.* Denver, CO: Hampton, 1996.

Gottfried Wilhelm Leibniz. *The Principles of Philosophy Known as Monadology.* Cambridge: Cambridge UP, 2010.

John Leslie. *Universes.* London: Routledge,1989.

Henry Margenau. *The Miracle of Existence.* Woodbridge, CT: Ox Bow, 1984.

Nitamo Federico Montecucco. "The unity of consciousness, synchronization and the collective dimension." *World Futures* 48 (1997):141–150.

———. "Coherence, brain evolution and the unity of consciousness." *World Futures* 62 (2006): 127–133.

Raymond A. Moody, Jr. *Life after Life.* New York: Bantam, 1975.

Raymond A. Moody, Jr. and Paul Perry. *The Light Beyond.* New York: Bantam, 1988.

H. Nomura and T. Okoshi. "Storage density limitation of a volume-type hologram memory." *Applied Optics* 15 (1976): 550–555.

Heinz Oberhummer, Attila Csoto, and Helmut Schlattl. "Bridging the mass gaps at A = 5 and A = 8 in nucleosynthesis." *Nuclear Physics A* 689:1-2 (2001): 269–279.

Clifford A. Pickover. *Black Holes: A Traveler's Guide.* New York: Wiley, 1996.

Raymond Frank Piper and Lila K. Piper. *Cosmic Art.* New York: Hawthorne, 1975.

Rita Pizzi, Andrea Fantasia, Fabrizio Gelain, et al. "Nonlocal correlations between separated neural networks." *Quantum Information and Computation II* 107 (2004). doi:10.1117/12.540785.

Giuliano Preparata, *QED Coherence in Matter.* Singapore: World Scientific, 1995.

Karl H. Pribram. *Languages of the Brain: Experimental Paradoxes and Principles in Neuropsychology.* Englewood Cliffs, NJ: Prentice-Hall, 1971.

Ilya Prigogine. *From Being to Becoming: Time and Complexity in the Physical Sciences.* San Francisco: W. H. Freeman, 1980.

Majid Rahnama, Jack A. Tuszynski, István Bókkon, et al. "Emission of mitochondrial biophotons and their effect on electrical activity of membrane via microtubules." *Journal of Integrative Neuroscience* 10:1 (2011): 65–88. Retrieved from arxiv.org/pdf/1012.3371.

Glen Rein and Rollin McCraty. "Local and nonlocal effects of coherent heart frequencies on conformational changes of DNA." *Proceedings of the Joint USPA/IAPR Psychotronics Conference.* Milwaukee, WI. 1993.

Kenneth Ring. *Life at Death.* New York: Coward, McCann and Geoghegan, 1980.

Stacy B. Schaefer and Peter T. Furst. *People of the Peyote: Huichol Indian History, Religion & Survival.* Albuquerque: U of New Mexico, 1996.

Benny Shanon. "Ideas and reflections associated with Ayahuasca visions." *MAPS Bulletin* 8 (1998): 18–21.

Rupert Sheldrake. *A New Science of Life: The Hypothesis of Formative Causation.* Los Angeles: J. P. Tarcher, 1981.

———. Scientific papers on telepathy, the sense of being stared at, Morphic Resonance. Accessed March 4, 2015. http://www.sheldrake.org/research.

Vladimir P. Skulachev. "Mitochondrial filaments and clusters as intracellular power-transmitting cables." *Trends in Biochemical Science* 26:1 (2001): 23–29.

Yan Sun, Chao Wang, and Jiapei Dai. "Biophotons as neural communication signals demonstrated by in situ biophoton autography." *Photochemical & Photobiological Sciences* 9:3 (2010): 315–322.

Roland Thar and Michael Kühl. "Propagation of electromagnetic radiation in mitochondria?" *Journal of Theoretical Biology* 230: 2 (2004): 261–270.

D.J. Triscker. *Spirits Alive: Confrontations with the Spirits of Brazil.* New York: Vantage, 1996.

Pirn van Lommel. *Consciousness Beyond Life*. New York: Harper One, 2010.

Pirn Van Lommel, Ruud van Wees, Vincent Meyers, and Ingrid Elfferich. "Near-death experience in survivors of cardiac arrest: a prospective study in the Netherlands." *The Lancet* 358:9298 (2001): 2039–2045.

Hank Wesselman and Jill Kuykendall. *Spirit Medicine: Healing in the Sacred Realms*. Carlsbad, CA: Hay House, 2004.

Alfred North Whitehead. *Process and Reality*. New York: Macmillan, 1929.

Carol Zaleski. *Otherworld Journeys: Accounts of Near-Death Experiences in Medieval and Modern Times*. Oxford: Oxford UP, 1988.

Biographical Notes on the Contributors

Alexander Laszlo is former president and currently chair of the Board of Trustees of the International Society for the Systems Sciences (ISSS) and Director of the Doctoral Program in *Leadership and Systemic Innovation* at ITBA, Argentina. As Professor of Systems Science and Evolutionary Development, he teaches on evolutionary leadership, collaboration, and systems thinking at a variety of MBA and Doctoral programs internationally, serves on the Honorary Board of Advisors of the World Complexity Science Academy (WCSA), as Vice-President for Education on the Board of Directors of Unity Foundation, and as the Advisory Editor at the Bertalanffy Center for the Study of Systems Science. He has worked for UNESCO, the U.S. Department of Education, has held visiting appointments with the London School of Economics and the European University Institute, and has been named a Level I Member of the National Research Academy of Mexico (SNI).

Dr. Laszlo is holder of a PhD in Science and Technology Policy from the University of Pennsylvania from where he also received his MA in History and Sociology of Science. He is the recipient of the Gertrude Albert Heller Award, the Sir Geoffrey

Vickers Memorial Award, and the *Förderpreis Akademischer Klub* award, and author of over seventy journal, book, and encyclopedia publications.

DEEPAK CHOPRA is the founder of The Chopra Foundation and co-founder of the Chopra Center for Wellbeing, is a world-renowned pioneer in integrative medicine and personal transformation, and is Board Certified in Internal Medicine, Endocrinology and Metabolism. He is a Fellow of the American College of Physicians, Clinical Professor in the Family and Preventive Medicine Department at the University of California, San Diego; Health Sciences Faculty and a member of the American Association of Clinical Endocrinologists. Additionally, Dr. Deepak Chopra also serves as Co-Founder of Jiyo, an Adjunct Professor of Executive Programs at Kellogg School of Management at Northwestern University and of Columbia Business School, Columbia University. *TIME* magazine has described Dr. Chopra as "one of the top 100 heroes and icons of the century." The Chopra Center for Wellbeing holds sought-after workshops and retreats, including programs such as Perfect Health, Seduction of Spirit, and Journey Into Healing.

Dr. Chopra is the author of more than 80 books translated into over 43 languages, including numerous *New York Times* best-sellers. His ground-breaking book, *Super Genes*, co-authored with Dr. Rudolph Tanzi, focuses on the new genetics and is revolutionizing how we understand ourselves and the health of those around us. For the last three years Greatistcom has recognized Dr. Chopra as one of "The 100 Most Influential People in Health and Fitness." The *World Post* and *The Huffington Post* global Internet survey ranked Chopra #17 influential thinker in the world and #1 in Medicine."

Stanislav Grof is a psychiatrist with over sixty years of research experience in non-ordinary states of consciousness and one of the founders and chief theoreticians of transpersonal psychology. He was born in Prague, Czechoslovakia, where he also received his scientific training: an M.D. degree from the Charles University School of Medicine and a Ph.D. degree (Doctor of Philosophy in Medicine) from the Czechoslovakian Academy of Sciences. His early research in the clinical uses of psychedelic substances was conducted at the Psychiatric Research Institute in Prague, where he was principal investigator of a program that systematically explored the heuristic and therapeutic potential of LSD and other psychedelic substances. In 1967 he was invited as Clinical and Research Fellow to the Johns Hopkins University and the Research Unit of Spring Grove Hospital in Baltimore, MD. In 1969, he became Assistant Professor of Psychiatry at Johns Hopkins University and continued his research as Chief of Psychiatric Research at the Maryland Psychiatric Research Center in Catonsville, MD. In 1973 Dr. Grof was invited to the Esalen Institute in Big Sur, California, where he developed, with his wife Christina Grof, Holotropic Breathwork, an innovative form of experiential psychotherapy that is now being used worldwide.

Dr. Grof is the founder of the International Transpersonal Association (ITA) and for several decades served as its president. In 1993 he received a Honorary Award from the Association for Transpersonal Psychology (ATP) for major contributions to and development of the field of transpersonal psychology, given at the occasion of the 25th Anniversary Convocation held in Asilomar, California. In 2007, he received the prestigious VISION 97 lifetime achievement award from the Foundation of Dagmar and Václav Havel in Prague, Czechoslovakia. In 2010, he received also the Thomas R. Verny Award from the Association for Pre- and Perinatal Psychology and Health for his contributions to this field.

NASSIM HARAMEIN PHD has spent over 30 years researching and discovering connections in physics, mathematics, geometry, cosmology, quantum mechanics, biology, and chemistry, as well as anthropology and ancient civilizations. These studies lead Haramein to ground-breaking theories, published papers, and patented inventions in unified physics, which are now gaining worldwide recognition and acceptance. Haramein's findings are focused on a fundamental geometry of space that connects us all, from the quantum and molecular scale to cosmological objects in the Universe. In Haramein's paper, Quantum Gravity and the Holographic Mass, a prediction of the charge radius of the proton, was confirmed with greater accuracy than any other theoretical framework. An experiment performed in 2013 by a team of scientists at the Paul Scherrer Institute, confirmed the prediction. In 2004, Haramein founded the Resonance Project Foundation, where as the Director of Research he leads physicists, mathematicians, and engineers in exploring unification principles and their implications in our world today and for future generations.

In fall of 2014 Haramein began The Resonance Academy Delegate Program, the first and only unified physics program of its kind, educating thousands of students from over 70 countries around the world. In 2015 Haramein founded Torus Tech LLC and opened a laboratory where he serves as the Executive Director of Research and Development. Here, Haramein leads teams of scientists and engineers applying his revolutionary theories and patents to resonate technologies that focus on vacuum energy and gravitational effects. Production of such technologies could provide indispensable energy and open up space exploration in a completely viable and safe manner. The Connected Universe, a feature length documentary film, was produced based on Haramein's discoveries.

Jude Currivan is a cosmologist, planetary healer and author and previously one of the most senior business women in the UK. Having grown up as the daughter of a coal miner in the north of England, she has since journeyed to nearly seventy countries around the world and for the last nearly twenty years has lived in the sacred landscape of Avebury. She has experienced multidimensional realities since early childhood and worked with the wisdom keepers of many traditions. She holds a PhD in Archaeology from the University of Reading in the UK researching ancient cosmologies and a Masters Degree in Physics from Oxford University specializing in cosmology and quantum physics. She is the author of five non-fiction books currently available in 15 languages and 25 countries including *CosMos: A Co-creator's Guide to the Whole-World* co-authored with Ervin Laszlo. Her first fictionalized e-book *Legacy,* is available at Amazon.

Dr. Currivan's corporate career culminated with her appointment as Group Finance Director of two major international businesses. She has extensive experience and knowledge of world events, international politics, and global economic and financial systems, and has spoken on transformational reforms in the UK, US, Europe, Japan, and South Korea. For the last sixteen years she has travelled around the world in service to planetary and collective healing, some of which is described in her books *The 8th Chakra*, *The 13th Step* and most recently *HOPE: Healing Our People & Earth.*

ALLAN COMBS is a transpersonal psychologist, consciousness researcher, neuropsychologist, and systems theorist. He holds appointments at The California Institute of Integral Studies (CIIS), the Saybrook Graduate School, and the Graduate Institute of Connecticut where he is the Director of the MA program in Conscious Evolution. He is also Professor Emeritus at the University of North Carolina-Asheville. He is author of over 200 articles, chapters, and books on consciousness and the brain, and is the Director of the Center for Consciousness Studies at CIIS and President of The Society for Conscious Studies. He is also co-founder of The Society for Chaos Theory in Psychology and the Life Sciences, a member of The General Evolution Research Group, and of the Club of Budapest. He is Co-Editor of the *Journal of Conscious Evolution*, and Editor of *CONSCIOUSNESS: Ideas and Research for the 21st Century.*

STANLEY KRIPPNER is professor of psychology at Saybrook University, Oakland, is a Fellow in five American Psychological Association (APA) divisions, and past-president of two divisions. Formerly, he was director of the Kent State University Child

Study Center, Kent OH, and the Maimonides Medical Center Dream Research Laboratory, Brooklyn NY. He is co-author of many books, including *Varieties of Anomalous Experience: Examining the Scientific Evidence.*

Professor Krippner received the Award for Distinguished Lifetime Contributions to Humanistic Psychology from Div 32 of the American Psychological Association in 2013, the Human Treasure Award from The Society for Clinical and Experimental Hypnosis in 2013, the Ashley Montagu Peace Award in 2003, the American Psychological Association Award for Distinguished Contributions to the International Development of Psychology in 2002, the Society for Psychological Hypnosis Award for Distinguished Contributions to Professional Hypnosis in 2002, and lifetime achievement awards from the Association for the Study of Dreams and the Parapsychological Association. He also holds Fellow status in several additional organizations, including the Association for Psychological Science, the Society for the Scientific Study of Religion, and the Society for the Scientific Study of Sexuality.

Stephan A. Schwartz is the columnist for the journal *Explore* and editor of the daily web publication Schwartzreport.net, in both of which he covers trends and social issues. He is a Distinguished Consulting Faculty of Saybrook University. Previous academic research appointments include: Senior Samueli Fellow of the Samueli Institute, founder and Research Director of the Mobius laboratory, Executive Director of the Rhine Research Center, Senior Fellow of The Philosophical Research Society, and Adjunct Professor John F. Kennedy University. Government appointments include: Special Assistant for Research and Analysis to the Chief of Naval Operations and r consultant to the Oceanographer of the Navy. For forty years he has been doing research in thee main areas: the dynamics of social transformation, trends shaping the future, and the role of consciousness in exceptional human performance. He is part of the group that founded modern Remote Viewing research and is the principal researcher studying the use of Remote Viewing in archaeology. Other areas of experimental study include research into creativity, meditation, and Therapeutic Intent/Healing.

Stephan Schwartz is the author of more than 130 technical reports and papers and 20 chapters in mutiauthored academic books. He wrote magazine articles for *Smithsonian, OMNI, American History Magazine*, American Heritage, *The Washington Post, The New York Times*, as well as other magazines and newspapers and produced and written a number of television documentaries. He is the author of five books: *The Secret Vaults of Time, The Alexandria Project, Mind Rover, Opening to the Infinite*, and his latest, *The 8 Laws of Change.*

EDE FRECSKA is Chief of Department at the National Institute of Psychiatry and Neurology in Budapest, Hungary. He received his medical degree in 1977 from the Semmelweis University in Hungary. He then earned qualifications as certified psychologist from the Department of Psychology at Lorand Eotvos University in Budapest. Dr. Frecska completed his residency training in Psychiatry both in Hungary (1986) and in the United States (1992). He is a qualified psychopharmacologist (1987) of international merit with 15 years of clinical and research experience in the United States. He is a member of several professional organizations (APA, ECNP, CINP), and has received grants and awards from a variety of sources.

Dr. Frecska's academic studies were devoted to research on schizophrenia and affective diseases. He published more than 50 scientific papers and book chapters on these topics, most recently on psychointegrator drugs and techniques. His theoretical work currently focuses on the interface between cognitive neuroscience and quantum brain dynamics with specific attention to the mechanism of initiation ceremonies and healing rituals.

Nitamo Federico Montecucco is researcher in neuroscience, psychosomatic and PNEI (Psycho-neuro-endocrine-immunology). He leads experiments on brain EEG coherence, as a measure of psychosomatic integrity, studying normal as well as sick people and meditators. He discovered the existence of "collective synchronization," measured by EEG coherence, between the brains of people in pairs and in groups. From this research he has developed a new field of clinical application of psychosomatic PNEI in medicine and psychology.

Dr. Montecucco taught psychosomatic medicin at the Master level in various institutions, including Complementary Medicines of the University of Medicine of Milan, Collaborating Center of Complementary Medicine of WHO (World Health Organization), and at the University of Medicine of Pavia, and at the University of Siena and Chieti. He is director of the Institute of Psychosomatics which has trained more than 1,000 doctors, psychologists and teachers. Since 1994 he developed an integrated neurophysiological map of self consciousness, the "*Psychosomatic*

Mindfulness Protocol" for global health and personal transformation. He has applied this Protocol to the "*Gaia Project*" a national scale education program for global consciousness and social health that reaches more than 15,000 students throughout Italy.

TULKU THONDUP RINPOCHE was born in a nomadic tribe in Eastern Tibet in 1937. At the age of four he was recognized as a Tulku, a reincarnatated Lama. He studied and trained in Tibetan Buddhism at Dodrupchen Monastery, a famous institution of learning in Golok province. In 1956, he went to India as a refugee and taught at the Lucknow University (1967–1976) and the Visava-Bharati University (1976–1980). In 1980, he went to Harvard University as a Visiting Scholar (1980–1983). Since 1980, he has been engaged in teaching and writing on Tibetan Buddhism under the auspices of The Buddhayana Foundation in the United States.

Tulku Thondup has authored a dozen books in English on Tibetan Buddhism, eight of which have been published in a number of foreign languages. Among his publications are *The Practice of Dzogchen*, *The Hidden Teachings of Tibet*, *Masters of Meditation and Miracles*, *The Healing Power of Mind* and *The Heart of Unconditional Love*.

NÁ ÁAK is a Mexican born Medicine Woman and Mystic who dedicates her life to the practice of indigenous wisdom as a spiritual path. She carries the understanding and experience of diverse indigenous traditions from Mexico, Latin America, Asia, and Europe. *Ná Áak* is a Mayan name and translates as "*Mother Turtle*." The person given this name by the elders is said to be a symbol of strength, permanence, and wisdom. There is no doubt that Ná Áak brings each of these qualities life in the heart of all those she works with, all those she brings healing to, and all those she reconnects to the heart.

In her life journey Ná Áak has trained as a Transpersonal Psychotherapist and is certified as a Holotropic Breathwork™ facilitator with Dr. Stanislav Grof and GTT Grof Transpersonal Training. She has also studied Western medicine, science and psychology. She studied Buddhist disciplines with the Kagyu lineage and Kriya yoga. The depth and power of Ná Áak' shamanic work has been influenced and nurtured by the Tibetian, Celtic, and Mayan wisdom.

For Ná Áak, the core of existence is *uncompromised compassion*. It is the active practice of compassion that guides us on the path of liberation from suffering afflictive states of consciousness.

She is the author of "Awakening Consciousness: Beyond 2012," a powerful insight into the human condition and the path of inner freedom.

Dr. Jean Houston, scholar, philosopher, and researcher in Human Capacities, is long regarded as one of the principal founders of the Human Potential Movement and one of the leading experts today in the field of human development and social change. She also leads an intensive program in social artistry with leaders coming from all over the world to study with her and her distinguished associates. Houston is well known for her studies and teaching on myth and archetype. She is a founder of Rising Woman, Rising World, a global initiative that empowers women's programs in many countries. As Chancellor of

Meridian University she directs doctoral and masters programs in leadership and social transformation. A past President of the Association of Humanistic Psychology and director of several foundations, she has taught in many universities and continues as Visiting Distinguished Scholar.

Dr. Houston has authored over thirty books. She has been a consultant to UN programs for many years, serving as advisor to UN agencies, principally UNICEF and the UNDP, and has done intensive training of leaders in developing countries in their own development in the light of dramatic social change. With other international agencies, she has implemented the social development of indigenous people through the integration of their unique cultural gifts into their health and educational systems. She has worked intensively in over forty cultures and one hundred and nine countries. She holds conferences and seminars with social leaders, educational institutions, and business organizations worldwide.

Jean Houston holds a BA from Barnard College, a PhD in psychology from the Union Graduate School, and a PhD in religion from the Graduate Theological Foundation. She has been the recipient of honorary PhDs as well as other awards

Christopher M. Bache is professor emeritus in the Department of Philosophy and Religious Studies at Youngstown State University where he taught for thirty-eight years. He is also adjunct faculty at CIIS and a Fellow at the Institute of Noetic Sciences where he served as Director of Transformative Learning from 2000 to 2002.

An award winning teacher, Dr. Bache's work explores the philosophical implications of non-ordinary states of consciousness, especially psychedelic states. He has written three books: *Lifecycles*, a study of reincarnation in light of contemporary consciousness research; *Dark Night, Early Dawn*, a pioneering work in psychedelic philosophy and collective consciousness; and *The Living Classroom*, an exploration of collective fields of consciousness and the transpersonal dimension of teaching. He is currently writing a book on his twenty year psychedelic odyssey, titled *Stealing Diamonds from Heaven*.

Master Zhi-Gang Sha is a Tao healer a revered spiritual teacher and an eleven-time *New York Times* best-selling author of twenty-one books. At the age of six, he was accepted by the first of several masters in Eastern martial arts. As a grandmaster of many ancient disciplines, including qigong, tai chi, kung fu, feng shui and the *I Ching*, Master Sha was named Qigong Master of the Year at the Fifth World Congress on Qigong in 2003.

Born in Shaanxi province, China, he became interested in healing as a young child as he observed with great concern and compassion people in his immediate and extended family suffering from a variety of illnesses. Master Sha became a conventional medical doctor in China and a doctor of traditional Chinese medicine in China and Canada. At the age twenty-two, even before completing his training as a physician, Master Sha began to combine the knowledge of energy development from his practice of martial arts with traditional Chinese acupuncture to create his own acupuncture system.

In 2005, he created Soul Mind Body Medicine, integrating conventional Western medicine and traditional Chinese medicine with spiritual wisdom, knowledge and techniques. As the founder of the Institute of Soul Healing and Enlightenmen and the Love Peace Harmony Foundation, Master Sha was honored in 2006 with the Martin Luther King, Jr. Commemorative Commission Award for his humanitarian efforts. In 2013, with quantum physicist Dr. Rulin Xiu, created Soul Mind Body Science, a new leading-edge way to integrate science and spirituality.

JOHN AUDETTE earned a Master of Science degree from Virginia Tech. His professional career spans over thirty-five years of senior executive level experience in hospital and hospice administration, physician practice management, public broadcasting and the performing arts. He has studied spiritually transformative experiences and nonlocal consciousness phenomena since 1974 and has worked closely with a number of leading figures in this field for over four decades. In 1977, he founded the International Association for Near-Death Studies, Inc. along with co-founders Drs. Raymond Moody, Kenneth Ring, Bruce Greyson, and Michael Sabom.

He currently serves as President & CEO of Eternea, Inc., an organization he co-founded with Eben Alexander, MD, in 2012, to continue his life-long commitment to help advance civilization by providing comprehensive resources, tools, and strategies to optimize consciousness, self, and society in the co-creation of an ideal future for Earth and all its inhabitants. John Audette served on active duty in the US Army Signal Corps during the

Vietnam era for more than three years. He is a native of South Florida, currently residing in Boca Raton.

Kingsley L. Dennis is a sociologist, researcher, and writer. He previously worked in the Sociology Department at Lancaster University, UK. Kingsley is the author of numerous articles on social futures; technology and new media communications; global affairs; and conscious evolution. He is the co-author (with Bente Milton & Duane Elgin) of the study 'New Media for a New Future: The Emerging Digital Landscape for a Planetary Society' produced as part of the Fuji Declaration for The Goi Peace Foundation, in collaboration with the renowned global think-tank The Club of Budapest. He currently serves as Director of Publications for the Laszlo Institute of New Paradigm Research.

Kingsley Dennis is the author of several critically acclaimed books including *Dawn of the Akashic Age* (2013 with Ervin Laszlo). He also publishes through his own imprint, Beautiful Traitor Books. He lives in Andalusia, Spain.

Gary Zukav is the author of *The Dancing Wu Li Masters; An Overview of the New Physics*, winner of The American Book Award for Science, *The Seat of the Soul*, a #1 *USA Today* Bestseller and a # 1 *New York Times* Bestseller thirty one times, and on the *New York Times* Bestseller list for three years; *Soul Stories*, a *New York Times* Bestseller; and with Linda Francis, *The Heart of the Soul: Emotional Awareness* and *The Mind of the Soul: Responsible Choice*, also *New York Times* Bestsellers. His books have sold six million copies and are published in thirty languages. He is a co-founder of the Seat of the Soul Institute with Linda Francis, his spiritual partner; Fellow of the World Business Academy, and Elder on the Council of Elders, Native American Earth Ambassadors. He served on the Editorial Board of the former *East-West Review: Business News for the Perestroika Era*; the Literary Advisory Board, Earth Day 1990; as chair of the Government and Politics Strategy Group, Campaign for the Earth; and on the Advisory Boards of EarthSave, Intuition Network, Humanity Federation, and LearnScience.

Dr. Zukav is a recipient of the World Business Academy *Pathfinder Award* and the *Einstein Award* from the Albert Einstein College of Medicine for Contributions to the Psychosocial Growth of Humanity, among others.

SHAMIK DESAI grew up in the San Francisco Bay Area and studied economics at Stanford University and Oxford. He worked as a banker at various institutions (Morgan Stanley in New York, Cisco Systems in the Silicon Valley, and the World Bank in Washington, DC) which gave him a window into some of the societal challenges pressing upon the world today. Following this, he pursued a master's degree in international public policy at Johns Hopkins University and wrote a satirical-philosophical novel. It has inspired a social giving app that encourages and measures people's attitudes toward giving. He is currently project manager of ConsciousWorld, a project that seeks to map and encourage conscious evolution in all branches of civilization, and serves as Director of Special Projects at the Laszlo Institute of New Paradigm Research in Italy.

Index

A

B

D

F

G

H

N

O

P

S

T

U

V

About the Author

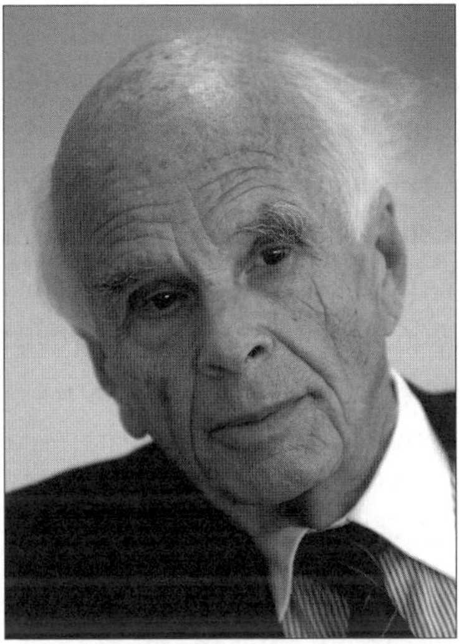

Ervin Laszlo spent his childhood in Budapest. He was a celebrated child prodigy, with public appearances as a concert pianist from the age of nine. Upon receiving a Grand Prize at the international music competition in Geneva, he was allowed to cross the Iron Curtain and begin an international concert career, first in Europe and then in the United States. At the request of Senator Claude Pepper of Florida, he was awarded US citizenship before his twenty-first birthday by an act of Congress,

Laszlo received the Sorbonne's highest degree, the Doctorat ès Lettres et Sciences Humaines in 1970. Shifting to the life of a scientist and humanist, he lectured at various universities in the United States, including Yale, Princeton, Northwestern University, the University of Houston, and the State University of New

York. The author, co-author or editor of ninety-one books that have appeared in a total of twenty-four languages, Ervin Laszlo has also written several hundred papers and articles in scientific journals and popular magazines.

He is a member of numerous scientific bodies, including the International Academy of Science, the World Academy of Arts and Science, the International Academy of Philosophy of Science, and the International Medici Academy. Laszlo received the Goi Award, the Japan Peace Prize in 2001, the Assisi Mandir of Peace Prize in 2006, the Polyhistor Prize of Hungary in 2015, and was nominated for the Nobel Peace Prize in 2004 and 2005. He was elected member of the Hungarian Academy of Science in 2010.

Laszlo is founder and president of the global think-tank The Club of Budapest and Founder and co-director of the Laszlo New Paradigm Research Center in Italy.